VI. Mechanics   93

25. Capitalization   96
26. Italics   99
27. Numbers   100
28. Abbreviations   102
29. Spelling   105

VII. Multilingual Speakers   109

30. American Style in Writing/ESL Resources   112
31. Verbs   114
32. Nouns (Count and Noncount)   118
33. Articles ("A," "An," and "The")   119
34. Prepositions   120
35. Omitted/Repeated Words   122
36. Idioms   123

VIII. Research   125

37. Finding a Topic   128
38. Searching for Information   131
39. Evaluating Print and Online Sources   154
40. Integrating Sources   161
41. Designing Documents   173

IX. Documentation   181

42. Documenting in MLA Style   183
43. Documenting in APA Style   216
44. *Chicago Manual of Style* (CM)   237
45. Council of Science Editors (CSE) Style   248

Glossary of Usage   253
Glossary of Grammatical Terms   261
Index   271

The Writer's FAQs

A POCKET HANDBOOK

FOURTH EDITION

MURIEL HARRIS
Purdue University

JENNIFER L. KUNKA
Francis Marion University

Prentice Hall

Boston Columbus Indianapolis New York San Francisco Upper Saddle River
Amsterdam Cape Town Dubai London Madrid Milan Munich Paris
Montreal Toronto Delhi Mexico City Sao Paulo Sydney Hong Kong
Seoul Singapore Taipei Tokyo

Editor-in-Chief: Joe Opiela
Senior Acquisitions Editor:
  Brad Potthoff
Senior Marketing Manager:
  Sandra McGuire
Editorial Assistant: Nancy C. Lee
Managing Editor: Linda Mihatov
  Behrens
Associate Managing Editor:
  Bayani Mendoza de Leon
Senior Operations Specialist:
  Nick Sklitsis

Operations Specialist: Mary
  Ann Gloriande
Art Director, Cover: Nancy
  Wells
Designer, Cover: Ilze Lemesis
**Production Coordination,
  Text Design, and Electronic
  Page Makeup:** GGS Higher
  Education Resources/PMG
Cover Image: Jupiter Images

Library of Congress Cataloging-in-Publication Data

Harris, Muriel
   The writer's FAQs : a pocket handbook / Muriel Harris and
Jennifer L. Kunka. — 4th ed.
      p. cm.
   Includes index.
   ISBN 978-0-205-77784-6
   1. English language—Rhetoric—Handbooks, manuals, etc.
   2. English language—Grammar—Handbooks, manuals, etc.
   I. Kunka, Jennifer L.   II. Title.
   PE1408.H3458 2011
   808'.042—dc22

                                                    2009040890

              10 9 8 7 6 5 4 3 2 1   RRD-IN   13 12 11 10

Prentice Hall
is an imprint of

                                    ISBN-13: 978-0-205-77784-6
www.pearsonhighered.com ISBN-10:   0-205-77784-8

How to Use This Book

This book has many ways to help you easily find the information you need:

- **Brief Contents:** This is on the inside front cover of the book and is the table of contents. It lists only the sections and chapter titles. Each section of the book begins with a more complete list of its contents.

- **Question and Correct:** This is a list of typical questions writers ask. Questions similar to the ones you have are paired with the section number and page to turn to. You won't need to know any terminology.

- **Sections of the Book:** Here you'll find detailed summaries of the contents of that part of the book to help you find the type of information you need.

- **HINT and TRY THIS Boxes:** Throughout the book, you'll find HINT boxes and TRY THIS strategies. They offer advice, mistakes to avoid, ways to remember rules, and strategies to try when planning and writing.

- **Questions at the Beginning of Each Part of the Book:** To help you find what you need in a section of the book, you'll find a list of more questions writers typically ask and the pages to turn to for answers.

- **Glossary of Usage:** This is an alphabetical list of words that can be confusing, such as when to write "may" and when to write "can" (or *your* or *you're*) or whether or not terms such as *could of* or *use to* are correct.

- **Glossary of Grammatical Terms:** This is an alphabetical list of grammatical terms and their definitions.

- **Index:** This is an alphabetical list of the topics in this book with the pages to turn to, to find explanations.

- **Correction Symbols:** This is a list of correction symbols many instructors use when reading student papers and the pages to turn to for information on how to revise what has been marked.

Sections of the Book

I **Writing and Speaking**
Here you'll find help with planning, writing, developing thesis statements, revising papers and portfolios, linking sentences and paragraphs, writing introductions and conclusions, using checklists for revising, writing about literature, and developing portfolios and oral and multimedia presentations.

II **Sentence Choices**
Here you'll find information about composing clear, effective sentences that have variety, don't overuse the passive voice, keep parallel structure, and use transitions that connect sentences and paragraphs smoothly.

III **Writing Style**
This section helps you write concisely, choose the appropriate level of formality, and use nonsexist language.

IV **Sentence Grammar**
This section explains rules of grammar and has HINT and TRY THIS boxes to help you avoid such errors as fragments, comma splices and fused sentences, subject-verb agreement errors, verb problems, pronoun and adjective/adverb errors, dangling and misplaced modifiers, and shifts in voice and number.

V **Punctuation**
This section has an overview of sentence punctuation patterns, and information on using commas, apostrophes, semicolons, quotation marks, and other punctuation.

VI **Mechanics**
Here you'll find information on when to capitalize words, use italics, write out numbers or use figures instead, abbreviate certain words, and learn rules for spelling correctly.

VII Multilingual Speakers (ESL)

For students whose first language is not English, this section includes a discussion of the American style of writing, a list of resources for learning English, explanations of English verbs, count and noncount nouns, articles, prepositions, words that should not be repeated or omitted, and idioms.

VIII Research

Here you'll find extensive help with the process of planning, researching, writing, and revising research papers. There is also advice and information about finding and narrowing a topic; formulating a thesis statement; searching for, evaluating, and documenting information, both in libraries and online; finding, evaluating, and documenting information; using search engines; integrating sources; and avoiding plagiarism.

IX Documentation

This section includes the most up-to-date information on how to document sources in MLA, APA, *Chicago Manual* (CM), and Council of Science Editors (CSE) style.

We hope that you find this book easy to use and that it becomes a writing friend to keep nearby as you write. Then you'll be more confident that you are writing correctly and effectively and are conveying your ideas in ways that others will appreciate and respect.

Muriel Harris

Jennifer L. Kunka

Question and Correct

Writing and Speaking   p. 1

+ What are some reminders and writing tips
  to keep in mind as I write?   1a
+ How do I write a good argument?   1a
+ What should I look for when I revise?   1a
+ How do I write about literature?   1a
+ What do I look for when I proofread?   1b
+ How do I plan a speech or a presentation
  with visuals?   2a,b

More questions about writing and revising: **p. 2**

Sentence Choices   p. 19

+ How do I make my sentences clearer and
  easier to read?   3
+ What's wrong with "The utilization of..."
  or "Her activation of the engine is..."?   3d
+ Are phrases like "It is a fact that..." OK to use?   3e
+ How can I make my sentences not sound all
  alike or choppy?   4, 8
+ What is passive voice, and when should I use it?   5
+ How do I fix sentences such as "He knows
  how to speak Spanish and fixing computers"?   6
+ Can I start sentences with "And" or "But"?   8

More questions about writing sentences: **p. 20**

Writing Style   p. 31

+ How can I make my writing less wordy?   9
+ How do I choose whether to sound formal
  or informal?   10
+ What is nonsexist language, and what words
  should I use?   11

More questions about style: **p. 31**

Sentence Grammar   p. 37

+ What's wrong with the following: "I'm a vegetarian.
  Because I don't want to eat animals." Why is it
  a fragment?   12

+ What are comma splices and fragments, and
  how do I fix them?   13
+ How should verb endings and subjects match?   14a
+ Which is correct: *between you and I* or
  between you and me?   15a
+ When do I use *who* or *whom* and *we* or *us*?   15a
+ Are these phrases correct: *real bad, talk loud*?   16
+ What's wrong with writing "She is so happy"?   16b
+ Where in the sentence should I put words like
  almost and *only*?   17b

More questions about sentence grammar: **pp. 38–41**

Punctuation   p. 69

+ What are most of the ways sentences
  are punctuated?   19
+ Where do the commas go in a list like *red,
  white and blue*?   20d
+ How do I punctuate dates and addresses?   20f
+ How do I punctuate quotations?   20h, 23a
+ When am I using too many commas?   20i
+ What's the difference between *it's* and *its*?   21b, d
+ Are these apostrophes correct: *his' car*
  and *the melon's are ripe*?   21c
+ Which is correct: *well-known speaker* or
  well known speaker?   24a
+ How do I show left-out words in a quotation?   24h

More questions about punctuation: **pp. 70–72**

Mechanics   p. 93

+ Which is correct?
  spring semester   (*or*)   Spring semester   25a
  April 1   (*or*)   April first   27
  6 million   (*or*)   6,000,000   28c
+ What are some problems with using
  spell-checkers?   29a

More questions about mechanics: **pp. 94–95**

Multilingual Speakers (ESL)   p. 109

+ How is academic writing in American English
  different from academic writing in my country?   30
+ What is the difference between *he ran* and
  he has run?   31a
+ Which is correct?
  She enjoys (to drink/drinking) coffee.   31e

two furnitures (*or*) some furniture 32
+ When do I use *the*, *a*, and *an*? 33
+ Do I write *in Tuesday* or *on Tuesday*? 34

More questions for ESL speakers: .... pp. 109–11

Research .... p. 125

+ How do I develop a topic sentence and narrow it? .. 37
+ How do I search library databases for articles
  and source materials? 38b
+ How do I start searching databases and
  the Internet for information? 38c
+ What are some useful Web sites to try? 38d
+ How do I know if a source is reliable? 39
+ How do I avoid plagiarizing? 40a
+ When do I cite a source? 40b,c,d
+ How do I set margins and spacing on papers? 41a
+ How and when should I use tables and charts? 41b

More questions about research: .... pp. 126–127

Documentation .... p. 181

+ What is MLA style? 42
+ Is there a list of examples for MLA style? 42c
+ What are some ways that APA and MLA are
  alike and different? 43
+ Is there a list of examples for APA style? 43c
+ How do I set up my paper (title, margins, etc.)
  –in MLA format? 42d
  –in APA format? 43d
+ How do I use *Chicago Manual of Style* (CM)
  or Council of Science Editors (CSE) format? 44, 45

**More questions about how to document
sources:** .... pp. 181–182

Glossary of Usage .... p. 253

+ What is the difference between *accept*
  and *except*? .... USAGE
+ Is it acceptable to write *a lot* or *and etc.*? .... USAGE
+ What's the difference between similar words
  such as *anyone* and *any one*, *awful*
  and *awfully*? .... USAGE
+ When do I use *that* or *which* and *who*
  or *whom*? .... USAGE

Glossary of Grammatical Terms .... p. 261

I

Writing and Speaking

Contents of this section

1 Checklist for Effective Papers and Portfolios　3
- **1a** Higher-Order Concerns (HOCs)　3
  - Purpose　3
  - Audience　4
  - Topic　4
  - Thesis　5
  - Organization　7
  - Paragraph development　7
  - Transitions　7
  - Introductions　7
  - Conclusions　8
- **1b** Arguments　9
- **1c** Writing about literature　11
- **1d** Portfolios　12
- **1e** Later-Order Concerns (LOCs)　13

2 Checklist for Oral and Multimedia Presentations　15
- **2a** Oral presentations　15
  - Planning　15
  - Content　16
  - Delivery　16
- **2b** Multimedia presentations　16
  - Organizing your presentation　17
  - Presenting with multimedia　18

Question and Correct

	SECTION	PAGE
✦ When I start planning or when I'm drafting my paper, what questions should I ask myself?	1a	3
✦ What are HOCs (Higher-Order Concerns), and why are they important?	1a	3
✦ What are different purposes for writing?	1a	3
✦ Why is it important to think about the audience of my paper?	1a	4
✦ How can I come up with a topic to write about?	1a	4
✦ What's a thesis statement, and how can I tell when I've phrased it appropriately?	1a	5
✦ How can I make my paper flow?	1a	7
✦ What should I put in my introduction and conclusion?	1a	7–8
✦ What are some ways to write a persuasive argument?	1b	9–10
✦ What are ways I can write about literature?	1c	11
✦ What is a portfolio, and how can I put one together?	1d	12
✦ What are LOCs (Later-Order Concerns), and why are they important?	1e	13
✦ How do I proofread the paper before I hand it in?	1b	14
✦ How can I use online tools to help me proofread?	1b	14
✦ How can I prepare for an oral presentation?	2a	15
✦ How should I deliver my presentation?	2a	16
✦ What is a multimedia presentation?	2b	18
✦ How should I design the slides for my multimedia presentation?	2b	18

Checklist for Effective Papers and Portfolios

HOCs (Higher-Order Concerns)

As you write, consider these Higher-Order Concerns (HOCs) to make your writing more effective.

Purpose

Your purpose shapes the writing you do. As you plan your writing, ask yourself what you want your audience to know, believe, or do after reading your paper. Also check to be sure your purpose fits your assignment. Consider these common purposes for writing:

- **Summarizing.** Stating concisely the main points of a piece of writing
- **Defining.** Explaining the meaning of a word or concept
- **Analyzing.** Breaking the topic into parts and examining how these parts work or interact
- **Persuading.** Offering convincing support for a point of view
- **Reporting.** Examining all the evidence and data on a subject and presenting an objective overview
- **Evaluating.** Setting up and explaining criteria for evaluation and then judging the quality or importance of the object being evaluated
- **Discussing or examining.** Considering the main points, implications, and relationships to other topics
- **Interpreting.** Explaining the meaning or implications of a topic
- **Exploring.** Considering a topic by putting mental notions into written form

Audience

Think about your readers. Is the audience you are writing to the appropriate audience for your assignment and purpose? The information you include, the tone you take, and the assumptions you make about your readers' level of interest or knowledge of a subject shape your writing.

CHECKLIST

Defining Audience

When you start to write, define your audience by asking these questions:

- **Who is my audience?** Peers? A potential boss? A teacher? Readers of a particular publication? People who are likely to agree with me? Readers who disagree with me?

- **What information should be included?** What do your readers already know about the subject? What will they need to know to understand what you are writing about? What do you want them to learn?

- **What is the audience's attitude?** Are readers already interested in the subject, or will you need to create some interest? Are they sympathetic, neutral, or inclined to disagree with your views? What will be needed to convince those who don't agree with you? Is there some common ground that can help those who disagree with you begin to consider your views?

- **What is the audience's background?** How would you describe your readers in terms of their education, specialized knowledge, religion, race, cultural heritage, political views, occupation, and age? Will this background determine in part what and how you write?

Topic

The topic of a piece of writing may be something the writer chooses, or it may be assigned. To choose a topic, try one or more of the strategies suggested here.

TRY THIS

To Find a Topic

- What is a problem you'd like to solve?

  _____ is a problem, and I think we should _____.

- What is something that pleases, puzzles, irritates, or bothers you?

  What annoys (or pleases) me is _____.

- What is something you'd like to convince others of?

  What I want others to agree on is _____.

- What is something that seems to contradict what you read or see around you?

  Why does _____? (or) I've noticed that _____, but _____.

- What is something you'd like to learn more about?

  I wonder how _____.

- What is something you know about that others around you may not know?

  I'd like to tell you about _____.

Thesis

A thesis statement is the main idea or subject of your paper. In an informative paper, your thesis statement summarizes your discussion about your topic. In an argumentative paper, your thesis communicates your primary position, solution, or interpretation to your audience. Thesis statements are often written as a single, concise sentence. For longer or more complex works, your thesis might be written in two or three sentences or even a short paragraph.

There are two parts to an effective thesis statement: the topic and a comment that makes an important point about the topic.

Topic	Comment
Effective document design	helps technical writers present complex material more clearly.
Lost	remains a popular television series because it combines action-packed plots with fascinating characters and innovative storytelling strategies.

An effective thesis statement should have a topic that will interest your readers, be as specific as possible, and be limited enough to make it manageable. It's important to make your thesis statement specific enough to be adequately discussed within the length of your paper. If a thesis statement is too general, it will be very difficult for you to decide what to write about. Consider this thesis statement:

Thesis statement: Education in the United States needs to improve.

Why does education need to be improved? What is inadequate about it? Think about of all the ways that education could be improved. For which subjects? Reading abilities? Music education? Financial education? And for whom? Elementary school? High school? College? And in what way? More funding for teachers? Smaller class sizes? Alternative curriculum strategies? Addressing all of these would be too much to cover effectively in a typical research paper.

This thesis needs to be narrowed down to provide more focus to this argument. Consider this revision:

Revised thesis statement: To keep the United States competitive in the global marketplace, local school districts need to provide American high school students with more exposure and hands-on training in technology, science, and engineering.

This thesis statement offers additional parameters, naming **who** (*local school districts* and *American high school students*), **what** (*improvement in technology, science, and engineering*), and **how** (*more exposure and hands-on training*) education can be improved. With these additional specifics, the writer of this paper will be able to provide a more focused argument.

If your assignment is to write a short paper, you will need to narrow down your thesis statement even further. Consider the thesis statement that follows.

Further revision of a thesis statement: To meet the global marketplace's demand for civil engineers, American high schools should offer college-prep courses that include hands-on training in engineering.

This revised thesis statement narrows the focus on **what** (*improvement in engineering*) and **how** (*hands-on training*) education needs to improve.

Organization

As you read over your draft, check to see whether your topic sentences clearly communicate the central idea of each paragraph. Then ask yourself if each paragraph contributes to the thesis in some way and if each paragraph leads logically to the next one. For example, you can order material chronologically to show historical development or explain a process. Cause-and-effect order can help you organize the relationship of one thing to another. Compare-and-contrast organization can help you decide how you will structure items you are discussing. With any organizational strategy, you want to avoid jumps in the development of your thesis that might confuse your reader.

For some writers, creating an outline, either before or after drafting, can be useful because it helps group related ideas together and rearrange material into the best logical structure. One way check your organization is to look at the topic sentences of your paper as an outline. Do those sentences, once collected, make a smooth, coherent outline? If some idea or subtopic doesn't seem to fit, it could be because it doesn't belong in the paper.

Paragraph development

A paragraph is well developed when it has enough details, examples, specifics, supporting evidence, and information to support your thesis. You may need to delete material that is no longer relevant or add material that will strengthen your thesis and help you achieve your purpose. Try to read your paper as an uninformed reader would, and ask yourself what else you'd need to know.

Transitions

Every paragraph should be written so that each sentence flows smoothly into the next. If your ideas, sentences, and details fit together clearly, your readers can follow along easily without getting lost. To help your reader, try repeating key terms and phrases and using synonyms, pronouns, and transitional devices between sentences and paragraphs. (See Chapter 8 for a list of transitions.) Also check for missing information that causes a break in your explanation or argument.

Introductions

The introduction brings the reader into your world, builds interest in your subject, and announces the topic. By the end of an effective introduction, your readers should have a clear sense of what your topic is and how the paper will be organized. Think of the introduction as a plan or map for your readers.

TRY THIS

To Write an Effective Introduction

- Cite an interesting statistic.
- Offer an analogy.
- Pose a question.
- Relate an anecdote.
- Make a surprising statement.
- Introduce a quotation.
- Acknowledge an opinion or approach that differs from yours.
- Suggest the long-term effects of your topic.

Conclusions

The conclusion signals that the paper is ending and helps put the whole paper in perspective. The conclusion is your opportunity to summarize your major points and make a memorable or persuasive final statement.

TRY THIS

To Write an Effective Conclusion

Look backward. If the paper has a complex discussion, try any of the following:

- *Summarize the main points* to remind the reader of what was discussed.
- *Emphasize important points* you don't want the reader to forget.
- *Refer to something in the introduction*, thus coming full circle.

Look forward. If the paper is short or doesn't need a summary, try the following:

- *Pose a question* for the reader to consider.

- *Offer advice.*
- *Call for action* the reader can take.
- *Consider future implications* of your topic.

Checking Your HOCs

Find writing strategies that are effective for you, such as the following:

Read your paper aloud to someone. Try reading your paper to a writing center tutor, instructor, friend, or even yourself. You'll see *and hear* problems that won't be as evident when you read silently.

Put the draft away for a while. Give yourself some time between drafting and revising. To revise effectively, you need to have some distance from the paper so that you can more easily recognize your readers' concerns.

Step into your readers' shoes. Think about what your readers would want to know, what they might object to in your arguments, what counterarguments they might make, and what questions they might have.

Review your topic sentences. On your computer, copy the topic sentences from each paragraph and put them in an outline. Check your organization by cutting and pasting your sentences to see if there are other arrangements that are more effective.

1b Arguments

Reading and writing persuasive arguments are parts of your everyday life. People actively persuade you to believe, act on, or accept their claims, just as you want others to accept or act on your claims. You might create arguments to justify your beliefs, solve problems, or evaluate products or works of art. Position papers, reviews of films and books, and literary analyses are all forms of argument.

Argumentation involves researching to find support for your claims as well as reasoning to explain and defend actions, beliefs, and ideas. To write a convincing persuasive paper, think about finding information that will prove that your view should be accepted. Also, think about how to present yourself as a knowledgeable or experienced person who deserves to be listened to.

CHECKLIST

Composing Persuasive Arguments

The following suggestions will help you plan your argument, establish yourself as someone who is credible and worth reading, and persuade your audience:

Show that your motives are reasonable and worthwhile.   Give your audience some reasonable assurance that you are arguing for a claim that is recognized as being for the general good or that shares the audience's motives.

Find common ground with your audience.   Consider the values, beliefs, interests, motives, or goals you share with your readers. Think about what you have in common with them. Rather than starting an argument by thinking about how you differ from your readers, try focusing on the goals or interests you share.

Incorporate various types of appeals.   Logical appeals are grounded in reason, data, and evidence. Emotional appeals arouse the audience's emotions: sympathy, patriotism, pride, anger, and other feelings based on values, beliefs, and motives. Ethical appeals act on the audience's impressions, opinions, and judgments about the person making the argument.

Use an appropriate tone.   Employing a serious tone when writing about serious issues can help your readers recognize your professionalism and trust your judgment. By contrast, writing in a mocking or lighthearted tone about serious issues might keep readers from considering your viewpoints.

Avoid vague and ambiguous terms and exaggerated claims.   Words such as *always, never, best,* or *worst* usually invite someone in your audience to find an exception. Vague arguments such as "everyone says" or exaggerations such as "no one cares about the farmers' problems anymore" are inflated opinions that weaken the writer's credibility.

Acknowledge that you have thought about opposing arguments by including them.   Readers who don't agree with you want to know that you aren't ignoring their views.

Rely upon knowledgeable, credible people as sources for your evidence.   Introduce your sources by indicating who they are and why they should be trusted.

Cite your source material. Documenting your sources in the proper documentation format for your assignment will help show your credibility. See Chapters 42–45 for information about documentation formats.

1c Writing about literature

When we write about various types of literature, such as stories, poems, and plays, we do so to enjoy the work, to think about it more closely, and to learn more about the world as seen through the eyes of the writer.

To analyze a text, begin by reading the work closely and considering its meaning. How can the work be interpreted? Think about its language, images, rhythms, use of dialogue, or symbolism.

TRY THIS

To Analyze and Write About Literature

Consider analyzing a work of literature in one of the following ways:

- **Analyze the theme.** What are some of the conflicts? Does the writer offer a lesson to be learned or a way of looking at life or the world?
- **Analyze characters.** Consider their behavior, how they are described, what they say, and how all this fits into the plot or theme of the work or its setting. Does your interpretation tell you anything more about the characters or the theme or the culture or time period in which the work is set? Do the characters change or stay the same?
- **Analyze the structure of the work.** Is it chronological? Does it skip around? Are you given clues by the writer as to what will happen?
- **Analyze the narrator.** Who is telling the story, someone outside the events or one of the characters? Does the narrator tell the reader the characters' thoughts? Does the narrator speak in the first person, using *I*? What is the narrator's tone or attitude?
- **Look at type or genre of the work.** Is it a tragedy, comedy, sonnet, mystery, or science fiction? How does it compare to others of its type? Does it blend several types of literature? Does it use elements common to this type of work?

- **Analyze the historical or cultural background.** How does the work reflect values and beliefs of the time and place in which it is set or in which it was written? What are some of the social or political forces that were at work at the time or that affected the author?

- **Analyze the work in terms of gender.** How does the work portray women or men? How does it define their roles in the family? In society? In the workplace?

- **Focus on the reactions of the audience to the work.** Why do readers respond as they do to this work? What would influence their reactions?

- **Research the life of the author.** What about the author's life is reflected in this particular work?

- **Resist the obvious meaning of the work.** Read skeptically, look for internal inconsistencies, and focus on ambiguities in the work. How would you interpret the work?

HINT

Avoiding Pitfalls in Writing About Literature

Students often make two kinds of errors in writing about literature.

- **Writing a plot summary instead of writing an analysis or doing research.** Unless you are specifically asked to write a plot summary, summarize only when you need to support a point.

- **Leaving out needed information.** Show your readers that you have read and understood the work. Demonstrate to your instructor that you have learned what has been taught in the course.

1d Portfolios

A portfolio is a collection of a writer's work. There are two key types of portfolios:

- **Process portfolio.** This portfolio type includes a series of rough drafts and final papers that are arranged chronologically to illustrate the growth of a writer's skills.

- **Presentation portfolio.** Presentation portfolios showcase a writer's best work. Writers may be asked to submit these portfolios for course or program evaluation. Sometimes job applicants also compile presentation portfolios that include an introductory statement, a résumé, and samples of their best work.

CHECKLIST

Revising Documents

When putting together your portfolio, you have a chance to revise your work and improve upon previous drafts. Consider the following questions as you review each paper:

- Does the overall message of your paper need to be expanded or narrowed?
- How can your thesis statement be stated more clearly and specifically?
- How can you make your introductory paragraph(s) more appealing?
- How can you improve on the logical connections in your argument?
- Would additional research help support your claims? If so, what kinds of evidence would help to back your thesis more effectively?
- Would reorganization make your argument more persuasive?
- Can you adjust your tone to appeal to your audience more effectively?
- Which word choices might communicate your message better?

1e LOCs (Later-Order Concerns)

When you edit and proofread, you attend to what are called the later-order concerns (LOCs)—details of grammar, usage, punctuation, spelling, missing words, format requirements, and other mechanics. These are "later-order" concerns in the sense that many writers wait until their paper is close to being finished before spending time on editing and proofreading. Some writers, though, prefer to edit and proofread as they write.

TRY THIS

To Edit and Proofread for Later-Order Concerns (LOCs)

- **Use online tools.** Use them as a guide, and check each adjustment you make carefully. Online spell-checkers and grammar-checkers catch some but not all spelling and grammar problems and can only offer suggestions. For example, spell-checkers cannot catch mistakes such as writing "your" for "you're" or when "there" instead of "their" is the appropriate word.

- **Edit on a hard copy.** It may be easier to print a draft and mark that for editing changes.

- **Put the paper aside for a bit.** It's easier to see problems when the paper is not as fresh in your mind.

- **Slide a card down each line as you reread.** This will help your eye slow down.

- **Keep in mind a list of the particular problems you tend to have when writing.** Which grammatical problems have teachers frequently marked on your papers? Here are some of the most common problems to look for in your papers:

Fragments	(see Chapter 12, p. 42)
Subject-verb agreement	(see Chapter 14a, p. 45)
Comma splices and run-on sentences	(see Chapter 13, p. 44)
Comma errors	(see Chapter 20, p. 75)
Verb tenses	(see Chapter 31a, p. 114)
Verb endings	(see Chapter 14b, p. 50)
Misplaced apostrophes	(see Chapter 21, p. 79)
Pronoun reference	(see Chapter 15, p. 52)
Omitted and repeated words	(see Chapter 35, p. 122)
Spelling errors	(see Chapter 29, p. 105)

2

Checklist for Oral and Multimedia Presentations

2a Oral presentations

Planning

Begin your planning as you would for writing a paper, thinking about your purpose, your audience, and your topic. Consider which strategies would be most effective in motivating your audience to agree with your opinions, act upon your suggestions, or become interested in your topic.

HINT

Preparing an Oral Presentation

Try these tips for planning your oral presentation.

Consider your mode of delivery. If you plan to read a paper or talk from an outline, print or type it out in a large font and double-space it so it will be easy for you to read.

Use visuals. Visuals can make your presentation more interesting. If you use a visual, make sure it is large enough for your audience to see. (See 2b on multimedia presentations.)

Plan your timing. To prepare for your talk, write out a couple of paragraphs. Then time yourself as you read them slowly and clearly. This should give you a fairly accurate estimate about how much material you can cover in your time limit. Also consider whether you need to leave time at the end for your audience's questions.

Practice your talk. Try delivering your oral presentation in front of a mirror or some friends. Pay attention to your expressions and eye contact.

Content

To help your audience see the organization of your talk, include an overview of what you will be speaking about and how it will be organized. This is easily done if you use hand-outs or visuals, but if that's not convenient, as you talk, indi-cate how each part of the presentation fits into the whole.

Be sure to emphasize your main point. If you present data, lists, or other information that the audience needs to understand or remember after your talk, don't be afraid to repeat your main ideas. Data and complex information can also be presented in a handout.

Delivery

As you deliver your presentation, try to engage your audience. Begin with a strong opening, perhaps using humor, a memorable quotation, a question, or an interest-ing anecdote. Maintain eye contact with your audience as much as possible. Rather than standing still behind a podium, move from one side of the room to the other so everyone can see you. Also, make natural gestures with your hands as you speak. If you prefer to read, look up occasionally and try to add remarks in addition to those written in the text of your talk.

2b Multimedia presentations

Multimedia software programs such as Microsoft PowerPoint have changed the ways writers deliver oral presentations. While they can enhance presentations, be aware that PowerPoint can limit the power of your mes-sage by oversimplifying complex ideas or reducing power-ful prose to bulleted items.

Organizing your presentation

A clear organizational structure can make the information you provide easy for your audience to follow.

1. *Title slide:* Provide the title of your presentation, your name, and your organization (if appropriate). An image can be added to increase your audience's interest in your topic.
2. *Introductory slide(s):* Grab the attention of your audience with questions, striking images, or an interesting quotation to lead into your main point.
3. *Thesis slide:* Use this slide to present your main point to your audience. Map out your supporting

Figure 2.1 Sample Slides

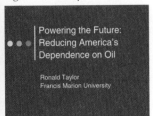

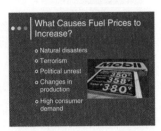

▲ **Title slide.** All of the slides in this presentation use consistent design elements. The dark green background is professional and complements the "green" message of the presentation.

▲ **Introductory slide.** With this introductory slide, the speaker can ask a question, pause, and invite responses from audience members, thereby investing them in the argument. The digital image provides evidence for the author's argument.

Photo source: © Exxon Mobil. Reprinted by permission.

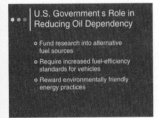

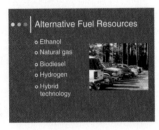

▲ **Thesis slide.** The thesis slide previews the supporting claims covered in the rest of the presentation. Note the parallel structure of the verb phrases in the bulleted items.

▲ **Body slide.** This body slide covers the first point listed in the thesis slide. Note how the digital photograph complements the topic of the slide.

claims or topics for discussion in short, bulleted statements.

4. *Body slides:* Prepare several slides to support claims listed on your thesis slide.
5. *Conclusion slide(s):* Complete your presentation by recapping your main points. Conclude with a strong written and visual statement that will make a lasting impression on your audience.
6. *Reference slide(s):* List all sources used in the presentation in the appropriate documentation style format.

CHECKLIST

Designing Multimedia Slides

Remember, *less is more* when designing multimedia slides.

Background. Choose backgrounds that complement the tone and content of your presentation. As a general rule, the simplest ones are the best.

Color. Use a dark-colored text on a light background or a light-colored text on a dark-colored background to make your presentation easy to read.

Font Type. Use fonts such as Times New Roman, Arial, Georgia, Tahoma, and Verdana that can be found on most computers. The fonts in your presentation rely on the font files stored on the computer where the slides were designed, so make sure your presentation computer has the fonts you used to create the presentation.

Font Size. Vary your font sizes. Titles should be somewhat larger (32–42-point font) than text on the body of the slide (20–32-point font). Words in fonts smaller than 20 point may be too difficult for your audience to read.

Graphics. Digital photographs can look professional, engage interest, and reinforce your points. Clip art, on the other hand, can look childish, so use it sparingly. If you use any visuals, be sure to cite your sources properly in your presentation.

Animations. Using one or two animation elements per presentation will help emphasize your key points and build interactions with your audience. Too many animations can be distracting to your audience.

Layout. Balance your use of text and images on each slide to emphasize main points. Words, descriptive phrases, or short sentences—known as *talking points*—should be set off in bullets so your audience members can easily follow your arguments.

Consistency. Don't switch background colors, font styles, or animation styles midway through your presentation. Set a tone with your opening slides, and stick with it throughout your presentation.

Presenting with multimedia

Use your slides as supplements to your speech. Instead of including the text of your speech on your slides and reading it word-for-word, list key talking points on the slides and follow them as you talk, using notes if necessary.

II

Sentence Choices

Contents of this section

3 **Clarity**   21
   3a   Positive instead of negative   21
   3b   Double negatives   21
   3c   Known/familiar information to new/unfamiliar
        information   22
   3d   Verbs instead of nouns   23
   3e   Intended subject as sentence subject   23

4 **Variety**   24

5 **Active/Passive Verbs**   25

6 **Parallelism**   26

7 **Predication**   27

8 **Transitions**   29

Question and Correct

	SECTION	PAGE
+ Why shouldn't I use negatives such as "no" and "not" in my writing?	3a	21
+ Why is "don't have no money" wrong?	3b	21
+ What is the best order for putting information in a sentence?	3c	22
+ Should I write "the consideration of" or "they consider"? Would "the completion of" or "they complete" be a better choice? Why?	3d	23
+ I sometimes start sentences with "It is" or "There is the issue that . . . ." How can I write sentences like this more effectively?	3e	23
+ How can I combine choppy sentences to make them smoother?	4	24

	SECTION	PAGE
✦ How can I add more variety to my sentences?	4	24
✦ What is active voice? What is passive voice?	5	25
✦ When should I use active verbs?	5	25
✦ When is it appropriate to use passive verbs?	5	25
✦ What is parallel structure?	6	26
✦ What's wrong with combining two phrases that have different verbs, such as "<u>to end</u> the book" and "<u>finishing</u> the novel"?	6	26
✦ When I connect two items with "both . . . and" or "either . . . or," what should I check to be sure I'm phrasing them the same way?	6	27
✦ What is faulty predication, and how can I avoid it?	7	28
✦ Why can phrases such as "is because" and "is where" cause confusion in my writing?	7	29
✦ What are transitions, and why do I need them in my writing?	8	29
✦ What are some ways to connect my sentences and paragraphs so that the paper flows?	8	29
✦ What are some of the connectors (like "however" and "furthermore") I can use?	8	29
✦ What kinds of words can I use to show a contrast or difference between two ideas?	8	29
✦ Can I start sentences with "But" and "And"?	8	30

3

Clarity

3a Positive instead of negative

Use positive statements because negative statements are harder for people to understand.

Unclear Negative: Less attention is paid to commercials that lack human interest stories.

Revised: People pay more attention to commercials that tell human interest stories.

Negative statements can also make the writer seem more evasive or unsure.

Evasive Negative: Senator Jamison does not disagree with the governor's entire proposal.

Revised: Senator Jamison agrees with the governor's proposed education funds but would like to see more tax cuts in his budget plan.

3b Double negative

Use only one negative at a time in your sentences. Using more than one negative word creates a double negative, which is grammatically incorrect and may be difficult to understand.

Double Negative: He did <u>not</u> have <u>no</u> money.

Revised: He had no money. (*or*) He did not have any money.

Double Negative: I <u>don't</u> think he did<u>n't</u> have money left after he paid for his dinner.

(This sentence is particularly hard to understand because it uses both a double negative and negatives instead of positives.)

TRY THIS

To Avoid Double Negatives

Watch out for contractions with negatives in them, like
doesn't, hasn't, and *couldn't.* If you use contractions, don't
use any other negatives in your sentence. Also, watch out
for negative words such as the following:

hardly	no one	nobody	nothing	scarcely
neither	no place	none	nowhere	

Sara hardly had ~~no~~ *any* popcorn left.

3c Known/familiar information to new/
unfamiliar information

Begin your sentences or paragraphs with something that
is generally known or familiar before you introduce new or
unfamiliar material.

Familiar ⟶ **Unfamiliar**

Familiar to unfamiliar:

Every semester, after final exams are over, I'm faced with the problem
of what to do with <u>lecture notes</u>. <u>They</u> might be useful someday,
         (OLD)   (OLD)

but <u>they</u> just keep cluttering <u>my computer's hard drive</u>. Someday,
(OLD)   (NEW)

<u>the computer</u> will crash with all the information I might never need.
(NEW)

> *These sentences should be clear as the discussion moves*
> *from old to new information.*

The next example is not as clear.

Unfamiliar to familiar:

<u>Second-rate entertainment</u> is my description of most <u>movies</u> I've
(NEW)   (OLD)

seen lately, but occasionally, there are some with <u>worthwhile themes</u>.
(NEW)

In the Southwest, the mysterious <u>disappearance</u> of an Indian culture
(NEW)

is the <u>topic</u> of a recent movie I saw that I would say has <u>a worthwhile</u>
(OLD)   (OLD)

<u>theme</u>.
(OLD)

> *These sentences are harder to follow because the familiar information comes after the new information.*

3d   Verbs instead of nouns

Actions expressed as verbs are more easily understood and more concisely stated than actions named as nouns.

TRY THIS

To Use Verbs Instead of Nouns

Try rereading your sentences to see which nouns could be changed to verbs.

Unnecessary Noun Form: <u>The decision was</u> to adjourn.

Revised: <u>They decided</u> to adjourn.

Some Noun Forms	**Verbs to Use Instead**
The negotiation of . . .	They negotiate . . .
The approval of . . .	They approve . . .
The preparation of . . .	They prepare . . .
The analysis of . . .	They analyze . . . .

3e   Intended subject as sentence subject

Be sure that the real subject (or the doer of the action in the verb) is the grammatical subject of the sentence. Sometimes the real subject of a sentence can get buried in prepositional phrases or other less noticeable places.

Subject buried in a prepositional phrase

For real music lovers, <u>it</u> is preferable to hear a live concert instead of an MP3.

> *(The grammatical subject here is* it, *which is not the real subject of this sentence.)*

Who prefers to hear a live concert? Music lovers, so "music lovers" is the real subject of this sentence.

Revised: <u>Music lovers</u> prefer to hear a live concert instead of an MP3.

Real subject buried in the sentence

It seems like playing games online is something Jonas spends too much time doing.

> (*If the real subject,* Jonas, *becomes the sentence subject, the entire sentence becomes clearer and more concise.*)

Revised: <u>Jonas</u> seems to spend too much time playing games online.

4

Variety

A series of short sentences or sentences with the same subject-verb order can be monotonous and sound choppy. Try these strategies for creating sentence variety.

- Combine two sentences (or independent clauses) into one longer sentence by using a comma and coordinating conjunction (see 73), or a semicolon (see 82).

  Comedians on *The Daily Show* mock politicians. ~~The~~ victims of the satire too often miss their point. *, but the*

- Combine the subjects of two independent clauses in one sentence when the verb applies to both clauses.

  Original: The Wabash River overflowed its banks. Wildcat Creek did the same.

  Revised: The Wabash River and Wildcat Creek overflowed their banks.

- Add a description, a definition, or other information about a noun after the noun.

  Professor Nguyen *,* is a political science teacher *,* ~~She~~ gives lectures in the community on current events.

- Turn a sentence into a *who, which,* or *what* clause.

  He was charged with breaking the city's newest law. ~~This law~~ states that motorcyclists must wear helmets. *, which*

- You can begin with dependent clauses that start with dependent markers such as the following words:

after	because	since	when
although	if	until	while

<u>After</u> the trial ended, the lawyers filed for an appeal.

<u>When</u> the stockholders met, they discussed the company's recent decline in profits.

5

Active/Passive Verbs

An active verb expresses the action completed by the subject. A passive verb expresses action done to the subject. Passive voice uses forms of "to be" (is, are, was, were) and sometimes by the use of "by."

Active: <u>Paulo</u> *wrote* the report.

(*The verb is* wrote, *and* <u>Paulo</u>, *the subject, did the writing.*)

Passive: The <u>report</u> *was written* by ***Paulo***.

(*The verb is* was written, *and the* <u>report</u>, *the subject, was acted upon.*)

Using active verbs often results in clearer, more direct, and more concise sentences than those with passive verbs. Active verbs clarify who is doing the action and add a strong sense of immediacy and liveliness to your writing.

Active: After the eye of the hurricane passed, <u>ambulance drivers</u> *rushed* injured patients to the hospital. (*more immediate and direct*)

Passive: After the eye of the hurricane passed, <u>patients</u> *were rushed* to the hospital by ***ambulance drivers***. (*wordy with weaker sense of action*)

However, there are occasions to use passive verbs:

- When the doer of the action is not important or is not known

  For the tournament game, more than five thousand tickets <u>were sold</u>.

- When you want to focus on the action or the receiver of the action, not the doer

  Lara <u>was chosen</u> to receive the scholarship.

- When you want to avoid blaming, giving credit, or taking responsibility

  The candidate conceded that the election <u>was lost</u>.

- When you want a tone of objectivity, particularly in science writing

  Ten grams of sugar <u>were added</u> to the solution.

6

Parallelism

Parallel structure involves using the same grammatical form or structure for equal ideas in a list or comparison. The balance of equal elements in a sentence helps your reader see the relationship between ideas. Often, the equal elements repeat words or sounds.

Parallel: The instructor carefully explained <u>how to start the engine</u>
(1)

and <u>how to shift gears.</u>
(2)

> (*Phrases 1 and 2 are parallel in that both start with* <u>how to</u>.)

Parallel: <u>Getting the model airplane off the ground</u> was even harder
(1)

than <u>building it from a kit</u>.
(2)

> (*Phrases 1 and 2 are parallel phrases that begin with -ing verb forms.*)

Parallelism is needed in the following constructions:

- Items in a series or list

Parallel: Our ideal job candidate will know how to

  - <u>manage</u> team projects
  - <u>troubleshoot</u> computer problems
  - <u>communicate</u> effectively with clients.

(parallelism with verbs)

- *Both . . . and, either . . . or, whether . . . or, neither . . . nor, not . . . but, not only . . . but also* (correlative conjunctions)

  Parallel: **Both** <u>his professional appearance</u> **and** <u>his knowledge of the company</u> suggested he wanted to make a good impression during his job interview.

(parallelism with noun phrases)

- *And, but, or, nor, yet, for, so* (coordinating conjunctions)

  Parallel: Job opportunities are <u>increasing</u> in the health fields **but** <u>decreasing</u> in many areas of engineering.

(parallelism using -ing verbs)

- Comparisons using *than* or *as*

  Parallel: The mayor noted that it was easier <u>to agree</u> to the new budget **than** <u>to veto</u> it.

(parallelism in a comparison with to + *verb)*

Nonparallelism (or faulty parallelism) is grammatically incorrect and can also lead to a lack of clarity.

When the investigator took over, he started his inquiry by <u>calling</u> the
(1)
requesting
witnesses back and ~~requested~~ that they repeat their stories.
(2)

The article looked at <u>future uses of computers</u> and ~~what their role~~
(1)   (2)

~~will be~~ in the next decade.

7

Predication

A logical sentence contains a subject and a predicate (the rest of the clause) that make sense together. Faulty predication occurs when the subject and the predicate are not logically connected.

Faulty Predicate: The <u>reason</u> for her rapid promotion to vice-president <u>proved</u> that she was talented.

(In this sentence, the subject, reason, *cannot logically prove "that she was talented.")*

Revised: Her rapid promotion to vice-president proved that she was talented.

Faulty predication often occurs with forms of the verb *to be* because this verb sets up an equation in which the terms on either side of the verb should be equal.

Subject		Predicate
2 x 2	is	4
Dr. Streeter	is	our family doctor.

Faulty Predication: Success is when you have your own swimming pool.

(The concept of success involves much more than having a swimming pool. Having a pool can be one example or a result of success, but it is not the equivalent of success.)

Revised: One sign of success is having your own swimming pool.

HINT

Avoiding Faulty Predication

Faulty predication often occurs in sentences that contain the following constructions:

is when . . . is why . . . is where . . . is because . . .

It is best to avoid these constructions in academic writing.

The reason I didn't show up is ~~because~~ ^{that} I overslept.

8

Transitions

Transitions are words and phrases that build bridges between sentences, parts of sentences, and paragraphs. These bridges build relationships and help smoothly connect sentences together.

There are several types of transitions you can use:

- Repetition of a key term or phrase

  Among the recent food fads sweeping America is the interest in **exotic foods**. While not everyone can agree on what **exotic foods** are, most of us like the idea of trying something new and different.

- Synonyms

  One food Americans are not inclined to try is **brains**. A Gallup poll found that 41 percent of the people who responded said they would never try **brains**. Three years later, the percentage of those who wouldn't touch animals' **gray matter** had risen to 49 percent.

- Pronouns

  In addition to brains, there are many other foods that some **Americans** now find more distasteful than **they** did several years
  (1)   (1)

  ago. For example, more people now say they would never eat **liver, rabbit, pigs' feet, or beef kidneys** than said so three
  (2)

  years ago. Even restaurant workers who are exposed to **these delicacies** aren't always wild about **them.**
  (2)   (2)

- Transitional words and phrases

  The state government is determined not to raise property taxes this year. <u>Whereas</u> some legislators advocated for an increase in the cigarette tax, the majority voted for a reduction in funding for educational programs. <u>As a result</u>, teachers, parents, and students protested in the state capital yesterday.

TRANSITIONS

Adding	and, besides, in addition, also, too, moreover, furthermore, next, first, second, third, likewise
Comparing	similarly, likewise, in like manner, at the same time, in the same way
Contrasting	but, yet, however, still, nevertheless, on the other hand, on the contrary, instead, rather, notwithstanding, though, whereas, although
Emphasizing	indeed, in fact, above all, and also, even more, in any event, in other words, that is, obviously
Ending	after all, finally, in sum, for these reasons
Giving examples	for example, for instance, to illustrate, that is, namely, specifically
Pointing to cause and effect, proof, or conclusions	thus, therefore, consequently, because of this, hence, as a result, then, so, accordingly
Showing place or direction	over, above, inside, next to, underneath, to the left, just behind, beyond, in the distance
Showing time	meanwhile, soon, later, now, in the past, then, next, before, during, while, at last, since then, presently, at the same time, in the meantime
Summarizing	to sum up, in conclusion, finally, as has been said, in general, to conclude, in other words

III

Writing Style

Contents of this section

9 **Conciseness** 32
10 **Voice and Formality** 32
11 **Nonsexist Language** 35

Question and Correct

	SECTION	PAGE
+ What does it mean to write concisely?	9	32
+ What are some ways to eliminate wordiness in my writing?	9	32
+ Sometimes I start sentences with "There is . . ." or "There are . . . ." How can I write sentences like these more smoothly?	9	32
+ What are fillers, and why should I avoid them?	9	32
+ When should writing be formal?	10	33
+ What's the difference between semiformal and informal tone?	10	33–34
+ Is it OK to use slang in my papers?	10	34
+ What is jargon, and when should I use it?	10	34
+ What is a euphemism?	10	35
+ What is sexist language?	11	35
+ What's wrong with using words like "policeman" and "mailman"?	11	35–36
+ Is it OK to write "<u>everyone</u> checked <u>his</u> cell phone"?	11	36
+ How can I make gender-neutral language less wordy?	11	36

9

Conciseness

To write concisely, omit

- what your readers do not need to know or already know
- whatever doesn't further the purpose of your paper

By writing concisely and eliminating wordiness, you will communicate to your readers more clearly and are more likely to keep your readers' interest. This often means resisting the impulse to include everything you know about a subject or to add words that sound more formal or academic.

Strategies to eliminate unnecessary words include the following:

- **Avoid repetition.** Some phrases, such as the following, say the same thing twice:

first beginning	6 p.m. in the evening
circular in shape	true facts
green in color	prove conclusively
positive benefits	each and every

- **Avoid fillers.** Some phrases, such as the following, say little or nothing:

there is (or) are	I am going to discuss
in view of the fact that	I think that
what I want to say is	it is my feeling that

He said ~~that there is~~ *is* a storm approaching

Artificial
~~I am going to discuss~~ artificial intelligence, ~~which~~ is an exciting field of research.

- **Combine sentences.** When the same nouns or pronouns appear in two sentences, combine the two sentences into one.

The data will be entered into the reports, ~~It will also be~~ *and* included in the graphs.

- **Eliminate** *who*, *which*, and *that*.

  The book ~~that is~~ lying on the piano belongs to her.

- **Turn phrases and clauses into adjectives and adverbs.**

  all applicants who are interested = all interested applicants

  spoke in a hesitant manner = spoke hesitantly

  the piano built out of mahogany = the mahogany piano

- **Turn prepositional phrases into adjectives.**

  the entrance to the station = the station entrance

- **Use active rather than passive.**

  research department   *the figures*

  The ~~figures were~~ checked ~~by the research department~~.
  　　　^　　　　　　　　　　　　　　　　　^

- **Remove excess nouns and change them to verbs whenever possible.**

  He ~~made the statement that he~~ agreed ~~with the concept~~ that inflation could be controlled.

  stores

  The ~~function of the~~ box ~~is the storage of~~ wire connectors.
  　　　　　　　　　　　　　^

10

Voice and Formality

In writing, an appropriate voice is one that fits the level of formality in your paper and your subject.

Formal tone contains sophisticated phrasing not commonly used in conversation. Third-person pronouns *he* or *she* or *one* are often used instead of *I* or *you*. Formal tone may be expected in professional and legal documents and research writing. Jargon or language appropriate to the field and intended readers may also be used.

Formal: *Slumdog Millionaire* provides a skillful dissertation on globalization, utilizing a postmodern narrative style that effectively juxtaposes starkly impoverished Mumbai neighborhoods against impossible hope fueled by Western influence and greed.

Medium/semiformal tone uses standard sentence structures and vocabulary. Contractions are generally avoided. This tone is appropriate for most college writing assignments.

> **Medium/semiformal:** *Slumdog Millionaire* uses a series of narrative flashbacks to spotlight the differences between the poverty of Mumbai and the hope provided by a Western-influenced television show.

Informal tone uses language common in daily conversation, include slang, colloquialisms, and regionalisms. Contractions and first- and second-person pronouns such as *I* and *you* are appropriate for this tone.

> **Informal:** I thought *Slumdog Millionaire* was a cool movie. You should've checked it out.

Slang

Slang terms are made up (such as *peeps, diss, or snarky*) or are given new definitions (such as *sick* for very skillful or impressive). Over time, some slang may enter the general vocabulary and dictionaries of standard written English. However, slang is generally considered informal and not appropriate for academic work.

Jargon

Jargon is the specialized language of various trades, professions, and groups. Specialists within the group use these terms to communicate with each other in a concise way when referring to complex concepts, objects, and techniques.

When you are writing about a specialized subject for a general audience and need to use a technical term, define the term in easily understandable language the first time you use it. You can then use the word later on and not lose the reader.

The term "jargon," however, is also sometimes applied to *inflated expressions,* which sound pompous, and *euphemisms,* which are terms used to disguise unpleasant realities.

> **Specialized Language:** subcutaneous hemorrhage, metabolic disorders, exhaust manifold, beta decay, data integrity, cloture

Inflated Expressions: learning facilitator (teacher), monetary remuneration (pay)

Euphemisms: revenue enhancement (taxes), preowned (used), nonmilitary collateral damage (dead civilians)

Unnecessary jargon reflects the writer's inability to write clearly. Note the wordiness and pompous tone of this example:

Original: Utilize this receptacle, which functions as a repository for matter to be removed.

Revised: Deposit litter here.

11

Nonsexist Language

English previously used male pronouns and *man* as "universals" that were understood to include members of both sexes. The fairness of such usage has come into question, and it is wise to avoid offending readers by using language that seems to favor one sex over the other. To create gender-neutral language, try the following strategies:

- Use alternatives to *man*:

Sexist Term	Neutral Alternatives
man	person, individual
mankind	people, human beings, humanity
man-made	machine-made, synthetic, artificial
manpower	staff, workforce
to man	to staff, to run, to work at

- Use neutral alternatives for job titles:

Sexist Term	Neutral Alternatives
chairman	chairperson, chair, coordinator
policeman, patrolman	police officer
congressman	congressional representative, member of Congress
businessman	business professional

| saleswoman/salesman | salesperson, salesclerk, sales specialist |
| Dear Sir | Dear Editor, Dear Service Representative, Dear Sir or Madam |

Note that we don't indicate the marital status of men when using *Mr.*, so when addressing women professionally, it is best to use *Ms.*, which does not indicate whether the woman is married.

● Use the plural.

Sexist: A nurse is trained to understand <u>her</u> patients' emotions and physical symptoms.

Revised: Nurses are trained to understand <u>their</u> patients' emotions and physical symptoms.

● Eliminate the pronoun or reword to avoid using a pronoun.

Sexist: If a taxpayer has questions about the form, <u>he</u> can call a government representative.

Revised: A taxpayer who has questions about the form can call a government representative.

● Replace the pronoun with *one, he or she,* or an article (*a, an, the*).

Sexist: The parent who reads to <u>her</u> infant helps increase the infant's sound discrimination.

Revised: The parent who reads to <u>an</u> infant helps increase the infant's sound discrimination.

● Address the reader directly in the second person.

Sexist: Each applicant must mail <u>his</u> form by Thursday.

Revised: Mail your form by Thursday.

HINT

Using "Everyone . . . His or Her"

There are different views when using the indefinite pronouns *everybody, anybody, everyone,* and *anyone.* Some people continue to use the singular pronoun (*everyone . . . his or her*) and consider the plural *they* to be wrong. However, the use of the plural pronoun (*everyone . . . their*) has become acceptable in many informal contexts. In formal writing, it is still advisable to avoid using either gender-specific or plural pronouns with these words.

IV

Sentence Grammar

Contents of this section

12	**Fragments**	42
	12a Unintentional fragments	42
	12b Intentional fragments	43
13	**Comma Splices and Fused Sentences**	44
	13a Comma splices	44
	13b Fused or run-on sentences	45
14	**Subjects and Verbs**	45
	14a Subject-verb agreement	45
	• Buried subjects	47
	• Compound subjects	47
	• *Or* and *either/or* in subjects	47
	• Clauses and phrases as subjects	48
	• Indefinites as subjects	48
	• Collective nouns and amounts as subjects	48
	• Plural words as subjects	48
	• Titles, company names, words, and quotations as subjects	49
	• Linking verbs	49
	• *There is/are, here is/are*, and it	49
	• *Who, which, that*, and *one of* as subjects	50
	14b Verbs	52
15	**Pronouns**	52
	15a Pronoun case	52
	• Pronouns in compound constructions	52
	• *Who/whom*	54
	• Pronoun case after *than* or *as*	55
	• Pronoun case *we* or *us* before nouns	55
	• Pronoun case with *to* + verb (infinitive)	55
	• Pronoun antecedents	56
	15b Pronoun reference	56
	• Pronoun number	57
	• Compound subjects	58

	• *Who/which/that*	58
	• Indefinite words	58
	• Indefinite pronouns	59
16	**Adjectives and Adverbs**	59
16a	Adjectives and adverbs	59
16b	Comparisons	61
17	**Modifiers**	62
17a	Dangling modifiers	62
17b	Misplaced modifiers	64
17c	Split infinitives	65
18	**Shifts**	65
18a	Shifts in person or number	65
18b	Shifts in verb tense	66
18c	Shifts in tone	67

Question and Correct

	SECTION	PAGE
✦ What is a sentence fragment, and how do I recognize one?	12	42
✦ Is "When I showed up for work" a sentence or a fragment?	12a	42
✦ Is "For example, the time she went to Mexico" a fragment?	12a	43
✦ How can I proofread for fragments in my writing?	12a	43
✦ When would I use a fragment on purpose?	12b	44
✦ How are comma splices, run-on sentences, and fused sentences different?	13	44
✦ How do I correct a comma splice?	13a	45
✦ Is a sentence like "I decided to take the job I start next month" a run-on?	13b	45
✦ What is subject-verb agreement?	14a	46
✦ Is it correct to write "The news are good"?	14a	47

	SECTION	PAGE
+ Is it correct to write "*All* of the students in my chemistry class *is* meeting for a study session tonight"?	14a	47
+ When I have two subject terms such as "Maya" and "her sisters," is the verb *have* or *has*?	14a	47
+ When I use *either/or* or *neither/nor*, should I use a singular or a plural verb? ("Either Francisco or his brothers is/are coming to the party.")	14a	47
+ When starting a sentence with *To work quickly* as the subject, would I use a singular or a plural verb?	14a	47
+ Do words like *each* or *some* go with singular or plural verbs?	14a	48
+ Do I use singular or plural verbs with collective nouns such as *team* and *family*? ("The team is/are winning.")	14a	48
+ Do I use singular or plural verbs with plural subjects such as *mathematics* and *eyeglasses*?	14a	48
+ Would a movie title like *Angels and Demons* go with a singular or plural verb?	14a	49
+ Are singular or plural verbs used with linking verbs? ("Their concern *is/are* polluted rivers.")	14a	49
+ Is it correct to write "There is good solutions to this problem"?	14a	49
+ Do I use singular or plural verbs with phrases and clauses that start with *who* or *which* in the middle of sentences (such as "She is a writer who like/likes to finish projects quickly."	14a	49
+ What are regular verb endings?	14b	50
+ What are irregular verb forms?	14b	50
+ What is the past tense of irregular verbs such as *swim*, *begin*, and *take*?	14b	50
+ Is it correct to write "He lies his pillow on his bed"?	14b	51

	SECTION	PAGE
+ What is the difference between active and passive voice?	14b	50
+ What does "verb mood" mean?	14b	52
+ Should I use an apostrophe with pronouns such as *his* or *hers*?	15a	52
+ Which is correct? "The bakers and *myself/I* went shopping for supplies."	15a	52
+ Should I write *between you and I* or *between you and me*?	15a	54
+ Should I write "*who* will win the election?" or "*whom* will win the election?"	15a	55
+ Would it be better to write *smarter than me* or *smarter than I*?	15a	55
+ Which is correct? "*We/Us* students filed a complaint."	15a	55
+ Should I write "Jenalee planned *to teach/teaching* me the violin"?	15a	56
+ Is it correct to say "The company submitted *their* report to the bank"?	15a	56
+ What is "vague pronoun reference," and how can I avoid it?	15b	56
+ Would it be appropriate to write "The family finished *its* dinner"?	15b	57
+ Which is correct? "The house and the neighborhood were nice, but *it was/they were* not what I expected."	15b	58
+ Should I write "The people *that* just left liked the play?"	15b	58
+ Which is correct? "Each of the girls hung up *her coat/their coats*."	15b	58
+ Is there a problem with writing "Everyone finished their paper"?	15b	59
+ What is the difference between adjectives and adverbs?	16a	59
+ When do I use *good*, and when do I use *well*?	16a	59
+ Which is correct? "Cara is the *taller/tallest* of the eight children"?	16b	61

	SECTION	PAGE
✦ How should I correct the following sentence? "Before watching the game, snacks were served."	17a	62
✦ When I use modifying words like *only*, *nearly*, and *just*, where should I place them in the sentence?	17b	64
✦ Is it incorrect to write "Priya will try to *quickly* finish her project"?	17c	65
✦ How should I correct the following sentence? "For most *people*, the career *we* decide on isn't always the major *they* had in college."	18a	65
✦ Is it OK to shift verb tenses in a sentence?	18b	66
✦ Why is it important to use a consistent tone in my writing?	18c	67

12

Fragments

A sentence fragment is an incomplete sentence.

To recognize a fragment, consider the basic requirements of a sentence:

● A sentence is a group of words with at least one independent clause.

● An independent clause has at least one subject and a complete verb, plus an object or complement if needed. An independent clause can stand alone as a thought, even though other sentences may be needed to clarify the thought or idea.

Independent clause: She saw the movie last night.

(We don't know who she is, but a pronoun can be a subject. And we don't know what movie she saw, but those bits of additional information can appear in accompanying sentences.)

Not an independent clause: Whenever I get too hot.

(Say that sentence out loud, and you will hear that it's not a complete sentence because we don't know what happens as a result of the when clause.)

12a Unintentional fragments

1. A fragment can occur when a subject or a verb is missing from the sentence.

   Fragment: The week I spent on the beach just relaxing with a good book and soaking up the bright sun every day we were there.

   (Week is probably the intended subject here, but it has no verb.)

2. A fragment can be caused by misplaced periods. This happens when a dependent phrase or dependent clause got detached from the sentence to which it belongs. Some writers do this when they worry about the sentence being too long. Such fragments can be corrected by removing the period between the independent clause and the fragment.

Fragment: She selected a current news item as the topic of her essay. <u>Then wondered if her choice was wise.</u>
(fragment)

(The second of these two word groups is a fragment with no subject for the verb wondered. *It is a phrase that got disconnected from the independent clause that came before it.)*

<u>Because he scored six three-point baskets during the game.</u>
(fragment)

Everyone applauded when he sat down on the bench before half-time.

(The word group Because he scored six three-point baskets during the game *is a dependent clause that was detached from the independent clause following it.)*

HINT

Finding Fragments

1. Read your paper backward, from the last sentence to the first. You will be able to notice a fragment more easily when you hear it without the sentence to which it belongs.
2. To find dependent clauses separated from the main clause, look at the marker word, such as *after, although, because, before, during, if, since, unless, when,* or *while.* If the clause is standing alone, attach it to the independent clause that completes the meaning.

If A happens ———▶ ?

12b Intentional fragments

Writers occasionally write an intentional fragment for its effect on the reader. However, intended fragments should be used only when the writing clearly indicates that the writer could have written a whole sentence but preferred a fragment.

Fragment: Dilek walked quietly into the room, unnoticed by the rest of the group. *Not that she wanted it that way.* She simply didn't know how to make an effective entrance.

13

Comma Splices and Fused Sentences

A comma splice and a fused sentence (also called a run-on sentence) are punctuation problems in compound sentences. (A compound sentence is one that contains two or more independent clauses.) There are three patterns for commas and semicolons in compound sentences:

1. Independent clause‿ and independent clause.
   > but
   > for
   > nor
   > or
   > so
   > yet

   No one has registered for that class yet‿**but** the deadline is approaching.

2. Independent clause‿ independent clause.

   Jamielle majored in American history‿**he** is now a high school history teacher.

3. Independent clause‿ however‿ independent clause.
   > therefore,
   > moreover,
   > consequently,
   > (etc.)

   Rami did agree to lend his computer to his roommate Matt‿**however**‿he clearly asked Matt to return it in an hour or two.

13a   Comma splices

The comma splice is a punctuation error that can occur in one of two ways:

- When independent clauses are joined only by a comma and no coordinating conjunction.

- When a comma is used instead of a semicolon between two independent clauses.

Comma Splice: In Econ 150, students meet in small groups for

and

an extra hour each week, this helps them learn from each other.

^

Comma Splice: The doctor prescribed a different medication,
however, it's not helping.

;

13b Fused or run-on sentences

The fused or run-on sentence is a punctuation error that
occurs when there is no punctuation between independent
clauses. This causes the two clauses to be "fused" or "run
on" into each other.

Fused or Run-on Sentence: I didn't know which job I

, and (or) ;

wanted I couldn't decide.

^

TRY THIS

To Fix Comma Splices, Fused Sentences, and Run-ons

- Between the two independent clauses, add a comma
  and then one of the seven joining words (*and, but, for,
  nor, or, so, yet*).
- Separate the independent clauses into two sentences.
- Change the comma to a semicolon.
- Make one clause dependent on the other clause.

14

Subjects and Verbs

14a Subject-verb agreement

Subject-verb agreement occurs when the subject and verb
(or helping verb) endings agree in number and person. The
subject of every sentence is either singular or plural, and

that determines the ending of the verb (or helping verb). Verb with singular subjects take singular endings, and verbs with plural subjects have plural endings.

Marco   doesn't   go there anymore.

(singular subject)   (singular verb)

doesn't
Marco ~~don't~~ go there anymore.

Singular nouns, pronouns, and nouns that cannot be counted, such as *news, time*, and *happiness* (see Chapter 32), take verbs with singular endings.

I chew.   Water drips.   Time flies.   You laugh.

Plural

Plural nouns and pronouns take verbs with plural endings.

We know.   The cups are clean.   They stretch.

TRY THIS

To Find the Subject and Verb

1. It's easier to find the verb first because the verb is the word or words that change when you change the time of the sentence, from present to past or past to present.

   Jaime <u>walks</u> to class.
   (verb—present tense)

   Yesterday, Jaime <u>walked</u> to class.
   (verb—past tense)

   Tomorrow, Jaime <u>will walk</u> to class.
   (verb—future tense)

2. Eliminate phrases starting with the following words because they are normally not part of the subject:

including	along with	together with
accompanied by	in addition to	as well as
except	with	no less than

   <u>Everyone</u> in our family, including my sister, <u>has taken</u>
   (subject)   (verb)

   piano lessons.

Buried subjects

It is sometimes difficult to find the subject word when it is buried among many other words. In that case, disregard prepositional phrases; modifiers; *who, which,* and *that* clauses; and other surrounding words.

> Almost <u>all</u> of Metha's many friends who are invited to her party
> (subject)
>
> <u>are bringing</u> gifts.
> (verb)
>
> (*In this sentence,* Almost *is a modifier,* of Metha's many friends *is a prepositional phrase, and* who are invited to her party *is a* who *clause that describes* friends.)

Compound subjects

Subjects joined by *and* take a plural verb (X *and* Y = more than one, plural).

> The dog and the squirrel <u>are</u> running around the tree.

Sometimes, though, the words joined by *and* act together as a unit and are thought of as one thing. If so, use a singular verb.

> Peanut butter and jelly <u>is</u> a popular filling for sandwiches.

Or and *either/or* in subjects

When the subject words are joined by *or, either . . . or, nei-ther . . . nor,* or *not only . . . but also,* the verb agrees with the subject word closer to it.

> Either Aleeza or her children <u>are</u> going to bed early.

> Not only the clouds but also the snow <u>was</u> gray that day.

Clauses and phrases as subjects

When a whole clause or phrase is the subject, use a singular verb.

> What I want to know <u>is</u> why I can't try the test again.

> Saving money <u>is</u> difficult to do.

> To live happily <u>seems</u> like a worthwhile goal.

However, if the verb is a form of *be* and the noun afterward (the complement) is plural, the verb has to be plural.

> What we saw <u>were</u> pictures of the experiment. [What we saw = pictures]

Indefinites as subjects

Indefinite words with singular meanings, such as *each, every*, and *any*, take a singular verb when they are the subject word or when they precede the subject word.

Each has her own preference.

Each book is checked in by the librarian.

However, when indefinite words such as *none, some, most*, or *all* are the subject, the number of the verb depends on the meaning of the subject.

Some of the book is difficult to follow.

(*The subject of the sentence is a portion of the book and is thought of as a single unit and has a singular verb.*)

Some of us are leaving now.

(*The subject of this sentence is several people and is thought of as a plural subject with a plural verb.*)

Collective nouns and amounts as subjects

Collective nouns are nouns that refer to a group or a collection (such as *team, family, committee*, and *group*). When a collective noun is the subject and refers to the group acting as a whole or as a single unit, the verb is singular.

Our family has a new car.

In most cases, a collective noun refers to the group acting together as a unit, but occasionally the collective noun refers to members acting individually. In that case, the verb is plural.

The committee are unhappy with each other's decisions.

When the subject names an amount, the verb is singular.

More than 125 miles is too far.   Six dollars is the price.

Plural words as subjects

Some words that have an *-s* ending, such as *civics, mathematics, measles*, and *news*, are thought of as a single unit and take a singular verb.

Physics is fascinating.   Modern economics shows contradictions.

Some words, such as those in the following list, are treated as plural and take a plural verb, even though they refer to one thing. (In many cases, there are two parts to these things.)

jeans are . . .   eyeglasses are . . .   thanks were . . .

riches are . . .   pants were . . .   shears are . . .

clippers have . . .   scissors cut . . .

Titles, company names, words, and quotations as subjects

For titles of written works, names of companies, words used as terms, and quotations, use singular verbs.

All the King's Men is a great book.

General Foods is hiring.

Thanks is not in his vocabulary.

"Cookies for everyone!" is what she said.

Linking verbs

Linking verbs agree with the subject rather than the word that follows (the complement).

Her problem is frequent injuries.

Short stories are my favorite reading matter.

There is/are, Here is/are, and *It*

When a sentence begins with *there* or *here*, the verb depends on the complement that follows the verb.

There is an excellent old movie on TV tonight.

Here are my friends.

However, *it* as the subject always takes the singular verb, regardless of what follows.

It was bears in the park that knocked over the garbage cans.

Who, which, that, and *one of* as subjects

When *who, which,* and *that* are used as subjects, the verb agrees with the previous word it refers to (the antecedent).

They are the students who study hard.

He is the student who studies the hardest.

In the phrase *one of those who* (or *which* or *that*), it is necessary to decide whether the *who, which,* or *that* refers only to the one or to the whole group. Only then can you decide whether the verb is singular or plural.

Chang is **one of** those shoppers **who** buy only things that are on sale.

(*In this case, Chang is part of a large group,* shoppers *who buy only things that are on sale, and acts like others in that group. Therefore,* who *takes a plural verb because it refers to* shoppers.)

The *American Dictionary* is **one of** the dictionaries on the shelf **that** <u>includes</u> Latin words.

(*In this case, the* American Dictionary, *while part of the group of dictionaries on the shelf, is specifically one that includes Latin words. The other dictionaries may or may not. Therefore,* that *refers to that* one *dictionary and takes a singular verb.*)

14b Verbs

Verbs that add *-ed* for the past tense and the past participle are regular verbs. The past participle is the form that has a helping verb such as "has" or "had."

For a guide to using verb tenses, see 31a.

Regular Verb Forms			
	Present	Past	Future
Simple	I walk.	I walked.	I will walk.
Progressive	I am walking.	I was walking.	I will be walking.
Perfect	I have walked.	I had walked.	I will have walked.
Perfect progressive	I have been walking.	I had been walking.	I will have been walking.

Some brief samples of irregular verb forms are shown in the following tables. Consult a dictionary for more verbs.

Irregular Verb Forms				
	Present		Past	
Verb	Singular	Plural	Singular	Plural
be	I am	we are	I was	we were
	you are	you are	you were	you were
	he, she, it is	they are	he, she, it was	they were
have	I have	we have	I had	we had
	you have	you have	you had	you had
	he, she, it has	they have	he, she, it had	they had
do	I do	we do	I did	we did
	you do	you do	you did	you did
	he, she, it does	they do	he, she, it did	they did

Some Irregular Verbs		
Base (Present)	Past	Past Participle
be (am, is, are)	was, were	been
become	became	become
begin	began	begun
bring	brought	brought
come	came	come
do	did	done
eat	ate	eaten
find	found	found
forget	forgot	forgotten
get	got	gotten
give	gave	given
go	went	gone
grow	grew	grown
have	had	had
know	knew	known
lay	laid	laid
lie	lay	lain
make	made	made
mean	meant	meant
read	read	read
say	said	said
see	saw	seen
sit	sat	sat
speak	spoke	spoken
stand	stood	stood
take	took	taken
teach	taught	taught
think	thought	thought
write	wrote	written

Lie/lay and sit/set

Two sets of verbs, *lie/lay* and *sit/set,* can cause problems. Because they are related in meaning and sound, they are often confused with each other, but each one of each set has a different meaning.

Lie (recline)   She lies in bed all day. (present)
She lay in bed all last week. (past)

Lay (put)   He lays his keys on the table. (present)
He laid his keys on the table. (past)

Sit (be seated)   Please sit here by the window. (present)
She sat by the window in class. (past)

Set (put)	Please <u>set</u> the flowers on the table. (present)
	He <u>set</u> the flowers on the desk before he left. (past)

Verb voice

Verb voice tells whether the verb is in the active or passive voice. In the active voice, the subject performs the action on the verb. In the passive voice, the subject receives the action. The doer of the action in the passive voice may be omitted or may appear in a "by the" phrase.

Active: The child sang the song.

Passive: The song was sung by the child.

Verb mood

The mood of a verb tells whether it expresses a fact, opinion, or question (indicative mood); expresses a command, request, or advice (imperative mood); or expresses a doubt, a wish, a recommendation, or something contrary to fact (subjunctive mood). In the subjunctive mood, present tense verbs stay in the simple base form and do not indicate the number and person of the subject. However, for the verb *be*, <u>were</u> is used for all persons and numbers.

Indicative: The new software <u>runs</u> well on this computer

Imperative: <u>Watch</u> for the rain to end.

Subjunctive: The doctor recommends that Amit <u>stop</u> smoking.
I wish I <u>were</u> rich.

15

Pronouns

15a Pronoun case

A pronoun is a word that substitutes for a noun. Pronouns change case according to their use in a sentence.

Subject case:	<u>She</u> told a story.
Object case:	Rosario told <u>them</u> a story.
Possessive case:	The children liked <u>her</u> story.

Pronoun Cases						
	Subject		**Object**		**Possessive**	
	Singular	Plural	Singular	Plural	Singular	Plural
First person	I	we	me	us	my, mine	our, ours
Second person	you	you	you	you	your, yours	your, yours
Third person	he	they	him	them	his, her	their, theirs
	she	they	her	them	her, hers	their, theirs
	it	they	it	them	it, its	their, theirs

HINT

Correcting Common Problems with Pronouns

HINT 1

Remember that *between, except,* and *with* are prepositions and take the object case.

between you and ~~I~~ _{me}

except Alexi and ~~she~~ _{her}

with ~~he~~ _{him}

and ~~I~~ _{me}

HINT 2

Don't use *them* as a pointing pronoun in place of *these* or *those.* Use *them* only as the object by itself.

He liked ~~them~~ _{those} socks.

He liked them.

HINT 3

Possessive case pronouns never take apostrophes.

The insect spread ~~it's~~ _{its} wings.

HINT 4

Use possessive case before *-ing* verb forms.

The crowd cheered ~~him~~ making a three-point basket.
^*his*

HINT 5

Use reflexive pronouns (those that end in *-self* or *-selves*) to intensify nouns they refer back to. Don't use reflexive pronouns in other cases because you think they sound more correct. They aren't.

Sarah puts too much suntan oil on herself.

They included ~~myself~~ in the group.
^*me*

Pronouns in compound constructions

To find the right case when your sentence has a noun and a pronoun, temporarily eliminate the noun as you read the sentence to yourself. You'll hear the case that is needed.

Jon and ~~him~~ went to the store.
^*he*

(*If Jon is eliminated, the sentence would be "Him went to the store." It's easier to notice the wrong pronoun case this way.*)

Mrs. Weg gave the tickets to **Lutecia** and ~~I~~.
^*me*

(*Try dropping the noun,* Lutecia. *You'll be able to hear that the sentence sounds wrong. ("Mrs. Weg gave the tickets to I.") Because* to *is a preposition, the noun or pronoun that follows is the object of the preposition and should be in the object case.*)

Using *we* or *us* before nouns

The lecturer told **~~we~~ students** to quiet down.
^*us*

(*When you drop the noun* students, *the original sentence would be "The lecturer told we to quiet down." Instead, the sentence needs the pronoun in the object case,* us, *because it is the object of the verb.*)

Who/whom

In informal speech, some people may not distinguish between *who* and *whom*. But for formal writing, the cases are as follows:

Subject	Object	Possessive
who	whom	whose
whoever	whomever	

Subject:	**Who** is going to the concert tonight? [*Who* is the subject of the sentence.]
	Give this to **whoever** wants it. [*Who* is the subject of *wants*.]
Object:	To **whom** should I give this ticket? [*Whom* is the object of the preposition *to*.]
Possessive:	No one was sure **whose** voice that was. [*Whose* is the possessive marker for *voice*.]

TRY THIS

To Choose Between *Who* and *Whom*

If you aren't sure whether to use *who* or *whom*, turn a question into a statement or rearrange the order of the phrase:

Question:	(**Who, whom**) are you looking for?
Rearranged order:	You are looking for **whom**.
	(Object of the preposition)
Sentence:	She is someone (**who, whom**) I know well.
Rearranged order:	I know **whom** well.
	(Direct object)

Pronoun case after *than* or *as*

In comparisons using *than* and *as*, choose the correct pronoun case by recalling the words that are omitted.

He is taller than (**I, me**). [The omitted words here are *am tall*.]
He is taller than **I** (am tall).

Our cat likes my sister more than (**I, me**). [The omitted words here are *he likes*.]
Our cat likes my sister more than (he likes) **me**.

Pronoun case *we* or *us* before nouns

When *we* or *us* is used before a noun, such as "we players" or "us friends," use the case appropriate for the noun. You can hear which to use by omitting the noun.

(*We, Us*) players paid for our own equipment.

> **Test:** Would you say "*Us* paid for the equipment" or "*We* paid for the equipment"? (*We* is the correct pronoun here.)

The barista gave (*we, us*) customers our coffee.

> **Test:** Would you say "The barista gave *we* our coffee" or "The barista gave *us* our coffee?" (*Us* is the correct pronoun here.)

Pronoun case with *to* + verb (infinitive)

When you use a pronoun after an infinitive (*to* + verb), use the object case.

> Mira offered to drive Orin and (*I, me*) to the meeting.
>
> (*Would you say "Mira offered to drive* I *to the meeting"? The correct pronoun is* me.)

Pronoun antecedents

Because pronouns substitute for nouns, they should agree with the nouns they refer to in number and gender.

> **Singular**: The <u>student</u> turned in *<u>her</u>* lab report.
>
> **Plural**: The <u>students</u> turned in *<u>their</u>* lab reports.

15b Pronoun reference

To avoid confusing your readers, be sure your pronouns clearly indicate the words they refer to (their antecedents).

> **Unclear reference:** Gina told Michelle that **she** took **her** bike to the library.
>
> (*Did Gina take Michelle's bike or her own bike to the library?*)
>
> **Revised:** When Gina took Michelle's bike to the library, she told Michelle she was borrowing it.

HINT

Avoiding Vague Pronouns

Watch out for the vague uses of *they, this, it,* or *which* that don't refer to any specific group, word, or phrase (antecedent).

the screenwriters and producers
In Hollywood, ~~they~~ don't know what the American public really
wants in movies.

(Who *are* the they *referred to here?*)

When the town board asked about the cost of the next political

the politicians
campaign, the board was assured that ~~they~~ would pay for **their**

own campaigns.

(To whom do they *and* their *refer? Most likely* they *refers to the politicians who will be campaigning, but* politicians *is only implied.*)

serving as a forest ranger
Martina worked in a national forest last summer, and ~~this~~ may be

her career choice.

(What does this *refer to? Because no word or phrase in the first part of the sentence refers to the pronoun, the revised version has one of several possible answers.*)

Many people who have cell phones let their musical ringtones go

and the loud ringing
off loudly when sitting in movies or lectures, ~~which~~ bothers me.

(What does which *refer to here? The fact that many people have cell phones, that they let their phones go off in movies or lectures, or maybe that the ringtones are so loud?*)

Pronoun number

For collective nouns, such as *group, committee,* and *family,* use either a singular or plural pronoun, depending on whether the group acts as a unit or acts separately as many individuals within the unit.

The committee reached **its** decision before the end of the meeting.

(*Here the committee acted as a unit.*)

The committee relied on **their** own consciences to reach a decision.

(*Here each member of the committee relied separately on his or her own conscience.*)

Be consistent in pronoun number. Don't shift from singular to plural or plural to singular.

> After **someone** studies the violin for a few months, **she** may
>
> *she*
> decide to try the piano. Then they can compare and decide which
> ^
>
> *she*
> instrument they may like better.
> ^

Compound subjects

Compound subjects with *and* take the plural pronoun.

> The **table** and **chair** were delivered promptly, but **they** were not the style I had ordered.

For compound subjects with *or* or *nor*, the pronoun agrees with the subject word closer to it.

> The restaurant offered either regular **patrons** or each new **customer** a free cup of coffee with **his** or **her** dinner.

Who/which/that

When *who, which*, or *that* begins a dependent clause, use the word as follows:

- *Who* is used for people (and sometimes animals).

  > He is a person **who** can help you.

- *Which* is used most often for nonessential clauses.

  > The catalog, **which** I sent for last month, had some unusual merchandise.

  (*The* which *clause here is nonessential.*)

- *That* is used most often for essential clauses.

  > When I finished the book **that** she lent me, I was able to write my paper.

  (*The* that *clause here is essential.*)

Indefinite words

Indefinite words such as *any* and *each* usually take the singular pronoun.

> **Each** of the boys handed in **his** uniform.

Indefinite pronouns

Indefinite pronouns are pronouns that don't refer to any specific person or thing, such as *anyone, no one, somebody,* or *each.* Some of them may seem to have a plural meaning, but in formal writing, treat them as singular. When another pronoun refers to one of these words, use *his or her*, switch to plural, use *they,* or use *a, an,* or *the.*

Everyone brought **his or her** coat.

(or)

All the people brought **their** coats.

(or)

Everyone brought **their** coats.
(*Some people view this as incorrect. Others, such as the National Council of Teachers of English, accept this as a way to avoid sexist language. See Chapter 11.*)

(or)

Everyone brought **a** coat.

16

Adjectives and Adverbs

16a Adjectives and adverbs

Adjectives and adverbs describe or add information about other words in a sentence.

- **Adjectives** modify nouns and pronouns:

red	house
(adjective)	(noun)

They	were **loud**.
(pronoun)	(adjective)

Order Of Adjectives

		Physical Description							
Determiner	Evaluation or Opinion	Size	Shape	Age	Color	Nationality	Religion	Material	Noun
a one her	lovely	big	round	old	green	English	Catholic	silk	purse

- the quiet Japanese rock garden
- a square blue cotton handkerchief
- my lazy old Siamese cat

- six excellent new movies
- many difficult physics problems
- every big green plant

- **Adverbs** modify verbs, verb forms, adjectives, and other adverbs:

danced	**gracefully**
(verb)	(adverb)

very	tall
(adverb)	(adjective)

ran	**very**	**quickly**
(verb)	(adverb)	(adverb)

Many adverbs end in -*ly*:

Adjective	Adverb
rapid	rapidly
nice	nicely
happy	happily

However, the -*ly* ending isn't a sure test for adverbs because some adjectives have an -*ly* ending (*early, ghostly*), and some adverbs do not end in -*ly* (*very, fast, far*). To be sure, check your dictionary to see whether the word is listed as an adjective or adverb.

To use adjectives and adverbs correctly:

- Use -*ed* adjectives (the -*ed* form of verbs, past participles) to describe nouns. Be sure to include the -*ed* ending.

used clothing   **painted** houses   **experienced** driver

- Use adjectives following linking verbs such as *appear, seem, taste, feel,* and *look.*

  The sofa seemed **comfortable**. [sofa = comfortable]

  The water tastes **salty**. [water = salty]

- Use adverbs to modify verbs.

  He ran quick. The glass broke sudden. She sang sweet.
  quickly   *suddenly*   *sweetly*

- Be sure to use the following adjectives and adverbs correctly:

Adjective	Adverb
sure	surely
real	really
good	well
bad	badly
surely	badly

surely   badly.   well

She sure likes to dance. The car runs bad. He sings good.

HINT

Using *Well*

Well is most common as an adverb, but *well* is an adjective when it refers to good health.

Despite her surgery, she looks **well**.

- When you use adverbs such as *so, such,* and *too,* be sure to complete the phrase or clause.

that she left the office early

Hailey was so tired.

that reservations are recommended

Malley's is such a popular restaurant.

16b Comparisons

Adverbs and adjectives are often used to show comparison, and their forms indicate the degree of comparison. In comparisons, most adjectives and adverbs add *-er* and *-est* as endings or combine with the words *more* and *most* or *less* and *least*.

- **Positive form** is used when no comparison is made.
  a **larger** box   an **acceptable** offer

- **Comparative form** is used when two things are being compared (with *-er, more,* or *less*).
  the **larger** of the two boxes the **less acceptable** of the two offers

- **Superlative form** is used when three or more things are being compared (with *-est, most,* or *least*).
  the **largest** of the six boxes
  the **least acceptable** of all the offers

Adjectives and Adverbs in Comparison		
Positive	Comparative	Superlative
(for one; uses the base form)	*(for two; uses -er, more, or less)*	*(for three or more; uses -est, most, or least)*
tall	taller	tallest
pretty	prettier	prettiest
cheerful	more cheerful	most cheerful
selfish	less selfish	least selfish
Curtis is **tall**.	Curtis is **taller** than Rachel.	Curtis is the **tallest** player on the team.

Irregular Forms of Comparison		
Positive	Comparative	Superlative
(for one)	*(for two)*	*(for three or more)*
good	better	best
well	better	best
little	less	least
some	more	most
much	more	most
many	more	most
bad, badly	worse	worst

HINT

Making Comparisons Correctly

Avoid double comparisons in which both the -er and more (or -est and most) are used.

the ~~most~~ farthest   ~~more~~ quicker

17

Modifiers

17a Dangling modifiers

A dangling modifier is a word or word group that refers to (or modifies) a word or phrase that has not been clearly stated in the sentence. When an introductory phrase does not name the doer of the action, the phrase then refers to (or modifies) the subject of the independent clause that follows.

Having finished the assignment, Jillian turned on the TV.

(Jillian, *the subject of the independent clause, is the doer of the action in the introductory phrase. She finished the assignment.*)

However, when the intended subject (or doer of the action) of the introductory phrase is not stated, the result is a dangling modifier.

Having finished the assignment, the TV was turned on.

(*This sentence says that the TV finished the homework. Since it is unlikely that TV sets can complete assignments, the introductory phrase has no logical word to refer to. Sentences with dangling modifiers say one thing while the writer means another.*)

Characteristics of dangling modifiers

- They most frequently occur at the beginning of sentences but can also appear at the end.

- They often have an *-ing* verb or a *to* + verb phrase near the start of the whole phrase.

Dangling modifier: After <u>getting</u> a degree in education, more <u>experience</u> in the classroom is needed to be a good teacher.

Revised: After <u>getting</u> a degree in education, Lu needed more experience in the classroom to be a good teacher.

Dangling modifier: <u>To work</u> as a lifeguard, <u>practice</u> in CPR is required.

Revised: <u>To work</u> as a lifeguard, you are required to have practice in CPR.

TRY THIS

To Revise Dangling Modifiers

1. Name the doer of the action in the dangling phrase.

Dangling modifier: Without <u>knowing</u> the guest's name, it was difficult for Marina to introduce him to her husband.

Revised: Because Marina <u>did</u> not <u>know</u> the guest's name, it was difficult to introduce him to her husband.

2. Name the appropriate or logical doer of the action as the subject of the independent clause.

Dangling Modifier: Having arrived late for practice, a written excuse was needed.

Revised: Having arrived late for practice, the team member needed a written excuse.

17b Misplaced modifiers

A misplaced modifier is a word or word group placed so far away from what it refers to (or modifies) that readers may be confused. Modifiers should be placed as closely as possible to the words they modify in order to keep the meaning clear.

Misplaced modifiers: The assembly line workers were told that they had been fired by the personnel director.

(*Were the workers told by the personnel director that they had been fired, or were they told by someone else that the personnel director had fired them?*)

Revised: The assembly line workers were told by the personnel director that they had been fired.

Single-word modifiers should be placed immediately before the words they modify. Note the difference in meaning in these two sentences:

I earned nearly $30.

(*The amount was almost $30 but not quite.*)

I nearly earned $30.

(*I almost had the opportunity to earn $30, but it didn't work out.*)

TRY THIS

To Avoid Misplaced Modifiers

When you proofread, check these words to be sure they are as close as possible to the words they refer to.

almost	hardly	merely	only
even	just	nearly	simply

17c. Split infinitives

Split infinitives occur when modifiers are inserted between "to" and the verb. Some people object to split infinitives, but others consider them grammatically correct. In some cases, inserting a modifier between "to" and the verb is the more natural phrasing.

> To *quickly* go
>
> (*Some people accept this, and others prefer to revise to "to go quickly."*)
>
> To *easily* reach
>
> (*Most writers prefer this as more natural than "He wanted easily to reach the top shelf."*)

18

Shifts

Consistency in writing involves using the same (1) pronoun person and number, (2) verb tense, and (3) tone.

18a Shifts in person or number

Avoid shifts between first, second, and third person pronouns and between singular and plural. The following table shows the three persons in English pronouns:

Pronoun Person	Singular	Plural
First person (the person or persons speaking)	I, me	we, us
Second person (the person or persons spoken to)	you	you
Third person (the person or persons spoken about)	he, she, it, him, her, it	they, them

Unnecessary shift in person

Once you have chosen to use first, second, or third person, shift only with a good reason.

he or she does

In <u>a person's</u> life, the most important thing <del>you do</del> is to decide
  (third)   (second)

on a type of job.

(*This is an unnecessary shift from third to second person.*)

Unnecessary shift in number

To avoid pronoun inconsistency, don't shift unnecessarily in number from singular to plural (or from plural to singular).

Women can face

<u>A woman faces</u> challenges to career advancement. When <u>they</u>
 (singular)   (plural)

take maternity leave, <u>they</u> should be sure that opportunities for
             (plural)

promotion are still available when they return to work.

(*The writer uses the singular noun* woman *in the first sentence but then shifts to the plural pronoun* they *in the second sentence.*)

18b Shifts in verb tense

Because verb tenses indicate time, keep writing in the same time (past, present, or future) unless the logic of what you are writing about requires a switch.

Necessary shift: Many people today <u>remember</u> very little about the Vietnam War except the filmed scenes of fighting they <u>watched</u> on television news at the time.

(*The verb* remember *reports a general truth in the present, and the verb* watched *reports past events.*)

Unnecessary shift: While we <u>were watching</u> the last game of the World Series, the picture suddenly <u>breaks up</u>.

(*The verb phrase* were watching *reports a past event, and there is no reason to shift to the present tense verb* breaks up.)

Revised: While we <u>were watching</u> the last game of the World Series, the picture suddenly <u>broke up</u>.

18c Shifts in tone

Once you choose a formal or informal tone for a paper, keep your use of that tone consistent in your word choices. A sudden intrusion of a formal phrase in an informal narrative or the use of slang in a formal report can disrupt the tone of your writing.

Unnecessary shift: The job of the welfare worker is to assist in a family's struggle to obtain funds for

children's

the kids' food and clothing.

(The use of the informal word kids' *is a shift in tone in this formal sentence.)*

V

Punctuation

Contents of this section

**19 Sentence Punctuation Patterns
(for Commas and Semicolons)**   73

20 Commas   75

  20a Commas between independent clauses   75

  20b Commas after introductory words, phrases,
and clauses   75

  20c Commas with essential and nonessential
words, phrases, and clauses   76

  20d Commas in series and lists   77

  20e Commas with adjectives   77

  20f Commas with dates, addresses, geographical
names, and numbers   77

  20g Commas with interrupting words or phrases   78

  20h Commas with quotations   78

  20i Unnecessary commas   78

21 Apostrophes   79

  21a Apostrophes with possessives   79

  21b Apostrophes with contractions   81

  21c Apostrophes with plurals   81

  21d Unnecessary apostrophes   81

22 Semicolons   82

  22a Semicolons in compound sentences   82

  22b Semicolons in a series   83

  22c Semicolons with quotation marks   83

  22d Unnecessary semicolons   83

23 Quotation Marks   84

  23a Quotation marks with direct and indirect
quotations   84

    • Quotation marks with prose quotations   84

    • Quotation marks in poetry   85

    • Quotation marks in dialogue   85

23b	Quotation marks for minor titles and parts of wholes	85
23c	Quotation marks for words	85
23d	Quotation marks with other punctuation	86
23e	Unnecessary quotation marks	86
24	**Other Punctuation**	**86**
24a	Hyphens	86
24b	Colons	88
24c	End punctuation	89
	• Periods	89
	• Question marks	90
	• Exclamation points	90
24d	Dashes	90
24e	Slashes	91
24f	Parentheses	91
24g	Brackets	91
24h	Omitted words (ellipsis)	91

Question and Correct

	SECTION	PAGE
✛ What are some general patterns for punctuating sentences?	19	73
✛ If I connect two sentences with "and" or "but," do I need a comma or a semicolon?	20a	75
✛ Do I need commas after introductory words such as "However," "On the other hand," or "Since we left"?	20b	75
✛ Does this kind of sentence, with some describing words in the middle of it, need commas? "My brother who lives in Wisconsin is an accountant."	20c	76
✛ When I write a list of items (such as "spotted owls, bald eagles, and hawks"), do I need a comma before the last "and"?	20d	77
✛ How do I know whether to put commas between descriptive words before a noun (such as "four soft gray kittens" or "hot humid weather")?	20e	77

	SECTION	PAGE
✦ Do I need a comma in a date such as "June 1 2009" or a location such as "Berlin Germany"?	20f	77
✦ Where might a comma be needed in this sentence? "The senator however voted for the bill."	20g	78
✦ Do commas go before or after the quotation marks when introducing a quote?	20h	78
✦ Does this sentence need the comma? "Many of our new employees, have excellent plans for improvements."	20i	78
✦ Where does the apostrophe belong? -Iris<u>'s</u> book _or_ Iris<u>'</u> book -Kate and Jon<u>'s</u> house _or_ Kate<u>'s</u> and Jon<u>'s</u> house -five pig<u>'s</u> tails _or_ five pigs<u>'</u> tails -one fox<u>'s</u> hole _or_ one fox<u>s'</u> hole	21a	79
✦ When should I write "it<u>'s</u>," and when should I write "it<u>s</u>"?	21b	81
✦ When are apostrophes used to form plurals?	21c	81
✦ Should I write "the dog is hers<u>'</u>" _or_ "the dog is her<u>s</u>"?	21d	81
✦ When should I use semicolons?	22	82
✦ Is this use of the semicolon correct? "This problem is serious<u>;</u> furthermore, it is very costly."	22a	82
✦ Is this use of the semicolon correct? "This magazine has lots of ads<u>;</u> especially for cosmetics and hair products."	22d	83
✦ When do I use quotation marks for quoting prose, poetry, and dialogue?	23a	84
✦ Are these uses of quotation marks for titles correct? -"The Star-Spangled Banner" -Alfred Lord Tennyson's "Lady of Shalott"	23b	85
✦ Do I put commas inside or outside of quotation marks?	23d	86

	SECTION	PAGE
✦ Should I use hyphens in words such as the following? -three fourths -five and ten year bonds -self motivated worker -father in law	24a	86
✦ Is the colon used correctly in this sentence? "I love sports such as: football, hockey, and snowboarding."	24b	88
✦ Which abbreviations do not need a period?	24c	89
✦ Do question marks go inside or outside of quotation marks?	24c	90
✦ What are dashes, and where should they be used?	24d	90
✦ How are slashes used when quoting poetry?	24e	91
✦ When would parentheses be used in a sentence?	24f	91
✦ What are brackets, and when are they used?	24g	91
✦ How do I indicate that words have been left out of a quotation?	24h	91

19

Sentence Punctuation Patterns (for Commas and Semicolons)

Commas and Semicolons in Sentences

- For simple sentences, use pattern 1.
- For compound sentences, use patterns 2, 3, and 4.
- For complex sentences, use patterns 5, 6, 7, and 8.

1. [Independent clause][.]

   This movie has a shocking ending.

2. [Independent clause][,] **coordinating conjunction:** [independent clause][.]

   and   or
   but   so
   for   yet
   nor

   The medication made Claire sleepy, so she went to bed.

3. [Independent clause][;] [independent clause][.]

   Jin is looking for a summer job; he wants to work in a hospital or a medical clinic.

4. [Independent clause][;] **independent clause marker:** [independent clause][.]

   however,
   nevertheless,
   therefore,
   consequently,
   (etc.)

   Fewer people are purchasing newspapers; however, more people are reading news on the Internet.

5.

| Dependent clause marker:
Because
Since
If
When
While
After
(etc.) | dependent clause | [,] | independent clause | [.] |

Since Olivia started her new job, she has had little time to spend with her friends.

6.

| Independent clause | dependent clause marker:
because
since
if
when
while
after
(etc.) | dependent clause | [.] |

Emergency vehicles arrived quickly after the police officer called for help.

7.

| Subject | [,] | nonessential dependent clause | [,] | verb/predicate | [.] |

[*Use commas before and after the dependent clause if it is nonessential.*]

Sayid, who is a talented mechanic, repaired the helicopter.

8.

| Subject | essential dependent clause | verb/predicate | [.] |

[*Do not use commas before and after essential clauses.*]

The fossils that the scientist discovered last month have been donated to a museum.

20

Commas

20a Commas between independent clauses

To use commas when you join independent clauses, you need to know the following:

Independent clause: a clause that can stand alone as a sentence

Compound sentence: a sentence with two or more independent clauses

Use the comma with one of the seven joining (coordinating) conjunctions. Some writers remember this list as "FAN BOYS," spelled out with the first letter of each word.

For And Nor But Or Yet So

(*Clause*), **and** (*clause*).

The television program was dull, but the commercials were entertaining.

Alternative: If one of the independent clauses has a comma, use a semicolon with the joining word instead.

Alesha, not Mateya, is the team captain; but Mateya assists the coach during practice.

Exception: A comma may be omitted if the two independent clauses are short and there is no danger of misreading.

We were tired so we stopped the game.

20b Commas after introductory words, phrases, and clauses

A comma is needed after introductory words, phrases, and clauses that come before the main clause in your sentence.

Introductory words

> Well,   In fact,   First,

> <u>Well</u>, perhaps he meant no harm. <u>In fact</u>, he wanted to help.

Introductory phrases and clauses

- Long phrases (usually four words or more) and clauses:

  <u>With the aid of a fast Internet connection</u>, he finished his project quickly.

  <u>While I was listening to my podcast</u>, I didn't hear my phone ring.

20c Commas with essential and nonessential words, phrases, and clauses

When you include words, phrases, or clauses that are not essential to the meaning of the sentences and could be included in another sentence, place commas before and after the nonessential element. If the word, phrase, or clause is essential, do not use commas.

> Dr. Tanar, who is a cardiac surgeon, retired after fifty years of practice.

HINT

Recognizing Essential and Nonessential Words and Clauses

You can decide if an element is essential by reading the sentence without it. If the meaning changes, that element is essential.

Essential: Apples <u>that are green</u> are usually very tart.

If you remove the clause "that are green," the statement changes to indicate that all apples are usually very tart.

Nonessential: Madison, who is my cousin, will move to Denver when she graduates college.

Whether or not Madison is my cousin, she will still move to Denver. "Who is my cousin" is not essential.

20d Commas in series and lists

Use commas when three or more items are listed in a series. The items can be words, phrases, or clauses. In a list of three items, some writers prefer to omit the comma before the "and."

> He first spoke to Julio, then called his roommate, and finally phoned me.

> Americans' favorite spectator sports are football, baseball, and basketball.

(*The comma after* baseball *is optional.*)

HINT

Using Commas with Lists

You need at least three items in a list in order to use commas. Some writers mistakenly put a comma between two items (often verbs) in a sentence.

Misused comma:	No one has ever been able to locate the source of the river, and follow it to its source.
Revised:	No one has ever been able to locate the source of the river and follow it to its source.

20e Commas with adjectives

Use commas to separate two or more adjectives that describe the same noun equally.

cold, dark water   happy, healthy baby

But when adjectives are not equal, do not use commas to separate them.

six big dogs   bright green sweater

20f Commas with dates, addresses, geographical names, and numbers

- **With dates listing month and day before the year:**

   In a heading or list: May 27, 2010   (*or*)   27 May 2010

   In a sentence: The order was shipped on March 18, 2009, but not received until April 14, 2009.

- **With addresses:**
  In a letter heading or on an envelope:

  Jim Johnson, Jr.
  216 Oakwood Drive
  Mineola, NM 43723-1342

  In a sentence:

  You can write to Senator Michael Johnson Jr.,1436 Westwood Drive, Birlingham, ID 83900, for more information.

- **With geographical names**
  Put a comma after each element in a place name.

  The conference next year will be in Chicago, Illinois, and in Washington, D.C., the year after that.

- **With numbers**
  4,300,150   27,000   4,401 (*or*) 4401

20g   Commas with interrupting words or phrases

Use commas to set off words and phrases that interrupt the sentence.

> The committee was, however, unable to agree.

> The weather prediction, much to our surprise, was accurate.

20h   Commas with quotations

Use a comma after expressions such as "he said."

> Everyone was relieved when the chairperson said, "I will table this motion until the next meeting."

> "I forgot," Serkan explained, "to complete the materials section of my lab report."

20i   Unnecessary commas

- Don't separate a subject from its verb.

  Unnecessary comma: An eighteen-year-old in most states, is now considered an adult.

- Don't put a comma between two verbs that share the same subject.

  Unnecessary comma: We laid out our music and snacks, and began to study.

- Don't put a comma in front of every *and* or *but*.

  Unnecessary comma: We decided that we should not lend her the money, and that we should explain our decision.

  (*The* and *in this sentence joins two* that *clauses.*)

- Don't put a comma in front of a direct object. (Remember that clauses beginning with *that* can be direct objects.)

  Unnecessary comma: He explained to me, that he is afraid to fly on airplanes because of terrorists.

- Don't put commas before a dependent clause when it comes after the main clause except for extreme or strong contrast.

  Unnecessary comma: She was late, because her alarm clock was broken.

  Extreme contrast: The movie actor was still quite upset, although he did win an Academy Award.

- Don't put a comma after *such as* or *especially*.

  Unnecessary comma: There are several kinds of dark bread from which to choose, such as, whole wheat, rye, oatmeal, pumpernickel, and bran bread.

21

Apostrophes

21a Apostrophes with possessives

The apostrophe shows ownership, but this is not always obvious.

TRY THIS

To Test for Possession
Turn the words around into an "of the" phrase.

Day's pay
the pay of the day

Mike's shoes
the shoes of Mike

- For singular nouns, use 's.

  the book's author   a flower's smell

- For a singular noun ending in -s, the s after the apostrophe is optional, especially if it would make pronunciation difficult.

  James's car   (or)   James' car

  Euripides' story (Trying to say *Euripides's story* is difficult.)

- For plural nouns ending in -s, add only an apostrophe.

  both teams' colors   six days' vacation

- For plural nouns not ending in -s (such as *children*, *men*, or *mice*), use 's.

  the children's game   six men's coats

- For indefinite pronouns (pronouns ending in *-body* and *-one*, such as *no one* and *everybody*), use 's.

  no one's fault   someone's hat

- For compound words, add 's to the last word.

  brother-in-law's job   everyone else's preference

- For joint ownership by two or more nouns, add 's after the last noun in the group. When individually owned, add 's after each noun.

Lisa and Vinay's house	(Lisa and Vinay own the house jointly.)
Lisa's and Vinay's houses	(Lisa and Vinay each own different houses.)

TRY THIS

To Use Apostrophes Correctly

For singular nouns that don't end in 's:

Word	Possessive Marker	Result
cup	's	cup's handle

When you aren't sure whether the word is plural or not, remember this sequence:

- Write the word.
- Then write the plural.
- Then add the possessive apostrophe.

Thus everything to the left of the apostrophe is the word and its plural, if needed.

Word	Plural Marker	Possessive Marker	Result
cup	s	'	cups' handles

21b Apostrophes with contractions

Use the apostrophe to mark the omitted letter or letters in contractions.

it's = it is   don't = do not   that's = that is   '79 = 1979
o'clock = of the clock   he's going = he is going

21c Apostrophes with plurals

Use apostrophes to form plurals of letters, abbreviations with periods, numbers, and words used as words. The apostrophe is optional if the plural is clear.

He earned all *A*'s last semester.

Torin's "you know's" in every sentence annoyed us.

Optional apostrophes: Ph.D.'s   (*or*)   Ph.D.s

21d Unnecessary apostrophes

Don't use the apostrophe with possessive pronouns (such as "hers" and "its") or with the regular plural forms of nouns.

Not correct:	it's edge	yours'	I bought five apples'.
Correct:	its edge	yours	I bought five apples.

22

Semicolons

The semicolon is a stronger mark of punctuation than a comma, and it is used with two kinds of closely related equal elements:

- between independent clauses
- between items in a series when any of the items contains a comma.

22a Semicolons in compound sentences

Use the semicolon when joining independent clauses not joined by the seven connectors that require commas: *and, but, for, nor, or, so, yet*.

Here are two patterns for using semicolons:

- Independent clause + semicolon + independent clause

  He often watched TV reruns; she preferred to read instead.

- Independent clause + semicolon + joining word or transition + comma + independent clause

  He often watched TV reruns; however, she preferred to read instead.

Transitional words or phrases are joining words that can be used to connect two independent clauses.

also	finally	instead
besides	for example	nevertheless
consequently	however	still
even so	in addition	therefore

A semicolon can be used instead of a comma with two independent clauses joined by *and, but, for, nor, or, so,* or *yet* when one of the clauses contains a comma.

- Independent clause with commas + semicolon + independent clause.

  Congressman Dow, who headed the investigation,
  (independent clause with commas)

  leaked the story to the press; but he would not answer
  (independent clause with commas)

  questions during an interview.

22b Semicolons in a series

For clarity, use semicolons to separate a series of items in which one or more of the items contain commas. Semicolons are also preferred if items in the series are especially long.

- Items with their own commas:

  Among her favorite Netflix rentals were old Cary Grant movies, such as *Arsenic and Old Lace;* any of Woody Allen's movies; and children's classics, including *The Sound of Music* and *The Wizard of Oz.*

- Long items in a series:

  When planning the trip, she considered the length of travel time between cities where stops would be made; the number of people likely to get on at each stop; and the times when the bus would arrive at major cities where connections would be made with other buses.

22c Semicolons with quotation marks

Place semicolons after quotation marks.

Her answer to every question I asked was, "I'll have to think about that"; she clearly had no answers to offer.

22d Unnecessary semicolons

Don't use a semicolon between a clause and a phrase or between an independent clause and a dependent clause.

Unnecessary semicolon: They wanted to see historical buildings; especially the courthouse. [should be a comma]

Unnecessary semicolon: He tried to improve his tennis serve; because that was the weakest part of his game. [should be no punctuation]

Don't use a semicolon in place of a dash, comma, or colon.

Incorrect semicolon: The office needed more equipment; a faster computer, another fax machine, and a paper shredder. [should be a colon]

23

Quotation Marks

23a Quotation marks with direct and indirect quotations

Quotation marks with prose quotations

Direct quotations:	the exact words said by someone you heard or read and are recopying. Enclose exact quotations in quotation marks.
Indirect quotations:	not someone's exact words but a rephrasing or summary of those words. Don't use quotation marks for indirect quotations.

If a quotation is longer than four lines, set it off as a block quotation by indenting one inch or ten spaces from the left margin. Use the same spacing between lines as in the rest of your paper, and don't use quotation marks.

- Direct quotation of a whole sentence: Use a capital letter to start the first word of the quotation.

  Mr. and Mrs. Yoder, farm owners, said, "We refuse to use that pesticide because it might pollute the nearby wells."

- Direct quotation of part of a sentence: Don't use a capital letter to start the first word of the quotation.

  Mr. and Mrs. Yoder stated that they "refuse to use that pesticide" because of possible water pollution.

- Indirect quotation:

  According to their statement, the Yoders will not use the pesticide because of potential water pollution.

- Quotation within a quotation: Use single quotation marks (' at the beginning and ' at the end) for a quotation inside another quotation.

  The agriculture reporter explained, "When I talked to the Yoders last week, they said, 'We refuse to use that pesticide.'"

If you leave some words out of a quotation, use an ellipsis (three spaced periods) to indicate omitted words. If you need to insert something within a quotation, use brackets [ ] to enclose the addition. (See 24g.)

Quotation marks in poetry

When you quote a single line of poetry, write it like other short quotations. Separate two lines of poetry with a slash (/) at the end of the first line. Leave a space before and after the slash. If the quotation is three lines or longer, set it off, indented one inch or ten spaces, like a longer quotation, and do not use quotation marks.

Quotation marks in dialogue

Write each person's speech, however short, as a separate paragraph. Use commas to set off *he said* or *she said*. Closely related bits of narrative can be included in the paragraph. If someone's speech goes on for several paragraphs, use quotation marks at the beginning of each paragraph but not at the end of any paragraph except the last one.

23b Quotation marks for minor titles and parts of wholes

Use quotation marks for the titles of parts of larger works (titles of book chapters, magazine articles, and episodes of television and radio series) and for short or minor works (songs, short stories, essays, short poems, and other literary works that are shorter than book length). Don't use quotation marks or italics for the titles of most religious texts and legal documents. For larger, more complete works, use italics. (See 26a.)

"The Star-Spangled Banner"

"The Mysteries of the Universe" (an episode of *Lost*)

The Bible

Hamlet

23c Quotation marks for words

Use quotation marks (or italics) for words used as words rather than for their meaning.

The word "accept" is often confused with "except."

23d Quotation marks with other punctuation

- Put commas and periods inside quotation marks. When a reference follows a short quotation, put the period after the reference.

  "Adonais," a poem by Percy Bysshe Shelley, memorializes John Keats.

  . . . after the stunning success" (252).

- Put a colon or semicolon after the quotation marks.

  . . . until tomorrow" ;

- Put a dash, a question mark, or an exclamation point inside the quotation marks when these punctuation marks are part of the quotation and outside the quotation marks when the marks apply to the whole sentence.

  He asked, "Do you need this book?"

  Does Dr. Lim tell all her students, "You must work harder"?

23e Unnecessary quotation marks

Don't put quotation marks around the titles of your essays, common nicknames, bits of humor, technical terms, and well-known expressions.

24

Other Punctuation

24a Hyphens

Hyphens have a variety of uses:

- **For compound words:**
  Some compound words are one word:

  | weekend | granddaughter | hometown |

  Some compounds are two words:

  | high school | executive director | turn off |

Some compounds are joined by hyphens:

father-in-law   president-elect   clear-cut

Fractions and numbers from twenty-one to ninety-nine that are spelled out have hyphens.

one-half   thirty-six   nine-tenths

For new words or compounds you are forming, check your dictionary. But not all hyphenated words appear there, especially new ones, and usage varies between dictionaries for some compounds.

e-mail (*or*) email   witch-hunt (*or*) witch hunt

wave-length (*or*) wavelength (*or*) wave length

For hyphenated words in a series, use hyphens as follows:

five- and six-page essays

- **For two-word units:**
  Use a hyphen when two or more words before a noun work together as a single unit to describe the noun. When these words come after the noun, they are not hyphenated.

  He needed up-to-date statistics. (*or*) He needed statistics that were up to date.

  They repaired the six-inch pipe. (*or*) They repaired the pipe that was six inches long.

  (Do not use a hyphen with adverbs ending in *-ly.*)

  That was a widely known fact.

- **For prefixes, suffixes, and letters joined to a word:**
  Use hyphens between words and prefixes *self-*, *all-*, and *ex-*.

  self-contained   all-encompassing   ex-president

  For other prefixes, such as *anti-*, *pro-*, and *co-*, use the dictionary as a guide.

  co-op   antibacterial   pro-choice

  Use a hyphen to join a prefix to a capitalized word or with figures and numbers.

  anti-American   non-Catholic   pre-1998

  Use a hyphen when you add the suffix *-elect.*

  president-elect

Use a hyphen to avoid doubling vowels and tripling consonants and to avoid ambiguity.

anti-intellectual   bell-like   re-cover   re-creation

- **To divide words between syllables when the last part of the word appears on the next line.**

  Every spring the nation's capital is flooded with tour-
  ists snapping pictures of the cherry blossoms.

- **When dividing words at the end of a line:**

  - Don't divide one-syllable words.

  - Don't leave one or two letters at the end of a line.

  - Don't put fewer than three letters on the next line.

  - Don't divide the last word in a paragraph or on a page.

  - Divide compound words between the parts of the compound. If a word contains a hyphen, break only at the hyphen.

  - Don't insert hyphens in Web addresses.

24b Colons

Use colons as follows:

- **To announce items at the end of the sentence**

  The company sold only electronics they could service: computers, printers, and television sets.

- **To separate independent clauses**
  Use a colon instead of a semicolon to separate two independent clauses when the second clause restates or amplifies the first.

  The town council voted not to pave the gravel roads: it did not have the funds for road improvement.

- **To announce long quotations**
  Use a colon to announce a long quotation (more than one sentence) or a quotation not introduced by words such as "said" or "stated."

  The candidate offered only one reason to vote for her: "I will not raise parking meter rates."

- **In salutations and between elements**

  Dear Dr. Philippa: 6:12 a.m.   Genesis 1:8

- **With quotation marks**
  When colons are needed, put them after closing quotation marks.

  "One sign of intelligence is not arguing with your boss": that was her motto for office harmony.

- **Unnecessary colons**
  Do not use a colon after a verb or phrases like "such as" or "consisted of."

Not correct:	The two most valuable players were: Timon Lasmon and Maynor Field.
Revised:	The two most valuable players were Timon Lasmon and Maynor Field.
Not correct:	The camping equipment consisted of: tents, lanterns, matches, and dehydrated food.
Revised:	The camping equipment consisted of tents, lanterns, matches, and dehydrated food.

24c End punctuation

Periods

Use periods at the ends of sentences that are statements, mild commands, indirect questions, or polite questions to which answers aren't expected.

Electric cars are growing in popularity. (statement)

Turn off your cell phones during class. (mild command)

Would you please let me know when you're done. (polite question)

Use a period with abbreviations, but don't use a second period if the abbreviation is at the end of the sentence.

R.S.V.P.   U.S.A.   Mr.   8 a.m.

A period is not needed after agencies, common abbreviations, names of well-known companies, and U.S. Postal Service state abbreviations.

NATO   NBA   CIA   YMCA   IBM   DNA   TX

Put periods that follow quotations inside the quotation marks. But if there is a reference to a source, put the period after the reference.

She said, "I'm going to Alaska next week."

Neman notes that "the claim is unfounded" (6).

Question marks

Use a question mark after a direct question but not after an indirect one.

> Did anyone see my laptop computer? (direct question)

> Jules wonders if he should buy a new stereo. (indirect question)

Place a question mark inside quotation marks if the quotation is a question. Place the question mark outside quotation marks if the whole sentence is a question.

> Drora asked, "Is she on time?"

> Did Eli really say, "I'm in love"?

Question marks may be used between parts of a series.

> Would you like to see a movie? go shopping? eat at a restaurant?

Use a question mark to indicate doubt about the correctness of a date, number, or other piece of information. But do not use it to indicate sarcasm.

> The ship landed in Greenland about 1521 (?) but did not keep a record of where it was.

> **Not correct:**   Matti's sense of humor (?) evaded me.

> **Revised:**   Matti's sense of humor evaded me.

Exclamation points

- Use the exclamation point after a strong command or a statement said with great emphasis or with strong feeling. But don't overuse the exclamation point.

> I'm absolutely delighted!

> **Unnecessary:**   Wow! What a great party! I enjoyed every minute of it!

- Enclose the exclamation point within the quotation marks only if it belongs to the quotation.

> As he came in, he exclaimed, "I've won the lottery!"

24d Dashes

The dash is informal but can be used to add emphasis or clarity, to mark an interruption or shift in tone, or to introduce a list. If you use a word processor without the dash, use two hyphens to indicate the dash with no space before or after the hyphens.

> The cat looked at me so sweetly—with a dead rat in its mouth.

24e Slashes

Use the slash to mark the end of a line of poetry and to indicate acceptable alternatives. For poetry, leave a space before and after the slash. For alternatives, leave no space. The slash is also used in World Wide Web addresses.

> He repeated Milton's lines: "The mind is its own place, and in itself / Can make a Heaven of Hell, a Hell of Heaven."

> pass/fail   and/or   http://www.whitehouse.gov

24f Parentheses

Use parentheses to enclose supplementary or less important material added as further explanation or example or to enclose figures or letters in a numbered list.

> The newest officers of the club (those elected in May) were installed at the ceremony.

> They had three items on the agenda: (1) the budget, (2) parking permits, and (3) election procedures.

24g Brackets

Use brackets to add your comments or additional explanation within a quotation and to replace parentheses within parentheses. The Latin word *sic* in brackets means you copied the original quotation exactly as it appeared, but you think there's an error.

> We agreed with Fellner's claim that "this great team [the Chicago Bears] will go to the Super Bowl next year."

> The lawyer explained, "We discussed the matter in a fiendly [*sic*] manner."

24h Omitted words (ellipsis)

Use an ellipsis (a series of three periods, with one space before and after each period) to indicate that you are omitting words or part of a sentence from the source you are quoting. If you omit a whole sentence or paragraph, add a fourth period with no space after the last word preceding the ellipsis.

"modern methods . . . with no damage."

"the National Forest System . . ." (Smith 9).

"federal lands. . . . They were designated for preservation."

If you omit words immediately after a punctuation mark in the original, include that mark in your sentence.

"because of this use of the forest, . . ."

VI

Mechanics

Contents of this section

25	**Capitalization**	96
	25a Proper nouns vs. common nouns	96
	25b Capitals in sentences, quotations, and lists	98
26	**Italics**	99
	26a Titles	99
	26b Other uses of italics	100
27	**Numbers**	100
28	**Abbreviations**	102
	28a Abbreviating titles	102
	28b Abbreviating places	103
	28c Abbreviating numbers	103
	28d Abbreviating measurements	103
	28e Abbreviating dates	104
	28f Abbreviating names of familiar organizations or other entities	104
	28g Abbreviating Latin expressions or documentation terms	104
29	**Spelling**	
	29a Proofreading	105
	29b Some spelling guidelines	106
	• *ie/ei*	106
	• Doubling consonants	107
	• Final silent *-e*	107
	• Plurals	107
	29c Sound-alike words (homonyms)	108

Question and Correct

	SECTION	PAGE
✦ Should I capitalize words such as "greek," "mother," "vice-president," and "summer"?	25a	96
✦ Which words do I capitalize in a quotation?	25b	98
✦ Should I capitalize the first word in each item of a list?	25b	98
✦ Are book titles underlined, or should I use italics?	26	99
✦ Should I use italics or quotation marks for names of movies, short stories, ships, and newspapers?	26a	99
✦ Should I use italics for words of foreign origin that are now considered part of English?	26b	100
✦ Should I write out "twenty" or use the numeral "20"?	27	100
✦ When do I write "June 4," and when do I write "June fourth"?	27	101
✦ Which titles of people can be abbreviated?	28a	102
✦ Do I write "U.S." or "United States"?	28b	102
✦ Should I write "five billion dollars" or "$5 billion"?	28c	103
✦ Should I write "forty-two percent" or "42%"?	28d	103
✦ Should I write "3 PM" or "3:00 p.m."?	28e	104
✦ Which is correct: "F.B.I." or "FBI"?	28f	104
✦ What do Latin abbreviations such as "e.g." and "et al." mean?	28g	104
✦ How can I work on improving my spelling skills?	29	105
✦ What are some strategies for proofreading my writing?	29a	106
✦ How useful is a spell checker?	29a	106
✦ What is the "ie/ei" rule in spelling? Should I write "receive" or "recieve"?	29b	106

	SECTION	PAGE
✦ Should I write "occurring" (with two "r's") or "occuring" (with one "r")?	29b	107
✦ How do I know when to drop the silent -*e* when adding a suffix, as in "lose" and "losing"?	29b	107
✦ Should I write "familys" or "families"?	29b	108
✦ What's the difference in meaning and spelling for these sound-alike words? -"there" and "their" -"its" and "it's" -"affect" and "effect" -"than" and "then"	29c	108

25

Capitalization

25a Proper nouns vs. common nouns

Capitalize proper nouns, which are words that name one
particular thing, most often a person or place rather than a
general type or group of things. Listed here are categories
of words that should be capitalized. If you are not sure
about a particular word, check your dictionary.

Proper noun	Common noun
James Joyce	man
Thanksgiving	holiday
University of Maine	state university
Macintosh	computer
May	month

- Persons

  Vincent Baglia   Rifka Kaplan   Masuto Tatami

- Places, including geographical regions

  Milwaukee   Alberta   Northeast

- Peoples and their languages

  French   Swahili   Portuguese

- Religions and their followers

  Buddhist   Judaism   Christianity

- Members of national, political, racial, social, civic, and
  athletic groups

  Democrat   African American   Green Bay Packers
  Danes   Friends of the Library   Olympics Committee

- Institutions and organizations

  Supreme Court   European Union   Lions Club

- Historical documents

  Declaration of Independence   Magna Carta

- Periods and events, but not centuries

  Middle Ages   Boston Tea Party   twentieth century

- Days, months, and holidays, but not seasons

  Tuesday   Thanksgiving   winter

- Trademarks

  Coca-Cola   Toyota   Google

- Holy books and words denoting the Supreme Being (pronouns referring to God may be capitalized or lowercased)

  Talmud   Bible   Lord

- Words and abbreviations derived from specific names, but not the names of things that have lost that specific association and now refer to general types

  Stalinism   Freudian   NBC
  french fries   pasteurize   italics

- Place words, such as *street, park,* and *city,* that are part of specific names

  New York City   Wall Street   Zion National Park

- Titles that precede people's names, but not titles that follow names

  Governor Charlie Crist   Aunt Selena   President Barack Obama
  Charlie Crist, governor Selena, my aunt Barack Obama, president

- Words that indicate family relationships when used as a substitute for a specific name

  Here is a gift for   Li Chen sent a gift to his
     Mother.   mother.

- Titles of books, magazines, essays, movies, plays, and other works, but not articles (*a, an, the*), short prepositions (*to, by, on, in*), or short joining words (*and, but, or*) unless they are the first or last word. With hyphenated words, capitalize the first and all other important words.

  The Taming of the Shrew   "The Sino-Soviet Conflict"
  The Ground Beneath Her Feet   "A Brother-in-Law's Lament"

- The pronoun *I* and the interjection *O*, but not the word *oh*

  "Sail on, sail on, O ship of state," I said as the canoe sank.

- Words placed after a prefix that are normally capitalized

  un-American   anti-Semitic   pro-Israeli

25b Capitals in sentences, quotations, and lists

- Capitalize the first word of every sentence.

- Capitalize the first word of a comment in parentheses when it is a full sentence but not when the comment is not a full sentence.

- Do not capitalize the first word in a series of questions in which the questions are not full sentences.

  What did the interviewer want from the rock star? gossip? news about her next single?

- Capitalize the first word of directly quoted speech, but not a continuation of an interrupted direct quotation or a quoted phrase or clause that is integrated into the sentence.

  She answered, "Everyone will know the truth."

  "Everyone," she answered, "will know the truth."

  When Bataglio declined the nomination, he explained that he "would try again another year."

- Capitalize the first word in a list after a colon if each item in the list is a complete sentence or if each item is displayed on a line of its own

  The rise in popularity of walking as an alternative to jogging has led to commercial successes of various kinds: (1) better designs for walking shoes, (2) an expanding market for walking sticks, and (3) a rapid growth in the number of manufacturers selling a variety of models of walking shoes.

  (*or*)

  The rise in popularity of walking as an alternative to jogging has led to commercial successes of various kinds:
  1. Better designs for walking shoes
  2. An expanding market for walking sticks
  3. A rapid growth in the number of manufacturers selling a variety of models of walking shoes

26

Italics

Italics have generally replaced underlining for titles of long works in word-processed documents. When you are writing by hand, use underlining (a printer's mark to indicate words to be set in italics) for the kinds of titles and names indicated in this section.

26a Titles

Use italics for titles and names of long or complete works, including the following:

Books	*Twilight*
Magazines	*Entertainment Weekly*
Newspapers	*The Washington Post*
Works of art (visual and performance)	*Swan Lake*
Pamphlets	*Saving Energy in Your Home*
Television/radio series (not titles of individual episodes)	*Lost*
Films and videos	*The Dark Knight*
Long plays	*Macbeth*
Long musical works	*Canon in D*
Long poems	*In Memoriam*
Software	*Adobe Dreamweaver*
Recordings	*Viva la Vida*
Web sites (not individual Web pages)	*The Daily Beast*
Ships, airplanes, and trains	*Orient Express*

- Do not use italics or quotation marks for references to the Bible and other religious works, the Internet or World Wide Web, and legal documents.

Genesis	Bible	Upanishads
Torah	U.S. Constitution	Internet
World Wide Web	Web site	Google

26b **Other uses of italics**

26b **Other uses of italics**

- Foreign words and phrases and scientific names of plants and animals

  de rigueur   *Felis domesticus*

- Trademarked names used as words

  Some words, such as *Kleenex*, are brand names for products.

- Letters used as examples or terms

  In English, the letters *ph* and *f* often have the same sound.

- Words being emphasized

  It *never* snows here at this time of year.

  (*Use italics for emphasis sparingly.*)

Do not use italics for the following

- Words of foreign origin that are now part of English

alumni	cliché	manga
blitz	chutzpah	karaoke

- Titles of your own papers

27

Numbers

Style manuals for different fields and companies vary. The suggestions for writing numbers given here are generally useful as a guide for academic writing.

- Spell out numbers that can be expressed in one or two words, and use figures for other numbers.

Words	Figures
eight pounds	284 days
six dollars	$49.99
thirty-seven years	8,962 bushels
forty-three people	3.43 liters

- Use a combination of figures and words for numbers that are close together when such a combination will make your writing clearer.

The club celebrated the birthdays of six 90-year-olds born in the city.

Use Figures for the Following

- Days and years

September 18, 2009	(or)	18 September 2009
A.D. 1066		
in 1931–1932	(or)	in 1931–32
the 1990's	(or)	the 1990s

- Time of day

8:00 A.M. (or) a.m.	(or)	eight o'clock in the morning
4:30 P.M. (or) p.m.	(or)	half past four in the afternoon

- Addresses

  15 Tenth Street

350 West 114 Street	(or)	350 West 114th Street
Prescott, AZ 86301		

- Identification numbers

Room 88	Channel 4
Interstate 95	Elizabeth II

- Page and division of books and plays

page 30	Book I
Act 3, sc. 2	Ch. 3

- Decimals and percentages

6.1 average	13½ percent
0.057 metric ton	

- Numbers in series and statistics

  two apples, six oranges, and three bananas
  115 feet by 90 feet

  Be consistent, whichever form you choose.

- Large round numbers

$14 billion	(or)	fourteen billion dollars
11.5 million	(or)	11,500,000

- Repeated numbers (in legal or commercial writing)

  Notice must be given at least ninety (90) days in advance.

Do not use figures for the following

- Numbers that can be expressed in one or two words

  in his forties   the twenty-first century

- Dates when the year is omitted

  June sixth

- Numbers beginning sentences

  Ninety-five percent of our students are from South Carolina.

28

Abbreviations

In writing government, business, social science, science, and engineering documents, abbreviations are used frequently. However, for writing in the humanities, only a limited number of abbreviations are generally used.

28a   Abbreviating titles

- *Mr., Mrs.,* and *Ms.* are abbreviated when used as titles before a name.

  Mr. Toyagama   Ms. Patuk   Mrs. Begay

- *Dr.* and *St.* ("Saint") are abbreviated only when they immediately precede a name; they are written out when they appear after the name.

  Dr. Marlen Chafonanda   Marlen Chafonanda, doctor of internal medicine

- *Prof., Sen., Gen., Capt.,* and similar abbreviated titles can be used when they appear in front of a full name or before initials and a last name but not when they appear before the last name only.

  Gen. R. G. Brindo   General Brindo

- *Sr., Jr., J.D., Ph.D., M.F.A., C.P.A.,* and other abbreviated academic titles and professional degrees can be used after the name.

  Leslie Lim, Ph.D.   Kim Takamota, C.P.A.

- *Bros., Co.,* and similar abbreviations are used only if they are part of the exact name.

  Bass & Co.   Warner Bros.

28b Abbreviating places

In general, spell out names of states, countries, continents, streets, rivers, and so on. But there are a few exceptions:

- Use the abbreviation *D.C.* in Washington, D.C.

- Use *U.S.* only as an adjective, not as a noun.

  U.S. training bases   training bases in the United States

- If you include a full address in a sentence, you must use the postal abbreviation for the state.

  For further information, write to us at 100 Peachtree Street, Atlanta, GA 30300, for a copy of our free catalog.

  The company's headquarters, on Peachtree Street in Atlanta, Georgia, will soon be moved.

28c Abbreviating numbers

- Write out numbers that can be expressed in one or two words.

  eighteen   fifty-six   345

- The dollar sign is generally acceptable when the written-out phrase would be three words or more.

  $29 million   thirty dollars

- For temperatures, use figures, the degree symbol, and F (for Fahrenheit) or C (for Celsius).

  10°F   25°C

28d Abbreviating measurements

Spell out units of measurement, such as *acre, meter, foot,* and *percent,* but use abbreviations for measurements in tables, graphs, and figures.

28e Abbreviating dates

Spell out months and days of the week. With dates and times, the following are acceptable:

57 B.C.   57 B.C.E.   329 C.E.   A.D. 329

[The abbreviations B.C., B.C.E. (before the common era), and C.E. (common era) are placed after the year, while A.D. is placed before.]

A.M., P.M. (*or*) a.m., p.m.   EST (*or*) E.S.T.

28f Abbreviating names of familiar organizations or other entities

Use abbreviations for names of organizations, agencies, countries, and things usually referred to by their initials.

IBM	NAACP	NASA	NOW
PTA	UNICEF	the former USSR	DVD

If you are using the initials for a term that may not be familiar to your readers, spell it out the first time and give the initials in parentheses. From then on, you can use the initials.

The study of children's long-term memory (LTM) has been difficult because of the lack of a universally accepted definition of childhood LTM.

28g Abbreviating Latin expressions and documentation terms

Some Latin expressions always appear as abbreviations.

Abbreviation	Meaning
cf.	compare
e.g.	for example
i.e.	that is
et al.	and others
etc.	and so forth
vs. (*or*) v.	versus

The following abbreviations are appropriate for bibliographies and footnotes, as well as in informal writing, but for formal writing, use the English phrase instead. The format for abbreviations may vary among style manuals, so use the abbreviations appropriate for the style you are following.

Abbreviation	Meaning
ed., eds.	editor (*or*) edited by, editors
n.d.	no date of publication given
n.p.	no place of publication given
n. pag.	no page number given
p., pp.	page, pages
vol., vols.	volume, volumes

29

Spelling

English spelling is difficult because it contains many words from other languages that have different spelling conventions. In addition, English has several ways to spell some sounds. But correct spelling is important, partly to be sure your words are understood correctly and partly because you don't want to signal your reader that are you are careless or not very knowledgeable.

29a Some spelling suggestions

- **Learn some rules.** Read the useful spelling rules on the following pages.

- **Make up some spelling aids.** Keep a list of words that cause you problems, and study that list. Also, make up memory aids for tricky words. For example, you could try remembering that "dessert" is the sweet treat you'd like seconds of. So it has an extra "s." And "desert," with one "s" is the one that refers to barren sandy places.

- **Use a spell checker.** Spell checkers are useful tools, but they can't catch all errors, such as the following:

  Omitted words.
  Sound-alike words (homonyms). Spell checkers cannot distinguish between words that sound alike (such as "there" and "their" or "brake" and "break").

Substitution of one word for another. If you meant to write "one" and typed "own" instead, the spell checker won't flag that.

Misspelled words. If you misspelled words or even well-known proper nouns, the spell checker may or may not be able to suggest the right word. If the spell checker does not have the right suggestion, use a dictionary to find the word.

● **Learn how to proofread.**

Slow down. Proofreading requires slowing down your reading rate so that you can see all the letters in each word.

Zoom in. If you proofread on your computer, set the display at 125 percent or more so that you can clearly see each word.

Focus on each word. One way to slow yourself down is to point a pencil or pen at each word as you say it aloud or quietly to yourself.

Read backward. Move backward through each line from right to left. In this way, you won't be listening for meaning or checking for grammatical correctness.

29b Some spelling guidelines

ie/ei

Write *i* before *e* / except after *c* / or when sounded like "*ay*" / as in *neighbor* and *weigh*.

This rhyme reminds you to write *ie* except under two conditions:

● When the two letters follow a *c*.
● When the two letters sound like *ay* (as in *day*).

Some *ie* Words		Some *ei* Words	
believe	field	ceiling	eight
chief	yield	receive	deceive

The following common words are exceptions to this rule:

conscience	foreign	neither	species
counterfeit	height	science	sufficient
either	leisure	seize	weird

Doubling consonants

One-Syllable Words If the word ends with a single short vowel and a consonant, double that last consonant when you are adding a suffix beginning with a vowel.

shop	shopped	shopping	shopper
wet	wetted	wetting	wettest

Two-Syllable Words For words with two or more syllables that end with a vowel and then a consonant, double the consonant when (1) you are adding a suffix beginning with a vowel, and (2) the last syllable of the base word is accented.

occur	occurred	occurring	occurrence
regret	regretted	regretting	regrettable

Final silent -e

Drop the final silent -e when you add a suffix beginning with a vowel. But keep the final -e when the suffix begins with a consonant.

line	lining	care	careful
smile	smiling	like	likely

Words such as "true/truly" and "argue/argument" are exceptions to this rule.

Plurals

- Most plurals are formed by adding -s. But add -es when words end in s, sh, ch, x, or z because another syllable is needed to make the ending easy to pronounce.

one apple	two apples
one box	two boxes

- With phrases and hyphenated words, pluralize the last word unless another word is more important.

one systems analyst	two systems analysts
one sister-in-law	two sisters-in-law
one attorney general	other attorneys general

- For words ending in a consonant plus -y, change the -y to -i and add -es. For proper nouns, keep the -y.

one company	four companies
a monkey	two monkeys
Mr. Henry	the Henrys

- For some words, the plural is formed by changing the base word. Other words have the same form for singular and plural. And other words, taken from other languages, form the plurals in the same way as the original language.

one child	several children
one woman	two women
one deer	nine deer
one medium	some media

HINT

Avoiding the use of apostrophes in plurals

Two books	NOT: two books'
four apples	NOT: four apple's

29c Sound-alike words (homonyms)

Word	Meaning	Example
accept:	to agree/receive	I have to accept the facts.
except:	other than	I called everyone except him.
affect:	to influence	Pollen affects my allergies.
effect:	a result	Sneezing is the effect.
its:	shows possession	Its hinge is loose.
it's:	it is	It's a problem.
than:	used to compare	He is smarter than I.
then:	indicates time	Then I read a book.
their:	shows possession	The kids lost their kite.
there:	indicates location	They found it over there.
they're:	they are	They're happy now.
your:	shows possession	Your suit looks great.
you're:	you are	You're ready for your interview.

VII

Multilingual Speakers

Contents of this section

30	**American Style in Writing/ESL Resources**	112
	30a American style	113
	30b Resources for learning English as a second language	114
31	**Verbs**	114
	31a Verb tenses	114
	• Present tense	115
	• Past tense	115
	• Future tense	115
	31b Helping verbs with main verbs	116
	31c Modal verbs	116
	31d Two-word (phrasal) verbs	116
	31e Verbs with *-ing* and *to* + verb form	117
32	**Nouns (Count and Noncount)**	118
33	**Articles (*A, An,* and *The*)**	119
34	**Prepositions**	120
35	**Omitted and Repeated Words**	122
	35a Omitted words	122
	35b Repeated words	122
36	**Idioms**	123

Question and Correct

	SECTION	PAGE
+ What are some characteristics of American style in writing?	30a	112
+ What kind of organizational style is expected in the American style of writing?	30a	112
+ Are conciseness and a clearly announced topic important for American audiences?	30a	112

	SECTION	PAGE
+ How important is it in American writing to cite sources?	30a	112
+ What are some Web sites that can help speakers of other languages learn English?	30b	113
+ What are the verb tenses in English, and how are they used?	31a	114
+ How do helping verbs such as "be," "do," and "have" combine with main verbs?	31b	116
+ How do modal verbs such as "may" and "could" combine with main verbs?	31c	116
+ What is a phrasal verb?	31d	116
+ How can words added to the main verb, as in "come <u>down</u>" or "come <u>around</u>," change the meaning of a phrase?	31d	116
+ Which is correct? "She plans <u>to finish/finishing</u> her paper tomorrow."	31e	117
+ Which is correct? "He means <u>to go/going</u> to the park this weekend."	31e	117
+ Is it correct to write "two furnitures" and "six chairs"?	32	118
+ When do I use "the," and when do I use "a/an"?	33	119
+ Should I write "<u>a</u> hour" or "<u>an</u> hour"?	33	119
+ Which is the correct preposition? -<u>in/on/at</u> Tuesday -<u>in/on/at</u> 4:00 a.m. -<u>in/on/at</u> home -<u>with/by</u> scissors -<u>on/at/in</u> the vase -six <u>of/for</u> the books -a gift <u>of/for</u> her -go <u>with/of</u> him	34	120
+ What is wrong with these sentences? -The child very smart. -Are going to beach today.	35a	122

	SECTION	PAGE

+ What is wrong with these sentences? 35b 122
  -The book we read it is very
   interesting.
  -The actor who is in that movie he is
   very talented.

+ What is an idiom? 36 123

+ Some phrases in English do not mean
  exactly what the words seem to mean
  (such as "put it on the table," "face the
  music," or "give me the bottom line").
  How do I learn what these mean? 36 123

American Style in Writing/ESL Resources

30a American style

If your first language is not English, you may have writing style preferences that are different from American style and questions about English grammar and usage. Your style preferences and customs will depend on what language(s) you are most familiar with, but in general, consider the following differences between the languages you know and academic style in American English.

	Language Styles of Other Cultures	American Academic Language and Style
Conciseness	In some cultures, writers try for a style with a variety of words and phrases. Ideas can be repeated in various ways.	Effective academic and public writing style in American English is concise and avoids unnecessary words.
Introduction of topic	In some languages, the topic is not immediately announced or stated at all. Instead, suggestions lead readers to develop the main ideas themselves.	In American English, there is a strong preference for announcing the topic in the opening paragraph or near the beginning of the paper.
Organization	Digressions, or moving off the main topic into related matters, are encouraged in some cultures because they add to the richness of ideas.	In American English, there is a preference for staying on the topic and not moving away, or digressing, from it.

(continued)

	Language Styles of Other Cultures	American Academic Language and Style
Pattern of reasoning	Writers in some cultures prefer inductive reasoning, moving from specifics to the more general conclusion.	American academic writing is usually deductive, beginning with general ideas and moving to more specific reasons or details.
Citation of sources	In some cultures, there is less attention to citing sources, ideas, or the exact words used by others. Ideas of great scholars, for example, can be used without citation because it is assumed that readers know the sources.	In American academic writing, writers are expected to cite all sources of information that are not generally known by most people. A writer who fails to credit the words or ideas of others is in danger of being viewed as a plagiarist.

30b Resources for learning English as a second language

Some Web sites where you can find useful resources for learning English as another language include the following:

dictionary.cambridge.org

This dictionary is especially useful for people learning English as another language. There are also links to dictionaries of idioms and two-word (phrasal) verbs.

esl.fis.edu

Frankfort International School's "Guide to Learning English" includes exercises on reading, writing, grammar, and vocabulary.

www.eslcafe.com

Dave Sperling's ESL Café provides discussion forums, links to jobs, help with pronunciation and slang, useful books, and many other aids.

owl.english.purdue.edu/owl/resource/678/01/

Purdue University's Online Writing Lab page includes links to handouts on ESL issues as well as other resources.

www.1-language.com

1-Language.com offers free English courses, an audio listening center, forums, real-time chat, job listings, and more.

www.englishforum.com/00

> Aardvark's English Forum includes dictionaries, interactive exercises, resources for teachers, world weather and news, and links to other useful sites.

http://a4esl.org

> The site contains quizzes, tests, exercises, and puzzles to help with ESL issues (a project of *The Internet TESL Journal*).

home.gwu.edu/~meloni/eslstudyhall

> Professor Meloni's ESL Study Hall at George Washington University lists resources for ESL students working on their reading, writing, vocabulary, grammar, and listening skills, as well as a section on U.S. culture.

31

Verbs

Unlike sentences in some other languages, verbs are required in English sentences because they indicate time and person (also see 14b for information about verb forms, voice, and mood).

31a Verb tenses

Progressive tenses: Use a form of *be* plus the *-ing* form of the verb, such as *going* or *running*.

She **is going** to the concert tonight.

Perfect tenses: Use a form of *have* plus the past participle, such as *walked* or *gone*.

They **have finished** the project.

Present tense

Simple Present:
- present actions or conditions

    She **feels** happy.

* a general action or literary truth

  The sun **sets** later during the summer.

* habitual actions

  I **take** my dog to the park every morning.

* future time

  The concert **begins** at 7:00 p.m. this evening.

Present Progressive: activity in progress, not finished, or continuing

He **is studying** Swedish.

Present Perfect: actions that began in the past and lead up to and include the present

She **has lived** in Alaska for two years.

Present Perfect Progressive: action that began in the past, continues to the present, and may continue into the future

They **have been building** that parking garage for six months.

Past tense

* **Simple Past:** completed actions or conditions

  They **ate** breakfast in the cafeteria.

* **Past Progressive:** past action that took place over a period of time or was interrupted by another action

  He **was swimming** when the storm began.

* **Past Perfect:** action or event completed before another event in the past

  No one **had heard** about the crisis when the newscast began.

* **Past Perfect Progressive:** ongoing condition in the past that has ended.

  I **had been planning** my trip to Mexico when I heard about the earthquake.

Future tense

* **Simple Future:** actions or events in the future.

  The store **will open** at 9:00 a.m.

- **Future Progressive:** future action that will continue for some time

  I **will be working** on that project next week.

- **Future Perfect:** action that will be completed by or before a specified time in the future

  Next summer, they **will have been** here for twenty years.

- **Future Perfect Progressive:** ongoing action or condition until a specific time in the future

  By tomorrow, I **will have been waiting** for the delivery for one month.

31b Helping verbs with main verbs

Helping or auxiliary verbs combine with other verbs.

Forms of Helping Verbs

be	be	am	is	are	was	were	being	been
have	have	has	had					
do	do	does	did					

31c Modal verbs

Modal verbs are helping verbs that indicate possibility, uncertainty, necessity, or advisability. Use the base form of the verb after the modal.

can	may	must	should	would
could	might	shall	will	ought to

Your car battery <u>can die</u> if you leave your headlights on all night.

<u>May</u> I <u>take</u> this?

31d Two-word (phrasal) verbs

Some verbs are followed by a second (and sometimes a third) word that combine to indicate the meaning. Many dictionaries will indicate the meanings of these phrasal verbs.

look over ("examine")	She **looked over** the contract.
look up ("search for")	I need to **look up** that phone number.

The second word of some of these verbs can be separated from the main verb by a noun or pronoun.

> Manuel told the team to <u>count</u> **him** <u>in</u>. (separable)

> The team could <u>count on</u> **him** to help. (cannot be separated)

31e Verbs with *-ing* and *to* + verb form

Some verbs combine only with the *-ing* form of the verb (the gerund), some combine only with the *to* + verb form (the infinitive), and some can be followed by either form.

Verbs Followed Only by *-ing* Forms (Gerunds)

admit	enjoy	recall
appreciate	finish	recommend
deny	keep	risk
dislike	practice	suggest

> He <u>admits spending</u> that money.

> She <u>risked losing</u> her scholarship.

Verbs Followed Only by *to* + Verb Forms (Infinitives)

agree	have	plan
ask	mean	promise
claim	need	wait
decide	offer	wish

> We <u>agree to send</u> an answer soon.

> They <u>planned to go</u> on vacation.

Verbs That Can Be Followed by Either Form

begin	like	remember
continue	love	start
hate	prefer	try

> They <u>begin to sing</u>. (*or*) They <u>begin singing</u>.

> I <u>tried to fix</u> the car. (*or*) I <u>tried fixing</u> the car.

Nouns (Count and Noncount)

Proper and common nouns

Proper nouns name specific places, things, and people. They begin with capital letters; all other names are **common nouns** and are not capitalized.

Count and noncount nouns

Common nouns are of two types: count and noncount nouns.

Count nouns name things that can be counted because those things can be divided into separate and distinct units. Count nouns have plurals and usually refer to things that can be seen, heard, touched, tasted, or smelled.

Count Nouns	
book	one book, two books
chair	a chair, several chairs
child	the child, six children

Noncount nouns name things that cannot be counted because they are abstractions or things that cannot be cut into parts. Noncount nouns do not have plurals and may have a collective meaning. Noncount nouns are used with singular verbs and pronouns. They are never used with *a* or *an,* but they can be used with *some.*

Noncount Nouns		
air	humor	oil
furniture	literature	weather

The names of many foods and materials are noncount nouns.

bread	corn	electricity
coffee	spaghetti	steel

To indicate the amount for a noncount noun, use a count noun first. If you use *some,* use a singular verb.

a pound of coffee	a loaf of bread
an ear of corn	a gallon of oil

Articles (*A, An,* and *The*)

A/An

A and *an* identify a noun in a general or indefinite way and refer to any member of a group. *A* and *an*, which mean "one among many," are generally used with singular count nouns (see Chapter 32).

> She likes to read <u>a</u> book before going to sleep.

> (*This sentence does not specify which book but refers to any book.*)

> He ordered <u>an</u> egg for breakfast.

The

The identifies a particular or specific noun in a group or a noun already identified in a previous phrase or sentence. *The* may be used with singular or plural nouns.

> She read <u>the</u> book that I gave her.

> (*This sentence identifies a specific book.*)

> **A** new model of computer was introduced yesterday. **The** model will cost much less than **the** older model.

> (*A introduces the noun the first time it is mentioned, and then* the *is used afterward whenever the noun is mentioned.*)

Some uses of *the*

- Use *the* when an essential phrase or clause follows the noun.

  <u>The</u> man who is standing at the door is my cousin.

- Use *the* when the noun refers to a class as a whole.

  <u>The</u> ferret is a popular pet.

- Use *the* with names that combine proper and common nouns.

  <u>the</u> British Commonwealth   <u>the</u> Gobi Desert   <u>the</u> University of Illinois

- Use *the* when names are plurals.

  <u>the</u> Netherlands   <u>the</u> Balkans

- Use *the* with names that refer to rivers, oceans, seas, points on the globe, deserts, forests, gulfs, and peninsulas.

  <u>the</u> Nile   <u>the</u> Pacific Ocean   <u>the</u> Persian Gulf

- Use *the* with superlatives.

  <u>the</u> best reporter   <u>the</u> most expensive car

No articles

Articles are not used with names of streets, cities, states, countries, continents, lakes, parks, mountains, languages, sports, holidays, universities and colleges without *of* in the name, and academic subjects.

He traveled to Botswana.   She applied to Brandeis University.
She is studying Mandarin.   My major is political science.

34

Prepositions

Prepositions in English show relationships between words. The following guide will help you choose among *on, at, in, of, for,* and *with* to indicate time, place, and logical relationships.

Prepositions of time

on   Use with days (**on** Monday).

at   Use with hours of the day (**at** 9:00 p.m.) and with *noon, night, midnight,* and *dawn* (**at** midnight).

in   Use with other parts of the day: *morning, afternoon, evening* (**in** the morning); use with months, years, seasons (**in** the winter).

They are getting married **on** Sunday **at** four o'clock **in** the afternoon.

Prepositions of place

on   Indicates a surface on which something rests

She put curtains **on** the windows.

at   Indicates a point in relation to another object

I'll meet you **at** Second Avenue and Main Street.

in   Indicates an object is inside the boundaries of an area or volume

She is **in** the bank.

Prepositions to show logical relationships

of   Shows relationship between a part (or parts) and the whole

One **of** her teachers gave a quiz.

of   Shows material or content

They gave me a basket **of** food.

for   Shows purpose

We bought seeds **for** our garden.

with   Shows a means used

He dug the hole **with** a shovel.

with   Shows cause or origin

Matt was sick **with** the flu.

with   Shows possession

The car **with** the Indiana license plate is mine.

35

Omitted and Repeated Words

35a Omitted words

Subjects and verbs can be omitted in some languages but are necessary and must appear in English sentences. The only exception in English is the command, which has an understood subject: "Move those chairs here." (The understood subject here is "you.")

Subjects

Include a subject in the main clause and all other clauses. *There* and *it* may sometimes serve as subject words. The subject is left out only when expressing a command (*Put that box here, please.*).

> *there*
> Certainly, are many confusing rules in English spelling.
> ^

> *It*
> is about ten miles from here to the shopping mall.
> ^

Verbs

Verbs such as *am, is,* and *are* and other helping verbs are needed in English and cannot be omitted.

> *is*
> Nurit studying to be a computer programmer.
> ^

> *has*
> She been studying ancient Mayan ruins in Mexico for many summers.
> ^

35b Repeated words

In some languages, the subject can be repeated as a pronoun before the verb. In English, the subject is included only once.

The plane that was ready for takeoff it stopped on the runway.

(Plane *is the subject of the verb* stopped, *and* it *is an unnecessary repetition of the subject.*)

When relative pronouns such as *who, which,* and *that* or relative adverbs such as *where* or *when* are the object of the verb, no additional word is needed.

The woman tried on the hat that I left it on the seat.

(That *is the object of the verb* left, *and* it *is an unnecessary repetition.*)

The city where I live there has two soccer fields.

(Where *is the object of the verb* live, *and* there *is an unnecessary repetition.*)

36

Idioms

An idiom is an expression that means something beyond the literal meaning of the words. An idiom such as *kick the bucket* (meaning "die") cannot be understood by examining the meanings of the individual words. Many idioms are used only in informal English. Dictionaries of American English, such as the *Cambridge International Dictionary of Idioms* (http://dictionary.cambridge.org) define many commonly used phrases.

Here are some typical idioms:

bottom line	the last figure on a financial balance sheet; the result or final outcome or ultimate truth
hand over fist	very rapidly, with rapid progress
hold water	be proved, be correct
on one's toes	eager, alert
on the table	open for discussion
see the light	understand something clearly at last, realize one's mistake

The meanings of two-word (phrasal) verbs (see 31d) also change according to the prepositions that follow the verbs. Note the difference in the meanings of the two-word (phrasal) verbs *look after* and *look over:*

look after take care of

Could you **look after** my dog while I am away on vacation?

look over examine something (briefly)

I'll **look over** the report you gave me.

VIII

Research

Contents of this section

37 Finding a Topic   128
   37a Selecting a topic   128
   37b Focusing your topic   128
   37c Researching your topic   130
   37d Formulating your thesis statement   130

38 Searching for Information   131
   38a Choosing primary and secondary sources   131
   38b Searching libraries and library databases   132
   38c Searching the Internet   136
   38d Using Web resources   140
        • Writers' resources   140
   38e Using firsthand research   145
        • Observations   146
        • Surveys   146
        • Interviews   147
   38f Taking notes   149
        • Starting a working bibliography   149

39 Evaluating Print and Online Sources   154
   39a Getting started   154
   39b Evaluating Internet sources   155
   39c Evaluating bibliographic citations   157
        • Author   157
        • Timeliness   159
        • Publisher, producer, sponsor   159
   39d Evaluating content   160

40 Integrating Sources   161
   40a Avoiding plagiarism   161
   40b Summarizing   165
   40c Paraphrasing   167
   40d Quoting   168
   40e Using signal words and phrases   170

41 Designing Documents   173
   41a Principles of document design   173
   41b Incorporating visuals   174
   41c Page preparation   177

Question and Correct

	SECTION	PAGE
+ How can I find a topic for my research paper?	37a	128
+ How do I narrow my topic?	37b	128
+ After I have my topic, how do I come up with a thesis statement?	37b	128
+ What is the difference between a primary source and a secondary source?	38a	131
+ What kinds of useful catalogs and reference sources might I find in the library?	38b	132
+ What is a library database, and what kinds of information does it have?	38b	132
+ When I'm researching in a specific field, which databases should I check?	38b	135
+ What are some strategies for searching the Web?	38c	136
+ What is a search engine?	38c	136
+ What are some useful Web sites I can use for research?	38d	140
+ How can I use firsthand observations in my research?	38e	145
+ What are some strategies for conducting a survey?	38e	146
+ How can I conduct an effective interview?	38e	147
+ What are some ways I can keep my research notes organized?	38f	149
+ How can I start evaluating the credibility of my sources?	39a	154
+ What should I look for to decide whether a Web site is credible or not?	39b	155
+ How can I evaluate a bibliographic citation to decide whether or not to spend time finding and reading it?	39c	157
+ What are some criteria to think about when I evaluate the content of a source?	39d	160

	SECTION	PAGE
+ What is plagiarism, and how can I avoid it?	40a	161
+ What is the difference between a summary and a paraphrase?	40b	165
+ How do I know whether my paraphrase is worded too closely to the original source?	40c	167
+ How do I smoothly insert a quotation into my paper?	40d	168
+ What are signal words and phrases, and how can I use them when including source material in my paper?	40e	170
+ What is document design, and why are the principles important when writing papers?	41a	173
+ What are some strategies for including visual elements in my papers?	41b	174
+ How and when do I use tables, graphs, and charts?	41b	174
+ How do I format the margins and layout of my paper?	41c	177

37

Finding a Topic

37a Selecting a topic

Selecting a topic is one of the most important decisions you will make in the research process. You'll want to find a topic that is interesting, fits the guidelines of your assignment, and can be researched effectively with the resources and time available to you.

TRY THIS

To Select a Topic

- **Read newspapers, magazines, and online news sites.** Issues covered in the news are often timely, debatable topics or are current developments you want to know more about, such as new technology or health news. (See Chapter 38 for links to news sites.)

- **Use Internet search engines and library databases.** Use a well-known search engine such as Google or Yahoo!, a library database such as InfoTrac or LexisNexis, or an electronic card catalog, and type in search terms for a topic interesting to you. (See Chapter 38 for a list of Internet search engines and library databases.)

- **Check reference guides.** Browse through any book or catalog of subject headings, such as the *Library of Congress Subject Headings* and the *Readers' Guide to Periodical Literature*.

Here are two examples of general subjects:

Topic: Human papillomavirus (HPV) vaccine

Topic: Narrative in Quentin Tarantino films

37b Focusing your topic

Once you have identified a general subject, you'll need to focus your topic so that it is specific and manageable. Consider these questions:

- How much time will you have to complete the research?

- Is there a specific number or type of sources required for this assignment?

- How long will your project need to be?

- Does your assignment specify a purpose for your writing? To inform? To persuade? To educate? To call to action?

- Who is the intended audience for your writing project? Your peers? A group of readers who resist your idea? A person or group who has the power to make the changes or solutions you suggest?

To focus your topic, start by thinking about how to make it more specific and manageable.

- **Narrowing Topics That Are Too Broad** As you begin, consider whether your topic idea is manageable for the time and resources you have. Often, your initial idea is too general and might need to be narrowed down. For example, what if you are interested in writing about America's over-reliance on oil? This is a big issue that has many political, economic, and scientific dimensions. Narrow that down to a more specific aspect of the problem, such as ways consumers can save energy when heating and cooling their homes. As you start your research, you may find that the topic still covers too much and may need to be narrowed even more.

- **Broadening Topics That Are Too Narrow** Sometimes a topic may be too narrow, especially when very little information or only specialized information exists on the topic. For example, perhaps you are wondering why you have to take twelve credits of a foreign language to complete your college's general education requirements. However, this question only affects you. How might you make your topic relevant for a wider audience? You might examine whether acquiring a foreign language is useful for law enforcement careers. After collecting more research, you will be in a better position to offer a credible judgment on this issue.

- **Avoiding Topics That Are Too Tired or Overdone** Topics that are too tired or overdone can result in boring, flat papers. Questions about legalizing marijuana, capital punishment, and abortion have been discussed so often that you may find the topic is worn out.

    To make those general topics of human papillomavirus (HPV) vaccine or narrative style in Quentin Tarantino

films more specific, narrow down to more focused subtopics
such as the following:

Narrowed topic: State laws requiring teenage girls to receive
the human papillomavirus vaccine

Narrowed topic: Use of narrative style in Quentin Tarantino's
Pulp Fiction

37c Researching your topic

When first starting your research process, try listing all of
the questions you need to answer so that you understand
your topic more fully. Thinking first about the journalist's
questions—*who*, *what*, *when*, *where*, *why*, and *how*—can
help you to gather basic information. Once you understand
the basics about your topic, you can work to develop more
specific questions that can lead you to your thesis.

After completing your research and reviewing your
sources, you should have enough information to create a
research question about your topic. A research question is
the main question you will answer in your paper. The
answer to your research question is the thesis, or main
point, of your paper.

These sample research questions focus the writer's
investigation into specific aspects of each topic.

Research Question: Should states legally require teenage
girls to get the HPV vaccine?

Research Question: What is the effect of *Pulp Fiction's*
narrative style on viewers' expectations?

37d Formulating your thesis statement

After completing your research and reviewing the information you've collected, you can begin to formulate a tenta-
tive thesis statement. Your thesis statement will answer
your research question, communicate the main idea of
your paper, and help you create a working outline. The thesis is more than a summary of information. It states your
position or the point you are arguing and researching and
shows what you, as a knowledgeable writer, have learned
about your topic. Your thesis may need to be revised further as you write and revise your paper.

These two thesis statements communicate the writer's
conclusions about each topic:

Thesis: States should not legally mandate that teenage girls
receive the HPV vaccine.

Thesis: *Pulp Fiction*'s narrative style forces viewers to create a chronological storyline in their own minds and take an active role in the storytelling process.

A good thesis statement will provide the main idea of the essay as well as suggest your purpose for writing (such as *to explain*, *to persuade*, or *to interpret*). And it will guide your writing as you compose the paper. See Chapter 1 for more about thesis statements.

38

Searching for Information

38a Choosing primary and secondary sources

Primary sources are original or firsthand materials. Primary sources include the following:

- Words written or spoken by the original author, such as essays, novels, or autobiographies (but not, for example, biographies *about* that person), narratives about the author's personal experiences, speeches, e-mails, blogs (journals that a person writes and posts on the Web for others to read), discussion group postings, or Tweets (posts on Twitter), if written by an authority on the subject

- Surveys, studies, or interviews that you conduct

- Any creative works by the original author (poems, plays, Web pages, art forms such as pictures and sculpture)

- Accounts of events by people who were present

Primary sources may be more accurate because they have not been distorted by others. Primary sources are not always unbiased, however, because some people present pictures of themselves and their accomplishments that may not be objective.

Secondary sources are secondhand accounts, information, or reports about primary sources written or delivered by people who weren't direct participants in the events or issues being examined. Typical secondary sources include the following:

- News articles, blogs, and other information written by people writing about the primary event or person

- Reviews

- Biographies

- Documentaries

- Encyclopedia entries

- Other material interpreted or studied by others

Although reading secondary sources may save time, we need to remember they are *interpretations* and may be biased, inaccurate, or incomplete. You may, though, find a more complete account by reading several secondary sources that disagree with each other. This can help demonstrate conflicting views.

HINT

Emphasizing the Writer's Views

While some cultures place more value on student writing that primarily brings together or collects the thoughts of great scholars or experts, readers of research papers in American institutions value the writer's own interpretations and thinking about the subject, based on the information found.

38b Searching libraries and library databases

Libraries have the types of scholarly resources your instructor will most probably want you to use for your research.

- **General Reference Sources** The library's reference section has encyclopedias, including those for specific areas of study. Other general sources include collections of biographies, yearbooks, and almanacs such as the *World Almanac and Book of Facts,* dictionaries, atlases, and government publications such as the *Statistical Abstract of the United States.* When you read an entry in a subject encyclopedia or other scholarly sources, you know you're reading information from authors who are selected because of their expertise.

- **Library Indexes and Catalogs**   Your library will have book indexes such as *Books in Print,* periodical indexes such as the *Readers' Guide to Periodical Literature,* and online indexes. Most library catalogs are computerized, so you can also do online searches of the library's holdings by author, title, keyword, and subject heading. When you request a *keyword search,* the search engine will look for the word in any part of the entry in the catalog (title, subtitle, abstract, etc.), whereas the *subject heading* has to match, word for word, the Library of Congress headings (listed in the *Library of Congress Subject Headings*). When doing a keyword search, you can also try synonyms for your topic or broader terms that might include it. For example, when searching for information about hybrid cars, you might also try **"fuel-efficient vehicles"** or **"alternative energy sources"** as keywords.

- **Library Databases and Subscription Services**   Many libraries subscribe to periodical databases and other services that have access to electronic versions of articles from journals, magazines, and newspapers. Sometimes these materials are available on CD-ROM in a library, but more often you'll find them online through links on the library's Web page. These databases are free for use by anyone registered with the college, and some databases can also be found on public library sites.

Resources in library databases are a good place to start because they are considered scholarly or newsworthy, don't contain advertisements, have current information about issues and events, and have already been fact-checked and edited. Some of the most widely used library databases include the following:

- *Academic Search Premier*—includes a wide range of newspaper, magazine, and journal articles.

- *Expanded Academic ASAP*—provides a wide range of newspaper, magazine, and journal articles.

- *General Business File ASAP*—offers articles on business news and research.

- *InfoTrac Custom Newspapers*—provides access to newspaper articles.

- *InfoTrac Health and Wellness Resource Center*—provides information on medical and health-related topics.

- *JSTOR*—contains full-text articles from a number of academic journals.

- *LexisNexis*—offers news articles, including transcripts of speeches, news shows, and other events.

- *MLA International Bibliography*—provides bibliographic information for literary criticism and research.

- *NewsBank*—contains newspaper articles.

- *OCLC FirstSearch*—contains a wide variety of articles on general academic subjects.

- *Project Muse*—provides full-text articles from several academic journals.

- *PsycARTICLES*—offers access to psychology research.

- *ScienceDirect*—specializes in science, technical, and medical articles.

Check your library's Web page or ask your reference librarians to find what other types of database resources your library offers as well as how to log in and access these materials. You will probably need your student ID or a school password to log in.

TRY THIS

To Conduct a Search on Library or Subscription Databases

- **Decide on starting with a search term or a keyword term.** When you begin, consider whether a subject search or keyword search would be more helpful for finding information on your topic.

- **Search by subject.** When you search a broad subject, like "**globalization**" or "**cancer**," some databases will connect you to a list of subdivided topics that allow you to narrow your search.

- **Search by keyword.** If you have a more narrow or specific topic, such as the laws needed to protect the nesting grounds of loggerhead turtles on the South Carolina coast, you might search by using a list of relevant keywords ("**loggerhead turtles**," "**nesting**," "**South Carolina**," and "**law**") to find relevant hits in the title or full text of articles.

- **Use Boolean terms.** Boolean terms can also sometimes help you narrow your search. For example, use words like **AND** to add items to your search. Use **OR** for choices between search terms and **NOT** to exclude certain items from your search.

- **Read the help section.** Start your database search by reading the directions for using the database's search engine. The help section of your database helps you find the ways that program works to narrow your search.

Many "full-text" databases provide the entire text of articles that originally appeared in journals, magazines, or newspapers. In many cases, you'll be able to see a Web page that shows the digitized text of the entire article. In other cases, you may be able to view a PDF file of the document. This allows you to see the article as it originally appeared in a journal, magazine, or newspaper with the same layout, colors, and photographs. In other cases, databases may provide just the bibliographic citations needed to locate relevant articles or an abstract, which is a brief summary of the article. To locate the full text of these materials, you should check your library's catalog to see whether the library has these resources in print form or on microfiche. You can also ask your reference librarians to see whether these materials are available through its interlibrary loan service.

HINT

Using Library Databases for Research in Various Disciplines

Try checking the following specialized databases for specific fields of study.

Art: *Art Full Text, JSTOR, Project Muse*

Business: *Business Source Premier, Business and Company Resource Center, Dun and Bradstreet's Million Dollar Database, General Business File ASAP, Standard and Poor's Net Advantage*

Communications and Journalism: *Communication and Mass Media Complete, Communication Abstracts, LexisNexis*

Computer Science/Technology: *Computer Source, INSPEC*

Education: *ERIC, Educator's Reference Complete*

Engineering: *Compendex, INSPEC*

History: *History Resource Center, America: History and Life, Historical Abstracts, JSTOR*

Law: *LegalTrac, LexisNexis*

Literature: *MLA International Bibliography, Literature Resource Center, JSTOR*

Mathematics: *Math SciNet*

Medicine: *Medline, Health Source, Cochrane Library, CINAHL, Nursing Resource Center*

Political Science: *International Political Science Abstracts (IPSA), Public Affairs Information Service International (PAIS), Worldwide Political Science Abstracts*

Psychology: *PsycARTICLES, PsycINFO, Psychology and Behavioral Sciences Collection*

Sciences: *Science Direct, Science Citation Index, Cambridge Scientific Abstracts*

Sociology: *Sociological Abstracts*

38c Searching the Internet

The Internet is particularly useful when searching for the kinds of sources and information listed here. But be cautious and remember that anyone can post anything on the Internet. That means you'll find biased, false, or distorted information and claims intended to entice you into buying products, changing your views, or donating money.

Despite the ocean of information you can access online, you are less likely to find older books, collections of reference works, the content of some journals, old archives of newspapers, and many other materials. For current events topics, searching your library's databases can be a better first research step than starting with the Internet.

For the Internet part of your search, you can find the sources described here.

- **Government Sources** The U.S. government offers huge quantities of information online, produced by various bureaus, agencies, and legislators. You can also check for references to government publications your library may have. For a list of government sites on the Internet, see 38d. There are also online city, county, and state sites with information of local concern. Governments outside the United States also post information on the Web about their countries.

- **Online Library Catalogs and Databases** You can search many libraries online, especially the Library of Congress, to find other materials on your topic, and your library may be able to borrow these resources for you. You can also read titles and abstracts to get a sense of what's available on the topic. Your library may also subscribe to full-text databases or online journals (see 38b for a list of popular library databases).

- **Current News and Publications** Most newspapers (including nationally circulated papers such as the *New York Times* and your local newspapers), television networks (such as ABC, CBS, CNN, Fox, and NBC), and print publications (such as *Time, Wired, The New Republic,* and some scholarly journals) maintain online databases. Here you'll find excerpts from current articles and news stories from their print sources or television programs. See the addresses listed in 38d. Some archives charge for copies, but you may be able to request copies through your library's interlibrary loan service. You may also be able to read full-text articles through your university account.

- **Newsgroups and E-Mail Lists** Newsgroups are open forums where anyone can post a message about forum topics. E-Mail lists are accessed by subscription, and messages sent by list members go to all subscribers. Many newsgroups and e-mail lists have very useful FAQs that may answer your questions, and some have archives of past discussions.

- **Blogs** Web logs or "blogs" are Web sites with dated entries listed in reverse chronological order so the most recent post is first. Some blogs are personal and informal, but others are written by journalists. Blogs may also have themes, such as politics, health care, or education. Some blogs are widely read and very influential because they are written by knowledgeable people whose writing is respected. Reading about the blog owner and writer(s) can help you determine the blog's credibility. And think about the quality of the content and whether it is reliable or not.

- **Older Books** Several sites, including Bartleby.com and Project Gutenberg, have posted older books with expired copyrights. Other projects are dedicated to making rare or hard-to-find older resources available online. See the addresses listed in 38d.

- **Other Online Sources** In addition, you'll find sites maintained by public-interest groups (such as environmental groups or consumer safety organizations) and nonprofit organizations (such as museums and universities) with information about their areas of interest, directories to help you locate companies and people, and company sites with information about the company's services and products (and discussion groups on the company site about its products and services). There are also biased sites that post propaganda to influence others to adopt their views. To sort out such sites from more trustworthy sites, evaluate your sources carefully (see Chapter 39).

- **Search Engines** Search engines scan huge numbers of Web sites and will help you find materials from a large variety of resources, including discussions of your topic on newsgroups, listservs, and blogs. Different search engines also allow you to indicate whether you want to search the Web, images, groups, news, audio, and so on. Google is the most powerful and most widely used search engine; it allows users to search the full text of Web sites, articles, and books, as well as images and video. By using Google's "Advanced Search," you can find results in book texts, government documents, and other languages. Yahoo!, MSN, Bing, AOL, and Ask.com are other commonly used search engines. You can also use metasearch engines, such as Dogpile and Mamma, to comb multiple search engines and view a limited number of the combined results. Many search engines include sponsored links (links that advertisers pay for) listed prominently on the first page of results.

TRY THIS

To Use Internet Search Engines Effectively

Keeping these suggestions in mind will make your search more efficient.

- Use phrases instead of single words to define your search more specifically.
- Think of a variety of keywords that apply to your topic. If your keyword doesn't turn up much that is useful, switch to a different one.
- Enclose the whole term (as a unit) in quotation marks to be sure that the entire term is the object of the search.
- When you find a useful site, look for links that connect you to related sites.
- Be sure your terms are spelled correctly.
- Use search engine directories or categories when they exist.

When you have two sets of keywords or phrases, combine them with some terms (known as *Boolean terms*) in combination with your topic or keywords to limit the results to what you are looking for.

HINT

Using Boolean Terms for Internet Searches

Each search engine has its own rules for the use of Boolean terms. Check the help section to understand how to use these terms effectively in your favorite search engines.

- (*or*) NOT

The minus sign or NOT can tell the database or search engine to find a reference that contains one term but not the other. For example, suppose you'd like information about coaches who have worked with the Chicago Bulls basketball team. However, the search phrase *"Chicago Bulls coaches"* will also bring up links to sites that sell coaches' series women's watches. To narrow that search and weed out links where such watches can be bought, you can include a minus sign directly in front of the word you want to exclude: *"Chicago Bulls coaches" -watches.*

OR

OR can help you combine terms in your search or find a search term that may appear two different ways. For example, if you want information on sudden infant death syndrome, try *"sudden infant death syndrome" OR SIDS*. Use OR if the comparative terms will help you find what you need more efficiently.

+ (*or*) AND

Many search engines, such as Google, Yahoo!, and Bing, automatically search for every keyword you list, so the word AND or a plus sign is often not needed. For some search engines and library databases, however, the plus sign or AND tells the search engine to find your first word or term *and* your second word or term (and perhaps a third word or term if it's relevant). That helps narrow the results list closer to what you want.

In some search engines like Google, however, the plus sign immediately in front of a word means that it is essential for the search. For example, if you are looking up the film *Rocky IV*, you can type in *Rocky +IV* to narrow your results.

Using Directories or Categories   Some search engines, such as Google (http://directory.google.com), have materials arranged by general subjects in directories (such as "business and economy," "education," "government," "health," and "society and culture"). Within each subject, you can find numerous related sites. For example, under "health," you may find the subheadings "diseases," "drugs," and "fitness." These can be very helpful to browse through when you are looking for a topic for a paper.

38d Using Web resources

This chapter provides you with a list of particularly useful Web sites to search. As you search, you'll need to collect bibliographic information about the Web sites you visit so you can locate them later as well as create entries for your Works Cited page (see 42c for MLA citation information) or References page (see 43c for APA citation information).

Writers' resources

These sites offer a variety of resources writers use, such as dictionaries, a thesaurus, instructional handouts, reference books, style guides, and a biographical dictionary. The Online Writing Labs (OWLs) are links to dozens of college and university writing centers with writing skills materials online.

Bartlett's Familiar Quotations	www.bartleby.com/100
Biographical Dictionary	www.s9.com
Cambridge Dictionaries Online	dictionary.cambridge.org
Dictionary.com/ Writing Resources	dictionary.reference.com/writing
IWCA Resources for Writers	writingcenters.org/resources
Merriam-Webster Online Dictionary	www.m-w.com
OWLs (Online Writing Labs)	writingcenters.org/owcdb
Purdue Online Writing Lab	owl.english.purdue.edu
Roget's New Thesaurus	www.bartleby.com/110
Strunk's *Elements of Style*	www.bartleby.com/141
Thesaurus.com	thesaurus.reference.com

Academic Databases and Online Resources Databases, as explained in 38b, are searchable indexes that offer either citations or the complete text of materials on a vast array of topics. Most academic libraries subscribe to some or all of these databases. You can search your own library's databases; however, often you can't search most other academic libraries because they pay for access to many of these databases and limit their use to students on their campus. You usually need a password or student identification to access these materials. The sites listed here, however, are available to all users. Public libraries also subscribe to databases that are usually open for public use.

Academic Info	www.academicinfo.net/digital.html
Directory of Open Access Journals	www.doaj.org
ERIC: Educational Resources Information Center	www.eric.ed.gov
Google Books	books.google.com
Google Scholar	scholar.google.com
Project Muse	muse.jhu.edu
Questia Online Library of Books and Journals	www.questia.com

Search Engines   Search engines, as explained in 38b, search millions of Web sites to find sites that match your search terms. Google is a very powerful search engine and is also a good starting point for most searches.

Google	www.google.com
Yahoo!	www.yahoo.com
Ask	www.ask.com
MSN	www.msn.com
Bing	www.bing.com

Metasearch Engines   Metasearch engines, as explained in 38b, collect the results of multiple search engines. As search engines such as Google have expanded their search capabilities, metasearch engines have generally become more limited in their coverage, but they can still provide useful results.

Dogpile	www.dogpile.com
Mamma	www.mamma.com

Libraries and Subject Directories   These online libraries can be searched by subject. Some also have the complete text of literary works online.

Academic Information Index	www.academicinfo.net
English Server	eserver.org

Internet Public Library	www.ipl.org
Libcat: A Guide to Library Resources on the Internet	www.librarysites.info
Library of Congress	www.loc.gov
Library Spot	www.libraryspot.com
Online Literary Resources	andromeda.rutgers.edu/ ~jlynch/Lit
U.S. Government Publications (GPO) Catalog	www.gpoaccess.gov
Voice of the Shuttle	vos.ucsb.edu/index.asp
WWW Virtual Library	www.vlib.org

Online Books (E-Books) These Web sites offer the complete text of previously printed books. See also the list of libraries and subject directories.

Bartleby.com	www.bartleby.com
Complete Works of William Shakespeare	thetech.mit.edu/ shakespeare
Google Books	books.google.com
Online Books Page	onlinebooks.library. upenn.edu
Project Gutenberg	www.gutenberg.org
Read Print	www.readprint.com
Scholars' Lab Digital Resources	www.lib.virginia.edu/ scholarslab/resources
Victorian Women Writers Project	www.indiana.edu/~letrs/ vwwp

Magazines, Journals, and News Media These Web sites are maintained by the major print, television, and online magazines, journals, and news media.

ABC News	abcnews.go.com
Arts and Letters Daily	www.aldaily.com
ArtsJournal.com	www.artsjournal.com
BBC News	news.bbc.co.uk
CBS News	www.cbsnews.com
CEO Express	www.ceoexpress.com
Chicago Tribune	www.chicagotribune.com
CNN News	www.cnn.com

Fox News	www.foxnews.com
Google News	news.google.com
London Times	www.thetimes.co.uk
Los Angeles Times	www.latimes.com
Metalinks.com	metalinks.com/usmedia.htm
MSNBC News	www.msnbc.com
New York Times Online	nytimes.com
NPR (National Public Radio) News	www.npr.org
Reuters	www.reuters.com
Roper Center for Public Opinion	www.ropercenter.uconn.edu
Salon	www.salon.com
SciTechDaily	www.scitechdaily.com
Slate	www.slate.com
United Press International	www.upi.com
USA Today	www.usatoday.com
Washington Post	www.washingtonpost.com
Washington Times	www.washtimes.com
Yahoo! News	news.yahoo.com

Government and Public Information

American Civil Liberties Union	www.aclu.org
American Recovery and Reinvestment Act	www.recovery.gov
Bureau of Labor Statistics	www.bls.gov
Census Bureau	www.census.gov
Census Bureau Fact Finder	factfinder.census.gov/home/saff/main.html?_lang=en
Census Bureau State and County QuickFacts	quickfacts.census.gov/qfd
Center for Urban Studies	www.cus.wayne.edu
Center on Budget and Policy Priorities	www.cbpp.org
Centers for Disease Control and Prevention	www.cdc.gov
Central Intelligence Agency	www.cia.gov
Childstats.gov	www.childstats.gov
CountryWatch	www.countrywatch.com
C-SPAN	www.c-span.org
Data.gov (*access to federal datasets*)	www.data.gov

Department of Commerce, Bureau of Economic Analysis	www.bea.gov
Department of Health and Human Services	www.hhs.gov
Department of Homeland Security	www.dhs.gov
Department of Housing and Human Development	www.hud.gov
Department of Justice, Bureau	www.ojp.usdoj.gov/bjs
Department of Transportation, Bureau of Transportation Statistics	www.bts.gov
Environmental Protection Agency	www.epa.gov
Federal Bureau of Investigation	www.fbi.gov
Fedstats	www.fedstats.gov
FedWorld.gov	www.fedworld.gov
Government Printing Office	www.gpoaccess.gov
National Aeronautics and Space Administration	www.nasa.gov
National Archives	www.archives.gov
National Atlas.gov	www.nationalatlas.gov
National Bureau of Economic Research	www.nber.org
National Center for Education Statistics	nces.ed.gov
National Institutes of Health	www.nih.gov
National Oceanic and Atmospheric	www.noaa.gov
NATO	www.nato.int
Regulations.gov	www.regulations.gov
Smithsonian Institution	www.si.edu
Stat-USA	www.stat-usa.gov
Supreme Court of the United States	www.supremecourtus.gov
THOMAS: Legislative Information	thomas.loc.gov
United Nations	www.un.org/english
United States House of Representatives	www.house.gov
United States Senate	www.senate.gov
White House	www.whitehouse.gov
World Health Organization	www.who.int/en

Online Media, Images, Art, and Photographs   Hundreds of Web sites, including news media archives, museums, historical sites, and libraries, have photographs. The following list of links is a good place to start searching for images to use in educational projects. Before you use any images you find online, check the Web site's permissions and copyright information.

Artcyclopedia	www.artcyclopedia.com
CDC Public Health Image Library	phil.cdc.gov/Phil/home.asp
FreeDigitalPhotos.net	www.freedigitalphotos.net
FreeFoto.com	www.freefoto.com
Free Public Domain Photo Database	pdphoto.org
FreeStockPhotos.com	www.freestockphotos.com
Library of Congress American Memory Map Collections	memory.loc.gov/ammem/ index.html/
Metropolitan Museum of Art	www.metmuseum.org
MorgueFile	www.morguefile.com
NASA Image Gallery	www.nasa.gov/multimedia/ imagegallery
NOAA Photo Library	www.photolib.noaa.gov
Openphoto.net	www.openphoto.net
U.S. Government Photos and Multimedia	www.usa.gov/Topics/ Graphics.shtml
Wikimedia Commons	commons.wikimedia.org/

Universities   This site provides links to colleges and universities in the United States and Canada.

Google's University Search	www.google.com/ universities.html

38e   Using firsthand research

Firsthand research involves investigating sources on your own. This can be done through taking notes on your own observations, conducting surveys, and interviewing people. These forms of information-gathering can add credibility and authority to your writing.

Observations

Conducting observations can help you gather information about your topic. You can learn a lot by watching a particular place and taking notes about what you see.

TRY THIS

To Conduct an Effective Observation

- **Ask permission, if necessary.** When observing in a public place, like a mall or a park, asking permission usually is not necessary. However, if you choose to observe in a place that has restricted access, such as a hospital emergency room or an elementary school class, be sure to ask the person in charge for permission.

- **Carry along something to write with and record your observations.** Bring some method of recording your observations with you, such as a pen or pencil, a notebook, or a video camera or audio recording equipment, such as a tape recorder or MP3 recorder.

- **Bring consent forms, if necessary.** Ask each person you wish to record to sign a consent form before you begin. A consent form should include a statement giving you permission to record each person as well as a blank line on which your subject can sign his or her name.

- **Answer basic questions.** In your notes, answer the basic journalistic questions: *who, what, when, where, why,* and *how.* Providing yourself with basic information first will help guide you to more specific questions as your observe.

- **Write detailed notes.** Jot down your impressions of the place you are visiting. Try using your senses, such as smelling and tasting, to gather information. It may be relevant to note the time order of events, what people are doing, how people are interacting, and what is said.

Surveys

Conducting surveys can be another effective method of gathering information about your topic. A survey can provide you with quantitative information, or numerical data, about the attitudes or beliefs of a group of people about a specific topic. There are two basic types of survey questions: closed questions and open questions.

Closed questions   Closed questions have a limited number of answers. Closed questions are easier to count than open questions, making it easier to show the results in graphs or charts. Closed questions include the following types:

- **True/false or yes/no:** These are best for gathering respondents' opinions on specific issues.

- **Multiple choice:** These are useful for asking respondents about their actions or practices regarding a topic. You can ask people to select one or all responses that apply.

- **Likert scales:** These give readers a range of responses to choose from. Responses can be selected from a numerical scale (i.e., 1 = most likely to 5 = least likely) or include descriptive phrases (i.e., strongly agree, agree, neutral, disagree, strongly disagree).

- **Rankings:** These types of questions ask readers to rate their preferences from strongest to weakest.

Open questions   Open questions ask for short-answer or narrative responses. This makes them harder than closed questions to count and represent in charts and graphs. But they can be helpful when you want individualized viewpoints on an issue. You can use quotations from the responses to these open questions to support points in your paper.

Analyzing and Presenting Your Results   Once you have your survey results, review them and think about their implications. Your readers will see that you are a credible researcher who has reviewed the data and presented the results fairly and accurately.

You can include pie charts or bar graphs to help your readers understand your results. Use pie charts to show the parts of a whole and bar graphs to show comparisons between items. See 41b for strategies for including visuals in your paper.

Interviews

Interviews are also a good method for gathering firsthand information. Talking with someone who is an authority or expert or has a specific connection to your topic may provide important information.

TRY THIS

To Conduct an Effective Interview

- **Do some preliminary searching.** Before conducting your interview, spend some time learning about the person. Then you'll have background on his or her expertise or position of authority.

- **Be prepared with questions.** Bring written questions with you to your interview. Include some open-ended questions that begin with *who, what, when, where, why,* and *how.* Having your notes to refer to can help you keep the conversation on track and gather the information you need for your paper.

- **Set up a time and place for your interview.** It's polite to contact your subject ahead of time to ask for and set up an interview. This ensures that the person will devote time to answering your questions.

- **Explain the purpose of your interview.** Make sure that the person you interview knows that his or her words may be used in your paper. If you eventually publish your paper in a newspaper or on the Internet, let the person know that others will read his or her words in a public forum.

- **Bring a pen, pencil, notebook, and/or recorder.** Because you'll want to take notes during the interview, consider using a tape recorder or MP3 recorder to record your conversation.

- **Have your subject fill out a consent form, if needed.** If you record your interview, ask your subject to sign a consent form before you begin recording. A consent form should include a statement giving you permission to record this person as well as a blank line on which to sign his or her name. Keep those signed consent forms for your records.

- **Be an interested listener.** During the interview, you'll want to show the person that you are actively listening. You can emphasize this by maintaining eye contact, sitting up in your seat, and nodding or responding to what the person says.

- **Use interview material responsibly.** When you include quoted or paraphrased material from your interview in your paper, you'll want to be sure you present the person's viewpoints fairly, accurately, and respectfully.

38f Taking notes

It's helpful to organize the information from your sources as you research. This will help you see the larger picture as you sort through your ideas and read through your sources.

TRY THIS

To Keep Your Research Notes Organized

These strategies will help you keep your notes organized as you proceed.

- Divide your major topics into subtopics, and save your research in separate file folders labeled by subtopic. Clearly named folders will help you keep your articles and notes organized.

- Save articles from library databases or Web sites on a flash drive, a CD-ROM, or the hard drive of your computer. You may want to go back later and reread them.

- If you make printouts, have some highlighters or colored pens handy so you can use different colors to highlight each subtopic. If you keep copies on your computer, try using fonts in different colors for highlighting.

- Keep a "researcher's notepad" to jot down ideas that come to you. That is likely to happen when you're doing other things and not consciously thinking about the research paper.

Keep track of the bibliographic information from each source so that you'll have it handy when you prepare your Works Cited or References page. See Figures 38.1–38.4 for maps that show how to find the information needed for your bibliographic citations.

Starting a working bibliography

As you begin to collect sources, build a working bibliography, a list of materials you plan to read. As you find more suggestions for sources, add them to the list. This working list can include Web sites, books, magazines, journals, and other sources you may find. Then, as you write your paper, you will have the ones you're using in your final bibliography ready to copy and paste in. Some of the materials in the working bibliography may not be used in your paper, so your working bibliography will be longer than your final bibliography.

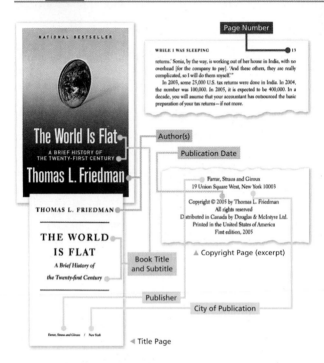

Page Number

WHILE I WAS SLEEPING   15

returns.' Sonia, by the way, is working out of her house in India, with no
overhead [for the company to pay]. 'And these others, they are really
complicated, so I will do them myself.'"
   In 2003, some 25,000 U.S. tax returns were done in India. In 2004,
the number was 100,000. In 2005, it is expected to be 400,000. In a
decade, you will assume that your accountant has outsourced the basic
preparation of your tax returns—if not more.

Author(s)

Publication Date

Farrar, Straus and Giroux
19 Union Square West, New York 10003

Copyright © 2005 by Thomas L. Friedman
All rights reserved
Distributed in Canada by Douglas & McIntyre Ltd.
Printed in the United States of America
First edition, 2005

▲ Copyright Page (excerpt)

Book Title and Subtitle

Publisher

City of Publication

◀ Title Page

MLA Works Cited Format

Friedman, Thomas L. *The World Is Flat: A Brief History of the Twenty-First Century.* New York, NY: Farrar, 2005. Print.

▲ Medium of Publication

APA References Format

Friedman, T. L. (2005). *The world is flat: A brief history of the twenty-first century.* New York, NY: Farrar, Straus & Giroux.

MLA Parenthetical Citation Example

The growing number of American tax returns prepared in India each year is reshaping the U.S. accounting industry (Friedman 13).

APA Parenthetical Citation Example

The growing number of American tax returns prepared in India each year is reshaping the U.S. accounting industry (Friedman, 2005, p. 13).

▲ Figure 38.1 **Citing a Book**

Source: *Jacket design and excerpts from* The World Is Flat: A Brief History of the Twenty-First Century (Updated and Expanded) *by Thomas L. Friedman. Copyright © 2005, 2006 by Thomas L. Friedman. Reprinted by permission of Farrar, Straus and Giroux, LLC.*

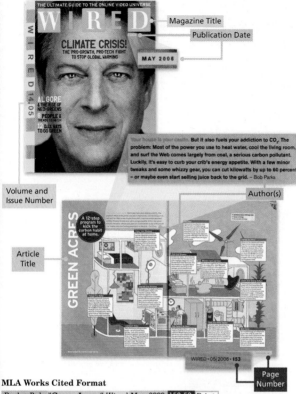

MLA Works Cited Format

Parks, Bob. "Green Acres." *Wired* May 2006: 152-53. Print.

APA References Format

Parks, B. (2006, May). Green acres. *Wired, 14*(5), 152–153.

MLA Parenthetical Citation Example

With some simple adjustments in power usage, homeowners "can cut kilowatts by up to 60 percent—or maybe even start selling juice back to the grid" (Parks 152).

APA Parenthetical Citation Example

With some simple adjustments in power usage, homeowners "can cut kilowatts by up to 60 percent—or maybe even start selling juice back to the grid" (Parks, 2006, p. 152).

▲ Figure 38.2 **Citing a Magazine Article**

Source: Wired *May 2006 cover with cover lines, photo by Martin Schoeller and pp. 152–153 "Green Acres" illustration by Steven Guarnaccia, text by Robert Parks, corner graphic by Marcel Laverdet. Originally published in* Wired. *Copyright © 1996 by The Condé Nast Publications Inc. Reprinted by permission.*

MLA Works Cited Format

Niederdeppe, Jeff, and Dominick L. Frosch. "News Coverage and Sales of Products with Trans Fat: Effects before and after Changes in Federal Labeling Policy." *American Journal of Preventive Medicine* 36.5 (2009): 395–401. *ScienceDirect.* Web. 1 Oct. 2009.

                  Medium of Publication ▲   ▲ Date of Access

APA References Format

Niederdeppe, J., & Frosch, D. L. (2009). News coverage and sales of products with trans fat: Effects before and after changes in federal labeling policy. *American Journal of Preventive Medicine,* *36,* 395–401. doi:10.1016/j.amepre.2009.01.023

MLA Parenthetical Citation Example

Niederdeppe and Frosch state that "news coverage influenced short-term consumer purchases of trans-fat products in LAC in the 1.5 years following the launch of the federally mandated labeling policy" (399).

APA Parenthetical Citation Example

Niederdeppe and Frosch (2009) state that "news coverage influenced short-term consumer purchases of trans-fat products in LAC in the 1.5 years following the launch of the federally mandated labeling policy" (p. 399).

▲ Figure 38.3 **Citing a Journal Article with a DOI from a Library Database**

Source: News Coverage and Sales of Products with Trans Fat: Effects Before and After Changes. In Federal Labeling Policy, by Jeff Niederdeppe, Ph.D. and Dominick L. Frosch, Ph.D. *American Journal of Preventative Medicine* Vol. 36, Issue 5, May 2009, pages 395–401. Copyright © 2006 *American Journal of Preventive Medicine* published by Elsevier, Inc. Reprinted with permission from Elsevier.

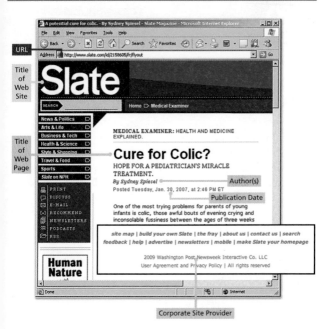

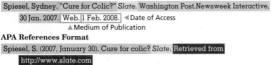

Corporate Site Provider

MLA Works Cited Format

Spiesel, Sydney. "Cure for Colic?" *Slate*. Washington Post.Newsweek Interactive,
30 Jan. 2007. Web. 1 Feb. 2008. ◄ Date of Access
▲ Medium of Publication

APA References Format

Spiesel, S. (2007, January 30). Cure for colic? *Slate*. Retrieved from
http://www.slate.com

MLA Parenthetical Citation Example
One recent study suggests that probiotic bacteria may be effective in treating
colicky infants (Spiesel).

APA Parenthetical Citation Example
One recent study suggests that probiotic bacteria may be effective in treating
colicky infants (Spiesel, 2007).

▲ Figure 38.4 **Citing an Article from an Internet Source**
Source: *"Cure for Colic? Hope for a Pediatrician's Miracle Treatment"* by Sydney
Spiesel, Slate. 1/30/07. © 2007 Washington Post.Newsweek Interactive, LLC. All
rights reserved.

Sometimes your online source or printout may be missing some information needed for the bibliography, such as
the date of publication or last revision or the sponsoring
organization. By checking for this information the first
time you visit a Web site, you will save time hunting for it
later.

39

Evaluating Print and Online Sources

We live in an age of such vast amounts of information that we can't know everything about a subject. All information that comes streaming at us from newspapers, magazines, the media, books, journals, brochures, Web sites, and so on is also of very uneven quality.

Evaluating sources, then, is a skill we rely on constantly, and applying that skill to research papers is equally important.

39a Getting started

To begin, ask yourself what type of information you are looking for and where you're likely to find appropriate sources for it.

- **What kind of information are you looking for?** Do you want facts? opinions? news reports? research studies? analyses? historical accounts? personal reflections? data? public records? scholarly essays reflecting on the topic? reviews?

- **Where would you find such information?** Which sources are most likely to be useful: the Internet? online library databases and subscription services? libraries with scholarly journals, books, and government publications? public libraries with popular magazines? newspapers? community records? people on your campus or in your town?

For example, if you're searching for information on some current event, a reliable newspaper such as the *New York Times* will be a useful source, and it is available on the Web and in a university or public library. If you need some statistics on the U.S. population, government census documents on the Web and in libraries are useful places to search. If you want to do research into local history, however, the archives and Web sites of local government offices and the local newspaper are better places to start.

Consider whether there are organizations that gather and publish the types of information you are seeking. For example, if you are seeking information about teen drinking and driving, a useful source would be a local office of Mothers Against Drunk Driving (MADD) if you want to know about local conditions. If you want national or regional information, the MADD Web site is also likely to be helpful. Be sure to ask yourself whether the sponsoring organization's goal for the site is to be objective, to gain support for its viewpoint, or to sell you something. For example, a tobacco institute, funded by a large tobacco company, is not likely to be an unbiased source of information about the harmfulness of cigarettes.

39b Evaluating Internet sources

Evaluate Internet sources the same way you evaluate sources elsewhere. But in addition, there are some special matters to consider when deciding whether to use Internet materials. Anyone can post anything from anywhere on the Internet. Although excellent sources of information exist on the Web, many sites or pages on sites can lead unsuspecting readers to accept as fact whatever biased, false, stolen, or fake information turns up in a search. No monitors, evaluators, or fact-checking organizations regulate or review what is posted on the Web. In addition, the sponsor or organization name on the site can be misleading.

TRY THIS

To Evaluate a Web Site

- Who is the site's author, organization, or sponsor? Try to find out through a link to the home page or by deleting the URL after the domain name (all the information after the first slash) to bring you to the home page. Then search the Web for references to this author or organization to learn more. Are the authors clearly identified? Is there a way to contact them? It's important to be very suspicious of an author or organization that wants to remain anonymous.

- What are the author's or organization's credentials? Why should you consider this a reliable source? If the domain name is .edu, be sure you are reading information the college or university posted. If you are reading a student's page, be aware that student pages are not always monitored by the institution.

- What evidence is there of the accuracy of the information? Are there any references cited or links provided to other sites or publications known to be reliable? Is there evidence that the information has been verified? Is there any evidence of bias? If a viewpoint is offered, are other viewpoints considered too?

- Is the information current? Is there a date of origin and any sign of the site being maintained and revised in the recent past? If there are links to other sites, are they live links or links that no longer work? Does the information sound dated, referring to "recent" events that actually occurred several years ago?

- Is there advertising (or pop-up windows) on the site? Does that interfere with the site's credibility? (Sites with .gov as the domain will not have advertising.)

- What is the site's goal: to inform? to persuade? to provide information or disinformation? Is there an "About Us" link to an explanation about the organization? Who is the intended audience?

- How did you access the site? Did you link to it from a reliable site? If you find the site through a search engine result, that means only that the site contains your search keywords; it says nothing about the trustworthiness or value of the site.

- How good is the coverage of the topic? Does the site have uniquely useful information? Does the site offer in-depth information?

HINT

Checking the Domain Name and Registrant

The domain is the last part of the URL or basic Web address, consisting of two or three letters that appear after the last dot. (Information after the domain name starts with a slash and links to pages on the site.) The domain can sometimes (though not always) give you clues about the Web site's source.

.gov	government sites (These are usually dependable.)
.edu	educational institutions (These are dependable, though personal student Web sites may not be.)

.org	organizations (These include nonprofit or public service organizations that may have their own biases.)
.com, .biz, .net	commercial sites (Business Web sites are likely to have a profit motive. Individuals, however, may also post their personal Web sites and blogs on corporate servers.)
.uk, .de, .ca, .jp	foreign sites (.uk = England; .de = Germany, .ca = Canada, .jp = Japan; there are two-letter abbreviations for all countries of the world.)

It is quite easy for businesses and individuals, however, to purchase most types of domain names (except .gov) for their corporate or personal Web sites. To check the names of people or groups who have registered their Web site domains, conduct a "whois" search at the following Web site:

www.networksolutions.com/whois

Some organizations and people pay to hide their names, so you won't find every Web site listed there, but it's worth a try because this search may help you learn more about who has created a particular Web site.

39c Evaluating bibliographic citations

Before you spend time searching for any type of source or reading it, look at the following information in the citation to evaluate whether it's worth your time. These suggestions apply to all types of sources, including those you find on the Web, in your library, and in your community.

Author

Credentials

- How reputable is the person listed as the author?

- What is the author's educational background? Is it appropriate for the type of expertise you want?

- What has the author written in the past about this topic? If this is the author's first publication in this area, perhaps the author isn't yet an expert.

- Why is this person considered an expert or a reliable authority? Who considers this person an expert? Would that source have any bias?

- If the author is an organization, what can you find out about it? How reputable is it?

You can learn more about an author by checking the Web and the Library of Congress catalog to see what else this person has written, and the *Book Review Index* and *Book Review Digest* may lead you to reviews of other books by this author. Your library may have citation indexes in the field that will lead you to other articles and short pieces by this person that have been cited by others.

For organizations, you can check databases or the Web to see what the organization publishes or who links to it. You don't want to spend time searching for a source from an organization that may be biased, have a profit motive, or be considered unreliable.

For biographic information about people, you can read the online *Biographical Dictionary* or, in the library, *Who's Who in America* or the *Biography Index*. There may also be information about the person in the publication, such as a list of previous works, awards, and notes about the author. Your goal is to get some sense of who this person is and why it's worth reading what the author wrote before you plunge in and begin reading. That may be important as you write the paper and build your case. For example, if you are citing a source to document the spread of AIDS in Africa, which of these sentences strengthens your argument?

Dr. John Smith notes that the incidence of AIDS in Africa has more than doubled in the last five years.

(or)

Dr. John Smith, head of the World Health Organization committee studying AIDS in African countries, notes that the incidence of AIDS in Africa has more than doubled in the last five years.

References

- Did a teacher, librarian, or other person knowledgeable about the topic mention this person or organization?

- Did you see the person or organization listed in other sources that you've already determined to be trustworthy?

When a person or group is an authority, you may find other references to the person or group. Decide whether this source's viewpoint or knowledge of the topic is important to read.

Institution or Affiliation

- With what organization, institution, or company is the author associated? If the name is not easily identified, perhaps the group is less than reliable.

- What are this group's goals? Is there a bias or reason for the group to slant the truth in any way?

- Does the group monitor or review what is published under its name?

- Why might this group be trying to sell you something or convince you to accept its views? Do its members conduct objective, disinterested research? Are they trying to be sensational or attention-getting to enhance their own popularity or ratings?

Timeliness

- When was the source published? (For Web sites, look at the "last revised" date at the end of the page. If no date is available, are all the links still live?)

- Is that date current enough to be useful, or might the site contain outdated material?

- Is the source a revision of an earlier edition? If so, it is likely to be more current, and a revision indicates that the source is sufficiently valuable to revise. For a print source, check a library catalog or *Books in Print* to see whether you have the latest edition.

Publisher, producer, or sponsor

- Who published or produced the material?

- Is that publisher or sponsor reputable? For example, a university press or a government agency is likely to be a reputable source that reviews what it publishes.

- Is the group recognized as an authority?

- Is the publisher or group an appropriate one for this topic?

- Might the publisher be likely to have a particular bias? (For example, a brochure printed by a right-to-life group is not going to contain much objective material on abortion.)

- Is there any review process or fact-checking? (If a pharmaceutical company publishes data on a new drug it is developing, is there evidence of outside review of the data?)

Audience

- Can you tell who the intended audience is? Is that audience appropriate for your purposes?

- Is the material too specialized or too popular or brief to be useful? (A three-volume study of gene splitting is more than you need for a five-page paper on some genetically transmitted disease. In contrast, a half-page article on a visit to Antarctica won't tell you much about research into the melting of glaciers going on there.)

39d Evaluating content

You can evaluate the content of print or online sources by considering the following important criteria:

- **Purpose** Read the preface, introduction, or summary. What does the author want to accomplish?

- **Audience** Are you the intended audience? Consider the tone, style, level of information, and assumptions the author makes about the reader. Are they appropriate to your needs? If there is advertising in the publication or on the Web site, it may help you determine the intended audience.

- **Type of Source** Is the content of the source fact, opinion, or propaganda? If the material is presented as factual, are the sources of the facts clearly indicated? Do you think enough evidence is offered? Does the author use a mix of primary and secondary sources?

- **Comprehensiveness** Is the topic covered in adequate depth, or is it too superficial or limited to only one aspect that overemphasizes only one part of the topic? Browse through the links to other pages on the site or the table of contents and the index. Is the topic covered in enough depth to be helpful?

- **Accuracy** What reasons do you have to think that the facts are accurate? Do they agree with other information you've read? Are there sources for the data given?

- **Credibility** Is the source of the material generally considered trustworthy? Does the source have a review process or do fact-checking? Is the author an expert? What are the author's credentials for writing about this topic? For example, is the article about personal perceptions of how bad this season's flu epidemic is, or is it a report by the Centers for Disease Control and Prevention?

- **Fairness** If the author has a particular viewpoint, are differing views presented with some sense of fairness, or are opposing views presented as irrational or silly? Are there broad, sweeping generalizations that over-state or simplify the matter? Are there arguments that are one-sided with no acknowledgment of other viewpoints?

- **Objectivity** Is the language objective or emotional? Does the author acknowledge differing viewpoints? Are the various perspectives presented fairly? If you are reading an article in a magazine or in an online publi-cation, do other articles in that source promote a partic-ular viewpoint?

- **Relevance** How closely related is the material to your topic? Is it really relevant or merely related? Is it too general or too specific? too technical?

- **Timeliness** Is the information current enough to be use-ful? How necessary is timeliness for your topic? Consider whether the source contains timely informa-tion or is outdated. Do some cross-checking. Can you locate more current information elsewhere?

- **References** Is there a list of references to show that the author has consulted other sources? Can the sources lead you to useful material?

40

Integrating Sources

40a Avoiding plagiarism

Plagiarism results when a writer fails to document a source and presents the words or ideas of someone else as the writer's own work. Plagiarism can occur in the follow-ing ways:

- Using someone's exact words without putting quotation marks around the words and without citing the source.

- Changing another person's words into your own words by paraphrasing or summarizing without citing the source.

- Stating ideas or research specifically attributed to another person or persons without citing the source.

- Claiming authorship of a paper written by someone else.

Why is avoiding plagiarism important?

- **Plagiarism is unethical.** When a writer uses someone else's words, information, or ideas and doesn't acknowledge using that work, that is considered an act of stealing, even if it happens because of carelessness or rushing too fast to write the paper.

- **Plagiarism means losing a learning opportunity.** Professors assign research projects to help students learn how to use sources as well as gain knowledge about their topics. If we plagiarize instead of researching and citing our sources, we lose the opportunity to learn about our topics and the chance to practice research skills needed in college and the workplace. Moreover, readers who want to find those sources mentioned in the paper so that they can learn more also lose when those citations are missing.

- **Plagiarism diminishes credibility.** Drawing upon other people's ideas and words is appropriate when writing research papers. Our arguments are more compelling when we cite the opinions of experts. To be considered credible writers, however, we need to let readers know where we located those ideas and words. Blending our own ideas and language with information from other sources is an important goal of the research process.

- **Plagiarism may result in serious penalties.** Plagiarism is considered a violation of academic honesty and may result in a variety of penalties, including expulsion. After college, plagiarism can negatively affect your career and reputation. Plagiarists can be sued for copyright violations or for use of intellectual property without permission.

HINT

Understanding Cultural Differences About Plagiarism

In some cultures, documenting something, particularly from a well-known work of literature, can be interpreted as an insult because it implies that the reader is not familiar with that work. In U.S. academic writing, however, it is very important to document sources. This may be a skill that is new or needs sharpening, but it is a vitally important skill.

Information that requires documentation

When we use the ideas, findings, data, conclusions, arguments, and words of others, we need to acknowledge that we are borrowing their work. We do that by documenting what we use. If you are arguing for a particular viewpoint and find someone who very clearly or very eloquently expresses that viewpoint, you may want to include it. Whenever you summarize, paraphrase, or quote someone else, provide documentation for those sources, including the author and the location of the source.

Common knowledge: information that does not require documentation

Common knowledge is that body of general ideas most people know and does not have to be documented. Common knowledge is sometimes slippery to identify, but generally it consists of standard information that is widely shared and can be found in numerous sources without reference to any source. For example, most people know that there is more water than land on earth. Common historical information in the United States, for example, includes knowing that the Declaration of Independence was adopted in 1776 and that George Washington was the first U.S. president. Among common physical or scientific knowledge is the fact that the earth is the third planet from the sun and the fact that water is composed of hydrogen and oxygen molecules. Specific details or statistics about these topics might not be considered common knowledge, however, so provide proper documentation to show where the ideas or study results came from.

Field research you conduct also does not need to be documented, though you should indicate that you are reporting your own findings. If you're reporting the results of your own study or survey, you should explain when and how the study or survey took place. However, if you include information from an interview, record the person's first and last name and the date of the conversation. For MLA documentation style, also note whether you spoke in person, by phone, or through e-mail.

Avoiding plagiarism: an example

Original source

The process of heating milk to kill bacteria has been common for nearly a century, and selling unpasteurized milk for human consumption is currently illegal in Canada and in half the U.S. states. Yet thousands of people in North America still seek raw milk. Some say milk in its natural state keeps them healthy; others just crave its taste. (Johnson 71)

Johnson, Nathanael. "The Revolution Will Not Be Pasteurized." *Harper's Magazine* Apr. 2008: 71-78. Print.

Plagiarized paraphrase

The procedure of heating milk to kill bacteria has been common for nearly a century. In Canada and half of the states in the United States, there are laws against selling unpasteurized milk for people to drink. But some people like the taste of raw milk and believe it keeps them healthy.

(This example illustrates plagiarism. In the first sentence, it is missing quotation marks around the direct quote and a parenthetical citation. A parenthetical citation is needed for all the material that is paraphrased from the original in the second and third sentences.)

Acceptable paraphrase

Even though pasteurization has been a standard practice for almost one hundred years and the distribution of unpasteurized milk is prohibited in many American states and Canada, some people still search for and purchase raw milk for its distinct flavor and perceived nutritional value (Johnson 71).

(The main ideas of the original are communicated here in the writer's own language and sentence structure. A parenthetical citation indicates where the original ideas came from.)

CHECKLIST

Checking Your Work for Plagiarism

- Read your paper and ask yourself whether your readers can properly identify which ideas and words are yours and which are from the sources you cite. Check to see that you cited all of the ideas that aren't your own and aren't considered common knowledge.

- Check to make sure your paper isn't a string of quotations from your sources. Even though you're using research and ideas from other sources, you should still show your own authority in the paper. Try paraphrasing some ideas, but use parenthetical citations to show where your ideas came from.

- Consider whether your paper predominantly reflects your words, phrases, and integration of ideas. Check to see whether your thesis unifies the ideas expressed in the full paper. Also check the topic sentences in your paragraphs to make sure they are clearly connected to the ideas in your paragraphs.

- Make sure all the sources on your Works Cited or References page are referenced in the body of the paper and vice versa.

40b Summarizing

A summary is a brief restatement of the main ideas in a source, using your own words.

Unlike paraphrases (see 40c), summaries are shorter than the original source because they convey only the main points of the source.

CHECKLIST

Identifying Characteristics of Summaries

- Summaries use fewer words than the source being summarized.
- Summaries include only the main points, omitting details, facts, examples, illustrations, direct quotations, and other specifics.
- Summaries are written in your own words, not copied from your source, and use your own sentence structures.
- Summaries are objective and do not include your own interpretation or reflect your slant on the material.
- Summaries represent the viewpoint of the author fairly and accurately.
- Summaries must be cited in the documentation format (MLA, APA, *Chicago Manual*, CSE, etc.) you are using for your paper.

Summary: an example

Original Source: book excerpt

The infectious diseases that visit us as epidemics, rather than as a steady trickle of cases, share several characteristics. First, they spread quickly and efficiently from an infected person to nearby healthy people, with the result that the whole population gets exposed within a short time. Second, they're "acute" illnesses: within a short time, you either die or recover completely. Third, the fortunate ones of us who do recover develop antibodies that leave us immune against a recurrence of the disease for a long time, possibly for the rest of our life. Finally, these diseases tend to be restricted to humans; the microbes tend to live in the soil or in other animals. All four of these traits apply to what Americans think of as the familiar acute epidemic diseases of childhood, including measles, rubella, mumps, pertussis, and smallpox (Diamond 202-03).

Diamond, Jared. *Guns, Germs, and Steel: The Fate of Human Societies.* New York: Norton, 2005. Print.

Unacceptable Summary: too close to original language and sentence structure and missing a parenthetical citation

Epidemics tend to be restricted to humans, generally spreading quickly and efficiently through communities. Those who contract an epidemic either die or recover completely within a short time. If they live, they may be immune against the disease for a long time, possibly for the rest of their lives.

(*The language and sentence structure of this example are too close to the original text and could be considered plagiarized. This example is also missing a parenthetical citation.*)

Acceptable Summary

Epidemics generally pass rapidly through human communities, either swiftly proving fatal or, in those who survive, causing illnesses of brief duration followed by protection against further sickness (Diamond 202-03).

(*The key idea of the original passage—the definition of "epidemic"—is communicated here in the writer's own language and sentence structure. A parenthetical citation indicates where the original idea came from.*)

40c Paraphrasing

A paraphrase restates information from a source, using your own words.

CHECKLIST

Identifying Characteristics of Paraphrases

- A paraphrase has approximately the same number of words as the source. (A summary, by contrast, is much shorter.)

- Paraphrases use your own words, not those of the source, and are written in your own sentence structures.

- Paraphrases are objective and do not include your own interpretation or slant on the material.

- Paraphrases represent the viewpoint of the author fairly and accurately.

- A paraphrase is approximately the same length as the passage from the original source and contains more detail than a summary would.

- Paraphrases must be cited in the documentation format (MLA, APA, *Chicago Manual*, CSE, etc.) you are using for your paper.

Paraphrase: an example

Original Source: article about college enrollment

Nationally, women's enrollment began to overtake men's in the early 1980's. In the last couple of years, the gap has widened enough to alarm state education boards, researchers, and higher-education policy wonks, who worry that men are falling behind even as women are succeeding.

Colleges are responding by trying to entice more young men to enroll—adding engineering programs and football teams, changing the color palette of their admissions brochures from pastel to primary, and quietly tweaking their standards to give male applicants a leg up. The gender gap is already changing classroom dynamics, rerouting social relationships, and paving a dangerous path toward a lopsided future, say some policy analysts.

Wilson, Robin. "The New Gender Divide." *The Chronicle of Higher Education* 26 Jan. 2007: A36-A39. Print.

Unacceptable Paraphrase: wording and sentence structure too close to the original source

Across the nation, female enrollment in college began to take over men's in the early 1980s. Recently, the divide has broadened enough to distress state education boards, researchers, and higher-education policymakers, who are concerned that males are dropping behind even as females are succeeding. Colleges are answering by working to attract more men— adding engineering programs and football teams, changing the colors of admissions brochures, and quietly changing standards to give male applicants a leg up. The gender gap is already altering classrooms, changing social relationships, and creating a negative path for the future (Wilson A36).

(The language and sentence structure of this example are too close to the original text and could be considered plagiarized.)

Acceptable Paraphrase

Policymakers and educational specialists are increasingly concerned about the decrease in the number of males enrolling in college, noting that the disparity in the percentages of men and women in college is beginning to reshape academic environments and may have adverse consequences in coming years. To reverse this trend, several colleges have adjusted their admissions standards, adopted male-oriented marketing strategies, and started new athletic programs in efforts to increase the number of men attending their institutions (Wilson A36).

(The main ideas of the original are communicated here in the writer's own language and sentence structures. A parenthetical citation indicates where the ideas originally came from.)

40d Quoting

A quotation is the record of the exact words of a written or spoken source, indicated by placing quotation marks directly before and after the quoted words.

CHECKLIST

Identifying Characteristics of Quotations

- Quotations are written exactly as they appear in the source.

- Quotations must be surrounded by quotation marks.
- Quotations are introduced by text that indicates the speaker of the quotation.
- Quotations must be cited in the documentation format (MLA, APA, *Chicago Manual*, CSE, etc.) you are using for your paper.

TRY THIS

To Use Quotations Effectively

- Use quotations as evidence, support, or further explanation of what you have written. Quotations are not substitutes for stating your point in your own words.
- Use quotations sparingly. Too many quotations strung together with very little of your own writing makes a paper look like a scrapbook of pasted-together sources, not a thoughtful integration of what is known about a subject.
- Use quotations that illustrate the author's own viewpoint or style, or quote excerpts that would not be as effective if rewritten in different words. Effective quotations are succinct or particularly well phrased.
- Introduce quotations with words that signal the relationship of the quotation to the rest of your discussion (see 40e).

HINT

Determining When to Use Quotations

Quote when

- the writer's words are especially vivid, memorable, or expressive.
- an expert's explanation is so clear and concise that a paraphrase would be confusing or wordy.
- you want to emphasize the expertise or authority of your source.
- the words the source uses are important to the discussion.

When you quote, use the exact words of the original source. Place the entire quotation within quotation marks, and use a parenthetical reference to give credit to your source.

40e Using signal words and phrases

When you summarize, paraphrase, or quote from outside sources in your writing, you need to identify each source and explain its connection to what you are writing about. You can do this by using signal words that tell the reader what to expect or how to interpret the material. They can help you integrate material smoothly into your writing.

TRY THIS

To Introduce Quoted, Paraphrased, or Summarized Words

To add variety to the verbs you use, try using the following signal words:

acknowledges	condemns	points out
adds	considers	predicts
admits	contends	proposes
agrees	describes	reports
argues	disagrees	responds
asserts	explains	says
believes	finds	shows
claims	holds	speculates
comments	insists	suggests
concedes	notes	warns
concludes	observes	writes

TRY THIS

To Integrate Sources Smoothly

To create smooth transitions and use sources effectively, try the following suggestions.

- **Explain how the source material is connected to the rest of the paragraph.** Show your readers the connection between the reference and the point you are making. Introduce the material by showing a logical link, or add a follow-up comment that integrates a quotation into your paragraph.

- **Use the name of the source and, if appropriate, that person's credentials as an authority.** Name your source's job title or professional affiliation as you introduce quoted, paraphrased, or summarized material ("According to Kathleen Sebelius, *Secretary of the United States Department of Health and Human Services*, the H1N1 flu virus . . .")

- **Use a verb to indicate the source's stance or attitude toward what is quoted.**
  - Does the source think the statement is very important ("Professor Mehta *stressed* . . . .")?
  - Does the source take a position on an issue ("The senator *argued* . . . .")?
  - Does the source remain neutral about what is stated ("The researcher *reported* . . . .")?

- **Use the appropriate verb tense.** When writing about literature and most other humanities subjects, use the present tense. Science writers generally use present tense verbs, except when writing about research that has been completed ("When studying the effects of constant illumination on corn seedlings, Jenner *found* that . . .").

- **Limit the use of quotations.** When a paragraph has a string of quotations and references to source material connected by a few words from the writer, the result can seem like a cut-and-paste scrapbook of materials from other people without much input from the paper's author. A few good quotations, used sparingly and integrated smoothly, will be much more effective.

- **Use signal words and phrases with quotations.** When you are quoting from sources, use words and phrases that prepare your reader for the quotation that will follow and that add smooth transitions from your words to the quotation.

- **Include each source on your Works Cited or References page.** See Chapters 42, 43, 44, and 45 for examples of citation formats.

In the following two examples, notice the difference in the way the source material is integrated into the text.

Unacceptable Paragraph: sources not introduced or explained well

People must pay for Internet access at home. President Barack Obama said, "It is unacceptable that the United States ranks 15th in the world in broadband adoption. Here, in the country that invented the Internet, every child should have the chance to get online" (qtd. in "Obama"). Diana G. Oblinger said, "Our nation must now extend these and the other benefits of broadband networking to all members of society as a critical matter of national policy" (qtd. in Fischman). "One study by the University of California at Santa Cruz in 2004 found that nearly half of high school graduates who had computers and Internet access at home went on to college. Among students who didn't have computers and Internet access, the college enrollment rate fell to one in four" (Hesseldahl).

(The quotations here are abruptly dropped into the paragraph without introductions and without clear indications from the writer as to how these statements connect together and relate to the main idea of the paragraph.)

Acceptable Paragraph: sources introduced and integrated effectively

Several key politicians and educators have voiced their support for free national broadband Internet service, particularly for lower-income families. Shortly before his inauguration, President Barack Obama declared, "It is unacceptable that the United States ranks 15th in the world in broadband adoption. Here, in the country that invented the Internet, every child should have the chance to get online" (qtd. in "Obama"). Providing families with free broadband access may yield long-term educational returns, including increased college enrollment rates for children from low-income households. Researchers at the University of California at Santa Cruz discovered in a 2004 study that nearly 50 percent of high school graduates with home Web access continued on to college, compared to only 25 percent of students without home Web access (Hesseldahl). Higher education officials also strongly support expanding broadband access to the public. Diana G. Oblinger, president of Educause, a nonprofit organization dedicated to effective use of technology in higher education, believes that the high-speed Internet access that has long been available to colleges should now be offered to all Americans: "Our nation must now extend these and the other benefits of broadband networking to all members of society as a critical matter of national policy" (qtd. in Fischman). To improve access to educational tools, Congress and the president must now work together to implement a national broadband plan.

(This revision creates a stronger connection between the main point of the paragraph and the source material. To avoid quoting too much, the Hesseldahl source is now paraphrased instead of quoted.)

Works Cited

Fischman, Josh. "Higher Education Groups Press Obama to Expand Broadband Access." *The Chronicle of Higher Education.* Chronicle of Higher Education, 9 Dec. 2008. Web. 11 Dec. 2008.

Hesseldahl, Arik. "Bringing Broadband to the Urban Poor."
Business Week. Business Week, 31 Dec. 2008. Web.
2 Jan. 2009.

"Obama Outlines Initiatives to Create 2.5 Million Jobs."
CNN.com. Cable News Network, 6 Dec. 2008. Web. 21
Dec. 2008.

41

Designing Documents

41a Principles of document design

Here are some principles to help you develop well-designed, readable pages.

- **Apply design elements consistently.** Use the design elements at the beginning of your document (such as bullets, white space, spacing, font types, and so on) consistently throughout your document.

- **Include white space.** Well-placed white space will make your documents more readable and offer some visual relief from heavy-looking blocks of text. White space in the margins helps to frame the text, leaves room for a reader to make notes, and indicates section breaks.

- **Avoid clutter.** With document design, less is more. Try to keep your pages uncluttered with no more than two or three different fonts.

- **Use contrasting design elements for emphasis.** Highlight selected elements of your text with variations in font size and type. Inserting indentations, graphics, and background shading can add emphasis to key parts of your document.

- **Insert headings and subheadings.** To announce new topics or subsections of your documents, use headings and subheadings. Make your headings and subheadings more noticeable by using a combination of bold, italics, and larger font sizes.

- **Create lists.** In research papers and professional writing documents, information can sometimes be presented more efficiently in lists than in long paragraphs. Use phrases or sentences containing key points and supporting details, and organize them with bullets, dashes, or numbers.

41b Incorporating visuals

Visuals such as images, graphs, charts, and tables can help you communicate clearly, concisely, and effectively.

- **Images** Images such as photographs, diagrams, maps, and illustrations add color, variety, and meaning to your documents. They can help your readers see a subject in a new perspective, follow steps in a process, or pinpoint a location. Multiple images placed next to each other can be used to show contrast or changes over a period of time (see Figure 41.1).

- **Graphs and charts** Use graphs and charts to illustrate data in visual form and explain relationships between items. You can produce these in a spreadsheet program such as Microsoft Excel. (See Figures 41.2–41.7.)

- **Tables** Create tables to show relationships between items. Use Microsoft Word or other word-processing software to create your tables.

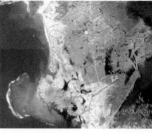

▲ Figure 41.1 **Comparing Images** These satellite photographs by NASA show the devastation of the Indonesian city of Lhoknga by the tsunami that struck on December 26, 2004. Placed next to each other, these before-and-after photos demonstrate the force of the tidal waves.

Figure 41.2 **Pie Chart**

Pie charts are used to show parts of a whole. They can be formatted to show numerical data, percentages, or both.

(**HINT:** Use contrasting colors or shading to distinguish between different slices of the pie.)

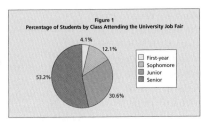

Figure 1
Percentage of Students by Class Attending the University Job Fair
4.1%
12.1%
30.6%
53.2%
First-year
Sophomore
Junior
Senior

Figure 41.3 **Bar Graph**

Bar graphs are primarily used to show relationships among items. They also may be used to illustrate increases or decreases over time.

The *X*- and *Y*-axes (horizontal and vertical axes) must be labeled to indicate the meaning of the data.

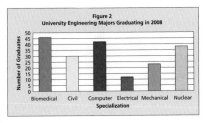

Figure 2
University Engineering Majors Graduating in 2008
Number of Graduates
50
45
40
35
30
25
20
15
10
5
0
Biomedical
Civil
Computer
Electrical
Mechanical
Nuclear
Specialization

Figure 41.4 **Line Graph**

Line graphs are used to show change over a period of time. The *X*- and *Y*-axes must be labeled to show data types.

(**HINT:** If the graph has multiple lines, use different colors or line types, such as dotted or dashed, to distinguish each from the others.)

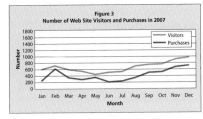

Figure 3
Number of Web Site Visitors and Purchases in 2007
Number
1800
1600
1400
1200
1000
800
600
400
200
0
Visitors
Purchases
Jan
Feb
Mar
Apr
May
Jun
Jul
Aug
Sep
Oct
Nov
Dec
Month

Figure 41.5 **Map**

Maps are used to identify locations. Thematic maps, such as this one from the U.S. Census Bureau, provide readers with a visual representation of demographic data.

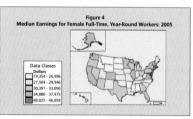

Always include a legend with your map to indicate spatial or thematic relationships.

Source: United States. Census Bureau. "M1902. Median Earnings for Female Full-Time, Year-Round Workers (in 2005 Inflation-Adjusted Dollars): 2005." *U.S. Census Bureau Factfinder.* United States, Census Bureau, 2005. Web. 26 Oct. 2006.

Figure 41.6 **Flowchart**

Flowcharts help readers follow a process or show options in making decisions.

(**HINT:** Use colors and shapes to differentiate levels of decision making.)

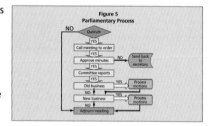

Figure 41.7 **Table**

Tables help summarize large amounts of data and help readers see relationships between and among items when the information is not easily reduced to numerical form.

Table 1 Growing Conditions for Rose Varieties				
Name	Height	Light Conditions	Soil Conditions	Growing Climate
English Roses	3–6'	Full sun to partial shade	Moist	Moderately cool to moderately warm
Musk Roses	4–6'	Full sun to partial shade	Moist	Warm
Rambler Roses	20–50'	Full sun	Moist	Moderately cool to warm
Tea Roses	4–7'	Full sun	Moist	Warm

Offer clear column headings in the table to categorize information.

Source: Roth, Susan A. *Better Homes and Gardens Complete Guide to Flower Gardening.* Des Moines: Meredith, 1995. 364-74. Print.

CHECKLIST

Adding Visuals to a Text

Visuals can add a great deal to a written text but need the proper context. Be sure to keep the following in mind when you include visuals:

- **Include a title.** Graphs, charts, and images are labeled as *figures*, and tables are labeled as *tables*. Add a title to each figure and table that explains its content, such as "Figure 1: Increases in Voter Registration" or "Table 5: Number of Registered Voters in Each Wisconsin County." Figures and tables should have separate numbering systems in your document.

- **Add labels.** In graphs and charts, provide a label on the X (horizontal) axis and Y (vertical) axis to specify values indicated in each area of the visual. Column headings in a table also need to be labeled clearly.

- **Place visuals in their appropriate location in the text.** In professional documents and MLA-formatted papers, be sure to place visuals in the body of a text, and introduce the visuals directly before you insert them in the text.

  Example: The number of people registering to vote has changed dramatically over the last decade (see Figure 1).

  After each visual, briefly explain the importance of the information.

  In APA-formatted papers, visuals appear on separate pages at the end of the paper, with tables first, then figures with their captions. Include a reference to each table or figure in the text.

- **Cite your sources.** To show that information has been gathered from outside sources, use the format appropriate for the documentation style you are using. (See Chapters 42–45 for documentation formats.)

41c Page preparation

- **Paper** Print on 8½-by-11-inch white paper, preferably the usual 20-lb. weight paper, and use only one side of each sheet.

- **Line spacing** Double-space throughout, including every line in the title, the text of the paper, headings, footnotes, quotations, figure captions, all parts of tables, and the bibliography section.

● **Margins**   Leave margins of one inch at the top and bottom and at both sides of the page, but put page numbers one-half inch from the top at the right side of the page. Justify margins at the left, but do not justify at the right margin unless that is the style your instructor requests.

● **Order of pages**

MLA Style
1. First page, with appropriate information followed by text of paper (see 42d)
2. Notes (optional section, starting on a separate page)
3. Works Cited (starting on a separate page)

APA Style
1. Title page (see 43d)
2. Abstract
3. Text of paper
4. References (start on a separate page)
5. Footnotes (list together, starting on a separate page)
6. Appendixes (optional, start each on a separate page)
7. Tables (optional, start each on a separate page)
8. Figures and figure captions (optional, place each figure with its caption on a separate page)

● **Titles and title pages**   In MLA format, research papers and reports do not need a title page unless your instructor asks for one. On the first page of your paper, leave a one-inch margin at the top. Then double-space and type your name, your instructor's name, the course number, and the date submitted at the left-hand margin. Then double-space and type the title, centered on the page. If you need more than one line for the title, double-space between these lines. Then double-space between the title and the first line of the text. Don't put your paper title in quotation marks, and don't use a period after the title. (See 42d for an example.)

In APA style, include a title page (all double-spaced) with the title centered between left and right margins and positioned in the upper half of the page. Depending on your instructor's preference, either include just your name and college (per APA guidelines and the sample page in 43d), or include your name, instructor's name, course, and date, with each line double-spaced and centered below the title.

- **Page numbers and identification**   In MLA style, number pages at the upper right of each page, one-half inch from the top and flush with the right margin. Include your last name before the page number (to prevent confusion if pages are misplaced), and don't use *page* or *p.* before the number (see the sample pages in 42d). In APA style, place the number one-half inch from the top and flush with the right margin. Include an abbreviated form of the paper's title (known as a "running head") flush with the left margin (see the sample pages in 43d).

- **Fonts**   Use 10- to 12-point type and a standard font that is easy to read, such as Times New Roman, Arial, or Palatino. Do not use fonts that resemble handwriting, appear unusually shaped, or are difficult to read.

- **Indentations**   Indent the first line of every paragraph one-half inch or five spaces from the left-hand margin. For long quotations (block quotations) within paragraphs, indent one inch or ten spaces from the left-hand margin in MLA style; indent one-half inch or five spaces in APA style.

- **Headings and subheadings**   Headings are the short titles that define sections and subsections in long reports and papers. Headings provide visual emphasis by breaking the paper into manageable portions that are easily seen and identified. For MLA style, use consistent phrasing and font style for headings and subheadings.

  In APA format, only one level of heading is recommended for short papers, centered on the page in bold font, with each word (except short prepositions and articles) capitalized. If multiple levels of headings are needed, use the following example as a guide.

APA Example

Level 1: **Bold, Centered Title**

Level 2: Bold Title on Left Margin

Level 3: **Indented title in bold.**

Level 4: ***Indented title in bold and italics.***

Level 5: *Indented title in italics.*

Contents of this section

42	**Documenting in MLA Style**	183
	42a Parenthetical references	184
	42b Endnotes (or notes)	189
	42c Works Cited list	189
	42d Sample pages	213
43	**Documenting in APA Style**	216
	43a In-text citations	217
	43b Footnotes	220
	43c References list	221
	43d Sample pages	234
44	***Chicago Manual of Style* (CM)**	237
45	**Council of Science Editors (CSE) Style**	248

Question and Correct

	SECTION	PAGE

For Modern Language Association (MLA) Format:

+ What are the major features of MLA style?	42	183
+ How do I refer to sources in the body of my paper in MLA style?	42a	184
+ What is a parenthetical reference?	42a	184
+ When do I use notes (or endnotes) in MLA, and what is the appropriate way to type them?	42b	189
+ What are the parts of a citation in the Works Cited list?	42c	189
+ How do I cite magazine and journal articles that I located on library databases?	42c	190

	SECTION	PAGE
+ How do I cite Internet sources in my Works Cited list?	42c	202
+ What do MLA-formatted pages of a research paper look like?	42d	213

For American Psychological Association (APA) Format:

	SECTION	PAGE
+ How do APA and MLA styles differ?	43	216
+ How do I refer to sources in the body of my paper in APA format?	43a	217
+ When do I use footnotes in APA, and what is the appropriate way to type them?	43b	220
+ What are the parts of a citation in a References list in APA format?	43c	221
+ What is a digital object identifier (DOI) on a journal article, and how do I cite this in my References list?	43c	222
+ How do I cite Internet sources in APA format?	43c	231
+ What do pages of an APA-formatted research paper look like?	43d	234

For Other Documentation Formats (*Chicago Manual*, CSE, etc.):

	SECTION	PAGE
+ How and when do I use *Chicago Manual* style for notes and a bibliography?	44	237
+ How and when do I use the two CSE styles for notes and the References list?	45	248

Documenting in MLA Style

For research papers in most of the humanities, use the format recommended by the **Modern Language Association (MLA)**. The latest style manuals published by the MLA are the following, but check to see whether more current guidelines have succeeded them (www.mla.org/style):

> Modern Language Association. *MLA Handbook for Writers of Research Papers.* 7th ed. New York: MLA, 2009. Print.

> Modern Language Association. *MLA Style Manual and Guide to Scholarly Publishing.* 3rd ed. New York: MLA, 2008. Print.

Major features of MLA style

- For parenthetical references, give the author's last name and the page number of the source at the end of the sentence and before the period. Parenthetical references placed after long quotations (which are indented one inch from the left margin) are placed after the sentence and after the period.

- In the Works Cited list, use full first and last names and middle initials of authors.

- Capitalize all major words in book and periodical titles, and put the titles in italics. Enclose article and chapter titles in quotation marks. If the title of a whole work appears within an italicized title, do not italicize the title of the whole work.

- In the Works Cited list at the end of the paper, give full publication information, alphabetized by author's last name.

HINT

The Three Parts of MLA Citation Format

1. **In-text citations.** In your paper, you need parenthetical references to acknowledge words, ideas, and facts you've taken from outside sources.

2. **Endnotes.** If you need to add material that would disrupt your paper if it were included in the text, include such notes at the end of the paper.
3. **Works Cited list.** At the end of your paper, include a list of the sources from which you have quoted, summarized, or paraphrased.

42a Parenthetical references

In-text citations, also referred to as "parenthetical references" because they are enclosed in parentheses, help your reader find the citation of the source in the Works Cited list at the end of the paper. You may have used footnotes in the past to cite each source as you used it, but MLA format recommends parenthetical citations, depending on how much information you include in your sentence or in your introduction to a quotation. Try to be brief, but not at the expense of clarity, and use signal words and phrases to introduce the citation (see 40d).

Examples of MLA In-Text Citations

1. Author's Name Not Given in the Text 184
2. Author's Name Given in the Text 185
3. Two or More Works by the Same Author 185
4. Two or Three Authors 185
5. More Than Three Authors 185
6. Unknown Author 185
7. Work in an Anthology 185
8. Corporate Author or Government Document 186
9. Entire Work 186
10. Literary Work 186
11. Biblical and Other Sacred Texts 186
12. Multivolume Work 187
13. Indirect Source 187
14. Two or More Sources 187
15. Work Listed by Title 187
16. Work from a Library Database 187
17. Work from an Online or Electronic Source 188
18. Long Quotation 188
19. Lecture, Speech, or Other Oral Presentation 189
20. E-Mail 189

1. **Author's Name Not Given in the Text** If the author's name is not in your sentence, put in parentheses the author's last name, a space with no punctuation, and the page number.

> Recent research on sleep and dreaming indicates that dreams move backward in time as the night progresses (Dement 72).

2. **Author's Name Given in the Text** If you include the author's name in the sentence, only the page number is needed in parentheses.

> Freud states that "a dream is the fulfillment of a wish" (154).

3. **Two or More Works by the Same Author** If you used two or more different sources by the same author in your paper and want to cite one of the sources, put a comma after the author's last name and include a shortened version of the title and then the page reference. If the author's name is in the text, include only the shortened title and the page reference. Put book titles in italics and enclose article titles in quotation marks.

> One current theory emphasizes the principle that dreams express "profound aspects of personality" (Foulkes, *Sleep* 144). Foulkes's investigation shows that young children's dreams are "rather simple and unemotional" ("Children's Dreams" 90).

4. **Two or Three Authors** If your source has two or three authors, either name them in your sentence or include the names in parentheses.

> Jeffrey and Milanovitch argue that the recently reported statistics for teen pregnancies are inaccurate (112).
>
> (*or*)
>
> The recently reported statistics for teen pregnancies are said to be inaccurate (Jeffrey and Milanovitch 112).

5. **More Than Three Authors** If your source has more than three authors, either use the first author's last name followed by *et al.* (which means "and others") or list all the last names.

> The conclusion drawn from a survey on the growth of the Internet, conducted by Martin et al., is that global usage will double within two years (36).
>
> (*or*)
>
> Recent figures on the growth of the Internet indicate that global usage will double within two years (Martin, Ober, Mancuso, and Blum 36).

6. **Unknown Author** If the author is unknown, use a shortened form of the title in your citation.

> More detailed nutritional information in food labels is proving to be a great advantage to diabetics ("New Labeling Laws" 3).

7. **Work in an Anthology** Cite the name of the author of the work, not the editor of the anthology, in the sentence or in parentheses.

When the author describes his first meeting with Narum, he uses images of light to show "the purity of the man's soul" (Aknov 262).

8. **Corporate Author or Government Document** Use the name of the corporation or government agency, shortened or in full. If the name is long, try to include it in your sentence to avoid extending the parenthetical reference.

The United Nations Regional Flood Containment Commission has been studying weather patterns that contribute to flooding in Africa (4).

9. **Entire Work** If you cite an entire work, it is preferable to include the author's name in the text.

Danino was the first to argue that small infants respond to music.

10. **Literary Work** If you refer to well-known prose works, such as novels or plays, that are available in several editions, you can help your readers by providing more information than just a page reference in the edition you used. A chapter number, for example, might help readers find the reference in any copy they find. In such a reference, give the page number first, add a semicolon, and then give other identifying information.

In *The Prince*, Machiavelli reminds us that although some people manage to jump from humble origins to great power, such people find their greatest challenge to be staying in power: "Those who rise from private citizens to be princes merely by fortune have little trouble in rising but very much trouble in maintaining their position" (23; ch. 7).

For verse plays and poems, omit page numbers and use act, scene, canto, and line numbers separated by periods. For lines, use the word *line* or *lines* in the first reference, and then afterward give only the numbers.

Eliot again reminds us of society's superficiality in "The Love Song of J. Alfred Prufrock": "There will be time, there will be time / To prepare a face to meet the faces that you meet" (lines 26-27).

11. **Biblical and Other Sacred Texts** Because sacred texts are available in several editions from various publishers, your reader needs more information than just a page reference. For the first reference in your document, give the shortened title of the work (italicized), followed by a comma. Then add the abbreviated title of the chapter. Add the verse number, followed by a period, and the line numbers. For additional references, give only the abbreviated chapter title, verse, and line numbers.

The Hebrew Bible emphasizes the seriousness of the passage to adulthood: "Banish anxiety from your mind, and put away pain from your body; for youth and the dawn of life are vanity" (*New Oxford Annotated Bible*, Eccles. 11.10). In his first letter, Paul echoes this sobering view of adulthood (1 Cor. 13.11-12).

12. **Multivolume Work** When you cite a volume number as well as a page reference for a multivolume work, separate the two by a colon and a space. Do not use the word *volume* or *page*.

> In his *History of the Civil War*, Jimmersen traces the economic influences that contributed to the decisions of several states to stay in the Union (3: 798-823).

13. **Indirect Source** Using original sources is preferable. But when you have to rely on a secondhand source— words from one source quoted in a work by someone else—start the citation with the abbreviation *qtd. in*.

> Although Newman has established a high degree of accuracy for such tests, he reminds us that "no test like this is ever completely and totally accurate" (qtd. in Mazor 33).

14. **Two or More Sources** If you refer to more than one work in the same parenthetical citation, separate the references by a semicolon.

> Recent attempts to control the rapid destruction of the rainforests in Central America have met with little success (Costanza 22; Kinderman 94).

15. **Work Listed by Title** For sources listed by title in your list of works cited, use the title in your sentence or in the parenthetical citation. If you shorten the title because it is long, use a shortened form that begins with the word you used to alphabetize it in your Works Cited list.

> The video excerpts revealed sophisticated techniques unknown in the early science-fiction movies ("Making Today's Sci-Fi Flicks" 27).

16. **Work from a Library Database** For works from library databases, start with the word you used to alphabetize the work in your Works Cited list. If you are able to view a PDF version of the original print file (meaning that it looks exactly the same as the original print publication), use the exact page numbers. If you are viewing the work in Web page format, do not use page numbers.

> Mountain biking has yet to be considered a full-fledged mainstream sport, due in part to the challenges faced by the advertising industry in marketing the mountain-biking lifestyle (Smith 66).

MLA

> Advertisers are now using custom-designed bottles, superheroes, and new flavors to market bottled water to children (Hein).

17. **Work from an Online or Electronic Source** For works from online or electronic sources, start with the word you used to alphabetize the work in your Works Cited list (see 42c). Because Web pages may vary in length when printed out on paper (due to printer settings, font settings, and computer preferences), page numbers for online sources in HTML format are not used for citations. But if the source contains numbered paragraphs, you may include paragraph numbers by adding *par.* or *pars.* and the paragraph number or numbers used. If your source is in PDF format, you may include page numbers.

> The World Wide Web is a helpful source for community groups seeking information on how to protest projects that damage the local environment ("Environmental Activism"). Electronic mailing lists can also provide activists with up-to-date local information (Stanzer).

> A number of popular romantic comedies from the late 1990s suggest that women can only succeed at maintaining their femininity by paying less attention to their careers (Negra, par. 6).

18. **Long Quotation** If a quotation runs more than four typed lines, set it off by indenting one inch or ten spaces from the left margin. Double-space the quotation, and do not use quotation marks. At the end of the quote, place the parenthetical citation after the period. Do not place another period after the final parenthesis.

> Thomas Friedman argues that Americans need to prepare today's students for tomorrow's challenges in the global marketplace:
>
>> Our fate can be different, but only if we start doing things differently. It takes fifteen years to train a scientist or advanced engineer, starting from when that young man or woman first gets hooked on science or math in elementary school. Therefore, we should be embarking immediately on an all-hands-on-deck, no-holds-barred, no-budget-too-large crash program for science and engineering education. They have to be educated through a long process, because, ladies and gentlemen, this really *is* rocket science. (359)

The bibliographic information for this long quotation would appear on the Works Cited page:

> Friedman, Thomas L. *The World Is Flat: A Brief History of the Twenty-First Century, Updated and Expanded.* New York: Farrar, 2006. Print.

19. **Lecture, Speech, or Other Oral Presentation** Use the name or word you used to alphabetize the source.

> The speaker indicated there would be no change in current student loan policies (Lefevre).

20. **E-Mail** Use the sender's last name.

> The Department of Natural Resources is reviewing the status of wild horses in national parks (Draheim).

42b Endnotes (or notes)

When you have additional comments or information that would disrupt the paper, cite the information in endnotes numbered consecutively through the paper. Put the number at the end of the phrase, clause, or sentence containing the material you are referring to, after the punctuation. Raise the number above the line, with no punctuation. Leave no extra space before the number.

> The treasure hunt for sixteenth-century pirate loot buried in Nova Scotia began in 1927,[3] but hunting was discontinued when the treasure seekers found the site flooded at high tide.[4]

At the end of your paper, begin a new sheet with the heading "Notes," but do not italicize the heading or put it in quotation marks. Leave a one-inch margin at the top, center the heading, double-space, and then begin listing your notes. For each note, indent five spaces, insert the note number and a period, and begin the note. Double-space, and if the note continues on the next line, begin that line at the left-hand margin. In your note, make reference to the author and, if the reference is specific, the page number(s) of the comment. This information should allow the reader to find complete information on the Works Cited page.

> 3. Some historians argue that this widely accepted date is inaccurate. See Flynn 29-43.

> 4. With better equipment and more funding, other treasure hunters continued to seek ways to locate the treasures. Information about these later efforts can be found in Jones and Lund.

Works Cited

Flynn, Jerome. *Buried Treasures.* New York: Newport, 1978. Print.

Jones, Avery, and Jessica Lund. "The Nova Scotia Mystery Treasure." *Contemporary History* 9.1 (1985): 81-83. Print.

42c Works Cited list

The list of works cited includes all sources you cite in your paper. Do not include other materials you read but didn't specifically refer to in your paper. Arrange the list alphabetically by the last name of the author; if there is no author, alphabetize by the first word of the title (ignore the articles *A, An,* and *The*).

For the Works Cited section, begin a new sheet of paper, leave a one-inch margin at the top, center the heading "Works Cited" (with no italicizing or quotation marks), and then double-space before the first entry. For each entry, begin at the left-hand margin for the first line, and indent five spaces (or one-half inch) for additional lines in the entry. Double-space throughout. Place the Works Cited list at the end of your paper after the notes, if you have any. Follow these basic formats for creating Works Cited entries. (Also see 42d for a sample Works Cited page.)

Books in Print

| Author Names. | | *Book Title.* | | Place of Publication: |

| Publisher, year of publication. | | Medium. |

(INDENT 5 SPACES)

Scholarly Journals

| Author Names. | | "Title of Article." | | *Journal Name* |

volume number.issue number (year of publication): page number(s). | | Medium. |

(INDENT 5 SPACES)

Magazines

| Author Names. | | "Title of Article." | | *Magazine Name* |

| day Mo. year: page number(s). | | Medium. |

(INDENT 5 SPACES)

Newspapers

| Author Names. | | "Title of Article." | | *Newspaper Name* |

day Mo. year, edition: page number(s). | | Medium. |

(INDENT 5 SPACES)

TRY THIS

To Format Names, Titles, Publishers' Names, and Media in MLA Style

Names of Authors

Use the author's full name: last name first, followed by a comma, and then the first name and any middle initial or name. End the name with a period and one space. If there is more than one name, place a comma after the first name of the first author, and insert *and*. Then add the second author's name: first name, middle initial or name (if any), and last name.

Titles

Give the full title, including the subtitle, if any. Put a colon and then a space between the title and subtitle. Italicize titles of books, magazines, newspapers, and Web sites. Place titles of articles, parts of books, and pages on Web sites in quotation marks. Capitalize all words except articles, prepositions, and coordinating conjunctions, unless they are the first or last words.

Publishers' Names

Shorten the names of publishers by omitting articles at the beginning of the name (*A, An, The*) and business names or descriptive words (*Books, Co., Press,* etc.). For university presses, use UP (Ohio State UP, U of Utah P). If more than one person's name is part of the company name, cite only the first name (Prentice, Simon, etc.), and if the company name is commonly known to your readers by an acronym, use the acronym (GPO, NCTE, IBM, etc.). If the work is published as an imprint, which is a name of a subdivision or specialized line of books printed by a publisher, list the name of the imprint, immediately followed by a hyphen and the name of the publisher (Viking-Penguin, Belknap-Harvard UP, etc.).

Media

All Works Cited entries should indicate the medium of the source. For print sources, the word *Print* appears at the end of the entry, followed by a period. Sources located on the Internet are indicated with the word Web, followed by a period, and then the date of access, followed by a period. MLA bibliographic format no longer includes the URL because these Web addresses change often and can be very lengthy and complex. However, include the URL when the reader isn't likely to be able to find the source otherwise or if your instructor requires that you include the URL. Other media tags include *DVD, Film, Television, Radio, Performance, JPEG file, Address,* and *Lecture*. Check your source to determine its media tag. Also see the examples in 40c.

Sources from online library databases or subscription services

| Author Names. | "Title of Short Work" (or) *Title of Book.* |

| Print publication information. | *Name of Database.* |

| Medium. | Date of access. |

(INDENT 5 SPACES)

Basic Web site sources

Author Names. | "Title of Web Page." | *Title of Web Site.*
Name of institutional or corporate site provider,
Date of publication, revision, or update.
Medium. | Date of access.

(INDENT 5 SPACES)

Print sources posted online

Author Names. | "Title of Article, Poem, or Short Work"
or *Title of Book or Long Work.*
Original print publication information. | *Title of Web Site.*
Medium. | Date of access.

(INDENT 5 SPACES)

Examples of MLA Works Cited Entries

BOOKS

1. One Author 194
2. Two or Three Authors 194
3. More Than Three Authors 194
4. More Than One Work by the Same Author 195
5. Work with a Publisher's Imprint 195
6. Republished Work 195
7. Anthology/Collected Works 195
8. Work in an Anthology/Collected Works 196
9. Two or More Works in the Same Anthology/Collected Works 196
10. Scholarly Collection/Work That Names an Editor 196
11. Article in a Scholarly Collection/Work That Names an Editor 196
12. Work with an Author and an Editor 197
13. Second or Later Edition 197
14. Work That Names a Translator 197
15. Work by a Corporate Author 197
16. Work That Has More Than One Volume 197
17. Article in a Dictionary, Encyclopedia, or Reference Book 197
18. Introduction, Foreword, Preface, or Afterword 198
19. Work with a Title within a Title 198
20. Work in a Series 198
21. Government Publication 199
22. Biblical and Other Sacred Texts 199
23. Graphic Novel 199

ARTICLES IN PERIODICALS

24. Scholarly Journal Article 199
25. Monthly or Bimonthly Magazine Article 199
26. Weekly or Biweekly Magazine Article 200

MLA

27. Newspaper Article 200

28. Unsigned Article 200

29. Editorial or Letter to the Editor 200

30. Review of a Work 200

31. Published Interview 201

ELECTRONIC SOURCES

32. Journal Article Located in a Library Database or Subscription Service 201

33. Magazine Article Located in a Library Database or Subscription Service 201

34. Newspaper Article Located in a Library Database or Subscription Service 201

35. Book Located in a Library Database or Subscription Service 201

INTERNET SOURCES

36. Entire Web Site 203

37. Page on a Web Site 203

38. Scholarly Project Accessed Online 203

39. Personal Home Page 203

40. Personal Page on a Social Networking Web Site 203

41. Entire Blog 204

42. Posting on a Blog 204

43. Entire Book Accessed Online 204

44. Poem Accessed Online 204

45. Article in an Online Journal 205

46. Article in an Online Magazine 205

47. Article in an Online Newspaper or Newswire 205

48. Article in an Online Dictionary, Encyclopedia, or Reference Database 205

49. Government Publication Online 205

50. Online Version of a Biblical or Other Sacred Text 206

51. E-Mail Communication 206

52. Real-Time Communication/Instant Messaging (IM) 206

53. Podcast 206

ADDITIONAL SOURCES IN PRINT, AUDIO, VIDEO, ONLINE, OR OTHER FORMATS

54. Publication on CD-ROM or DVD 206

55. Computer Software/ Video Game 206

56. Television Program 207

57. Online Television Program 207

58. Radio Program 207

59. Online Radio Program 207

60. Sound Recording/CD 207

61. Sound Recording/ MP3/Music Download 208

62. Film Viewed in a Theater 208

63. Film, Emphasis on the Director 208

64. Video Recording on Videocassette or DVD 208

65. Video Recording Posted Online 208

66. Live Performance of a Play 208

67. Musical Composition 209

68. Work of Art 209
69. Online Work of Art 209
70. Photograph 209
71. Online Photograph 210
72. Personal Photograph 210
73. Letter or Memo 210
74. Personal, Telephone, or E-Mail Interview 210
75. Radio or Television Interview 211
76. Online Radio or Television Interview 211
77. Map or Chart 211
78. Online Map or Chart 211
79. Cartoon or Comic Strip 211
80. Online Cartoon or Comic Strip 211
81. Advertisement 212
82. Lecture, Speech, or Address 212
83. Online Lecture, Speech, or Address 212
84. Pamphlet 212
85. Online Pamphlet 213
86. Comic Book 213
87. Online Comic Book 213
88. Online Published Dissertation 213
89. Abstract of a Dissertation 213

Examples of MLA Works Cited

Please note that all entries should be double-spaced on your Works Cited page.

Books

1. **One Author** To cite books from online library databases, see entry 35. To cite books accessed online, see entry 43.

   > Zakaria, Fareed. *The Post-American World*. New York: Norton, 2008. Print.

2. **Two or Three Authors** Reverse the name of the first author only.

   > Roizen, Michael F., and Mehmet C. Oz. *You: The Owner's Manual*. New York: Harper, 2005. Print.

   > Israel, Susan E., Dorothy A. Sisk, and Cathy Collins Block. *Collaborative Literacy: Using Gifted Strategies to Enhance Learning for Every Student*. Thousand Oaks: Corwin, 2007. Print.

3. **More Than Three Authors** For more than three authors, you may list only the first author's name and add *et al.* (for "and others"), or you may give all names in full in the order in which they appear on the title page.

   > Orlik, Peter B., et al. *Exploring Electronic Media: Chronicles and Challenges*. Malden: Blackwell, 2007. Print.

   (*or*)

MLA

Orlik, Peter B., Steven D. Anderson, Louis A. Day, and
W. Lawrence Patrick. *Exploring Electronic Media:
Chronicles and Challenges*. Malden: Blackwell, 2007.
Print.

4. **More Than One Work by the Same Author** Use the
author's name in the first entry only. From then on,
type three hyphens and a period, and then begin the
next title. Alphabetize by title.

Amis, Martin. *The Information*. New York: Harmony, 1995.
Print.

---. *Yellow Dog*. New York: Miramax, 2003. Print.

5. **Work with a Publisher's Imprint** Publishers sometimes
put books under imprints or special names that
usually appear with the publisher's name on the title
page. Include the imprint name, a hyphen, and the
name of the publisher.

Waters, Sarah. *The Little Stranger*. New York: Riverhead-
Penguin, 2009. Print.

6. **Republished Work** State the original publication
date after the title of the book. In the publication
information that follows, put the date of publication
for the current version.

Greene, Graham. *The Comedians*. 1965. New York:
Penguin, 2005. Print.

7. **Anthology/Collected Works** An *anthology* is a book
that contains several smaller works. If the anthology
contains works from several authors, list the editor or
editors first. Use the abbreviation *ed.* for one editor
and *eds.* for more than one editor. If the anthology
contains works by a single author, list the author first
and include the editor or editors after the title. When
adding the name of an editor or editors after the title
of the work, use the abbreviation *Ed.* (which means
"Edited by"). To cite one or more works in an
anthology, see entries 8 and 9.

Tuma, Keith, ed. *Anthology of Twentieth-Century
British and Irish Poetry*. New York: Oxford UP, 2001.
Print.

James, Henry. *The Complete Notebooks of Henry James*.
Ed. Leon Edel and Lyall H. Powers. New York: Oxford
UP, 1987. Print.

8. **Work in an Anthology/Collected Works** State the author and title of the work first, and then give the title and other information about the anthology, including the pages on which the selection appears. Include the original publication date after the title of the work if it is different from the publication date of the anthology or collected works.

> Alexie, Sherman. "Ghost Dance." *McSweeney's Mammoth Treasury of Thrilling Tales*. Ed. Michael Chabon. New York: Vintage-Random, 2003. 341-53. Print.

9. **Two or More Works in the Same Anthology/Collected Works** If you cite two or more works from the same collection and wish to avoid unnecessary repetition, you may include a complete entry for the collection and then cross-reference the works to that collection. In the cross-reference, include the author and title of the work, the last name of the editor of the collection, and the page numbers. For previously published material, you may include the original date of publication after the title of the work.

> Grand, Sarah. "A New Sensation." 1899. Richardson 231-43.

> Richardson, Angelique, ed. *Women Who Did: Stories by Men and Women, 1890-1914*. New York: Penguin, 2005. Print.

> Wharton, Edith. "The Reckoning." 1904. Richardson 296-317.

10. **Scholarly Collection/Work That Names an Editor** Use the abbreviation *ed.* for one editor and *eds.* for more than one editor.

> Kunka, Andrew J., and Michele Troy, eds. *May Sinclair: Moving towards the Modern*. Burlington: Ashgate, 2006. Print.

11. **Article in a Scholarly Collection/Work That Names an Editor** Include the author's name, and add the article title (in quotation marks). Then name the scholarly collection and the editor or editors. If a selection has been published before, give that information and then use *Rpt. in* (for "Reprinted in") with the anthology information.

> Brantlinger, Patrick. "What Is 'Sensational' about the 'Sensation Novel'?" *Nineteenth-Century Fiction* 37 (1982): 1-28. Rpt. in *Wilkie Collins*. Ed. Lyn Pickett. New York: St. Martin's, 1998. 30-57. Print.

> Kail, Harvey. "Separation, Initiation, and Return: Tutor
> Training Manuals and Writing Center Lore." *The
> Center Will Hold: Critical Perspectives on Writing
> Center Scholarship*. Ed. Michael A. Pemberton and
> Joyce Kincaid. Logan: Utah State UP, 2003. 74-95.
> Print.

12. **Work with an Author and an Editor** If there is an editor
in addition to an author, but it is not an anthology
(see entry 7), give the editor's name after the title.
Before the editor's name, put the abbreviation *Ed.*
(for "Edited by").

> Kolakowski, Leszek. *My Correct Views on Everything*.
> Ed. Zbigniew Janowski. South Bend: St. Augustine's,
> 2005. Print.

13. **Second or Later Edition**

> Wolfram, Walt, and Natalie Schilling-Estes. *American
> English*. 2nd ed. Malden: Blackwell, 2006. Print.

14. **Work That Names a Translator** Use the abbreviation
Trans. (for "Translated by").

> Changeux, Jean-Pierre. *The Physiology of Truth:
> Neuroscience and Human Knowledge*. Trans.
> M. B. De Bevoise. Cambridge: Belknap-Harvard UP,
> 2004. Print.

15. **Work by a Corporate Author**

> Microsoft Corporation. *Inside Out: Microsoft—In Our Own
> Words*. New York: Warner, 2000. Print.

16. **Work That Has More Than One Volume** If you are
citing two or more volumes of a work in your paper,
put references to volume and page numbers in the
parenthetical citations. If you are citing only one of
the volumes in your paper, state the number of that
volume in the Works Cited list, and give publication
information for that volume alone.

> Spodek, Howard. *The World's History*. 3rd ed. 2 vols.
> Upper Saddle River: Prentice, 2006. Print.

> Lewis, C. S. *The Collected Letters of C. S. Lewis*. Ed.
> Walter Hooper. Vol. 3. San Francisco: Harper, 2007.
> Print.

17. **Article in a Dictionary, Encyclopedia, or Reference Book**
Treat an encyclopedia article or a dictionary entry
from a well-known reference book like a piece in an

anthology, but do not cite the editor of the reference work. If the article is signed, give the author first. If it is unsigned, give the title first. If articles are arranged alphabetically, omit volume and page numbers. When citing familiar reference books, list only the edition and year of publication. For less familiar reference books, especially those that have been published only once, give all publication information, but omit page numbers if arranged alphabetically.

> "Bioluminescence." *Columbia Encyclopedia*. 6th ed. 2001. Print.

> Miller, Catherine. "Informed Consent." *Encyclopedia of Psychotherapy*. Ed. Michel Hersen and William H. Sledge. 2 vols. San Diego: Academic, 2002. Print.

18. **Introduction, Foreword, Preface, or Afterword** Start the entry with the author of the part you are citing. Then add the information about the book, followed by the page numbers where that part appears. If the author of the part is not the author of the book, use the word *By* and give the book author's full name. If the author of the part and the book are the same, use *By* and the author's last name only.

> Annan, Kofi A. Foreword. *In His Own Words*. By Nelson Mandela. New York: Little, 2003. xiii-xiv. Print.

> Langland, Elizabeth. Introduction. *Telling Tales: Gender and Narrative Form in Victorian Literature and Culture*. By Langland. Columbus: Ohio State UP, 2002. xiii-xxiii. Print.

19. **Work with a Title Within a Title** If a title that is normally italicized appears within another title, do not italicize it or put it inside quotation marks.

> Welsh, Alexander. *Dickens Redressed: The Art of* Bleak House *and* Hard Times. New Haven: Yale UP, 2000. Print.

20. **Work in a Series** If the title page or a preceding page of the book you are citing indicates that it is part of a series, include the series name, without italicizing or quotation marks, and the series number, followed by a period, before the publication information.

> Haimo, Ethan. *Schoenberg's Transformation of Musical Language*. Music in the Twentieth Century 22. Cambridge: Cambridge UP, 2006. Print.

21. **Government Publication** Use the abbreviation *GPO* for publications from the Government Printing Office. If a specific author is not named, list the government agency issuing the work as the author. To cite a government publication consulted online, see entry 49.

> United States. Office of the President. *Budget of the United States Government, Fiscal Year 2007*. Washington: GPO, 2006. Print.

> United States. Dept. of Education. *Tutor-Trainer's Resource Handbook*. Washington: GPO, 1973. Print.

22. **Biblical and Other Sacred Texts** To cite an online text of a sacred text, see entry 50.

> *The Bible: Authorized King James Version with Apocrypha*. Ed. Robert Carroll and Stephen Prickett. Oxford: Oxford UP, 1998. Print.

> *The Jewish Study Bible: Tanakh Translation, Torah, Nevi'im, Kethuvim*. Trans. Jewish Publication Society. Ed. Adele Berlin, Marc Zvi Brettle, and Michael Fishbane. Oxford: Oxford UP, 2003. Print.

23. **Graphic Novel** Writers and artists are co-creators of graphic novels. Start your entry with the creator whose work is most central to your project, following it with a label identifying the person's role.

> Sale, Tim, artist. *Batman: Dark Victory*. Jeph Loeb, writer. New York: DC, 2001. Print.

> Vaughan, Brian K., writer. *Pride of Baghdad*. Art by Niko Henrichon. New York: Vertigo-DC, 2006. Print.

Articles in Periodicals

24. **Scholarly Journal Article** Provide the volume and issue number after the title of the journal.

> Goode, Mike. "Blakespotting." *PMLA* 121.3 (2006): 769-86. Print.

25. **Monthly or Bimonthly Magazine Article** For a magazine published every month or every two months, give the month or months (abbreviated except for May, June, and July) and year, plus the page numbers. Don't add the volume and issue numbers. If the article does not appear on consecutive pages, give the first page followed by a plus sign.

> Bardach, Ann Louise. "Twilight of the Assassins." *Atlantic* Nov. 2006: 88+. Print.

Nelson, Michael J. "Snob Classics." *Cracked* Nov.-Dec. 2006: 60-61. Print.

26. **Weekly or Biweekly Magazine Article** For a magazine published every week or every two weeks, give the complete date, beginning with the day and abbreviating the month (except for May, June, or July). If the article does not appear on consecutive pages, give the first page followed by a plus sign.

Drumming, Neil. "High Wire Act." *Entertainment Weekly* 22 Sept. 2006: 54-57. Print.

27. **Newspaper Article** Provide the author's name and the title of the article. Then add the name of the newspaper as it appears on the masthead, omitting any introductory article such as *The*. If the city of publication isn't included in the name, add the city in square brackets after the name: *Journal-Courier* [Trenton]. If the paper is nationally circulated, such as the *Wall Street Journal*, don't add the city of publication. Abbreviate all months except for May, June, and July. Give any information about the edition, and follow it with a colon and page numbers. If the article is not printed on consecutive pages, give only the first page number followed by a plus sign.

Steel, Emily. "Novel Program Blends Charity and Marketing." *Wall Street Journal* 20 Dec. 2006: B1+. Print.

Stech, Katy. "Congress Gives $36.8M for Hospital." *Post and Courier* [Charleston] 17 Dec. 2006: B1. Print.

28. **Unsigned Article**

"The System of Down." *Esquire* Jan. 2007: 48. Print.

29. **Editorial or Letter to the Editor** If you are citing an editorial, add the word *Editorial* after its title. Use the word *Letter* after the author of a letter to the editor.

"The Story of the Numbers." Editorial. *New York Times* 16 Dec. 2006, late ed.: A16. Print.

Salisbury, Alan B. Letter. *Washington Post* 15 Dec. 2006: A34. Print.

30. **Review of a Work** Include the reviewer's name and title of the review, if any, followed by the words *Rev. of* (for "Review of"), the title of the work being reviewed, a comma, the word *by,* and then the author's name. If the work has no title and isn't signed, begin the

entry with *Rev. of*, and in your list of works cited, alphabetize under the title of the work being reviewed.

> Gleiberman, Owen. "Of Human Bondage." Rev. of *Casino Royale*, dir. Martin Campbell. *Entertainment Weekly* 24 Nov. 2006: 79-80. Print.

> Rev. of *The Beak of the Finch*, by Jonathan Weiner. *Science Weekly* 12 Dec. 1995: 36. Print.

31. **Published Interview** For interviews published, recorded, or broadcast on television or radio, begin with the name of the person interviewed, the title of the interview in quotation marks (if there is no title, use the word *Interview*), the interviewer's name if known, and any relevant publication information.

> Brown, Peter. "Just Say No to Direct to Video." Interview with Lucas Graves. *Wired* Apr. 2006: 44. Print.

Electronic sources

32. **Journal Article Located in a Library Database or Subscription Service**

> Miller, Christopher R. "Jane Austen's Aesthetics and Ethics of Surprise." *Narrative* 13.3 (2005): 238-60. *MLA International Bibliography*. Web. 27 Mar. 2009.

33. **Magazine Article Located in a Library Database or Subscription Service**

> Boo, Katherine. "The Best Job in Town." *New Yorker* 5 July 2004: 56+. *Expanded Academic ASAP Plus*. Web. 7 June 2009.

34. **Newspaper Article Located in a Library Database or Subscription Service**

> Davis, Mark. "Baby Giant Panda Takes the Next Step." *Journal-Constitution* [Atlanta] 22 Dec. 2006: F2. *Custom Newspapers*. Web. 29 Dec. 2008.

35. **Book Located in a Library Database or Subscription Service**

> Day, Gary. *Class*. New York: Routledge-Taylor, 2001. *NetLibrary*. Web. 29 Apr. 2009.

Internet sources

MLA distinguishes between works located only on the Internet and works with print publication information that are reproduced on the Internet.

When citing works located only on the Internet, provide standard information such as the names of authors and titles of works. The title of a work is italicized if it is the title of the whole content. But if the work is part of a larger whole, such as a page or article on a Web site, then enclose the title in quotation marks and do not use italics. Then list the following:

- Title of the Web site (in italics), followed by a period.
- Name of the corporation, publisher, or organization that sponsors the site, followed by a comma. If none is named, write *N.p.*
- Date of publication (day Mo. year), followed by a period. If no date is listed, write *n.d.*
- Medium (all sources located on the Internet are indicated by *Web*), followed by a period.
- Date of access (day Mo. year), followed by a period.

When print publication works are reproduced online, provide all of the standard information for print sources, such as the names of authors, titles of works, and appropriate publication information for books or periodicals. Then add the following:

- Title of the Web site (in italics), followed by a period.
- Medium (all sources located on the Internet are indicated by *Web*), followed by a period.
- Date of access (day Mo. year), followed by a period.

HINT

Knowing When to Add a Web Address to an Online Source Citation

Most online sources can be easily located by typing relevant information into an online search engine such as Google. Consequently, a Web address (also known as a URL) should only be added to your citation for an online source in cases where your instructor requests it or the reader would be unable to find the source without this information. If you need to include a Web address in your citation, add it after the date of access. Enclose the entire URL in angle brackets, and end the entry with a period, as shown on the next page.

Emery, Gene. "Study Tracks Big Growth in Drug Ads." *ABC News*. ABC, 15 Aug. 2007. Web. 19 Aug. 2007. <http://abcnews.go.com/Health/Drugs/wireStory?id=3483903>.

36. **Entire Web Site** List the name of the author or editor, if available. Then list the name of the site (italicized). Next list the institution, publisher, or corporation that sponsors the site, followed by a comma. If no sponsor is listed, write *N.p.*, followed by the date of publication or revision. If no date is provided, write *n.d.* Then indicate the medium of publication by writing *Web*. Then add the date of access.

> *The Feed*. G4TV, 2008. Web. 23 June 2008.

> *International Spy Museum*. Intl. Spy Museum, 29 May 2009. Web. 29 May 2009.

> Nee, Brendan. *Brendan Nee*. N.p., Nov. 2002. Web. 18 June 2009.

37. **Page on a Web Site** A Web page is a single page on a Web site. Think of a Web page on a Web site like a chapter in a book—it is a small part of the entire work. After the author's name (if available), place the name of the Web page in quotation marks.

> Johnson, Stephen. "Obama, McCain Face off on Twitter." *The Feed*. G4TV, 23 June 2008. Web. 23 June 2008.

> "Language of Espionage." *International Spy Museum*. Intl. Spy Museum, 29 May 2009. Web. 29 May 2009.

> Nee, Brendan. "Urban Sprawl: A Case Study of La Crosse, WI." *Brendan Nee*. N.p., Nov. 2002. Web. 18 June 2009.

38. **Scholarly Project Accessed Online**

> Sapir, J. David. "Ethnographic Photography." *Fixing Shadows: Still Photography*. U of Virginia Dept. of Anthropology, Apr. 2009. Web. 1 May 2009.

39. **Personal Home Page**

> Timberlake, Justin. Home page. *Justin Timberlake*. Tennman Entertainment, 2009. Web. 4 Apr. 2009.

40. **Personal Page on a Social Networking Web Site**

> Panettiere, Hayden. *MySpace: Hayden Panettiere*. MySpace, 22 Apr. 2009. Web. 29 Apr. 2009.

41. **Entire Blog** List the blog owner as the author. If the
    blog owner uses a pseudonym or handle, use that name.

    > Little Professor. *The Little Professor*. Typepad, n.d. Web. 5
    > June 2009.

    > Sims, Chris. *Chris's Invincible Super-Blog*. N.p., 2009.
    > Web. 2 May 2009.

    > Zúniga, Markos Moulitsas. *Daily Kos: State of the Nation*.
    > Kos Media, n.d. Web. 17 June 2009.

42. **Posting on a Blog** Include the title of the posting
    in quotation marks after the name of the blog owner.
    If the posting is from a writer other than the blog
    owner, list the author of the posting, the title of
    the posting (in quotation marks), the blog title
    (italicized), and then *By* and the blog owner.

    > BarbinMD. "What You (and the Fly) Missed." *Daily Kos:
    > State of the Nation*. By Markos Moulitsas Zúniga.
    > Kos Media, 17 June 2009. Web. 17 June 2009.

    > Little Professor. "Rules for Writing Neo-Victorian Novels."
    > *The Little Professor*. Typepad, 15 Mar. 2006. Web.
    > 5 June 2009.

    > Sims, Chris. "Hold the Garlic." *Chris's Invincible Super-
    > Blog*. N.p., 20 Apr. 2009. Web. 2 May 2009.

43. **Entire Book Accessed Online** Provide the name of the
    author and text. Include the original date of the text,
    if available. Add the editor's name, publication
    information, and the date of the edition of the text, if
    available. Then list the name of the site (italicized),
    Web., and the date of access.

    > Christie, Agatha. *The Mysterious Affair at Styles*. 1920.
    > *Project Gutenberg*. Web. 3 June 2009.

    > Fitzgerald, F. Scott. *This Side of Paradise*. New York:
    > Scribner, 1920. *Bartleby.com*. Web. 21 Dec. 2008.

44. **Poem Accessed Online** Provide the name of the
    author and text. Include the original date of the text,
    if available. If print publication information is listed,
    add the editor's name, publication information, and
    the date of the edition of the text, if available. If page
    numbers are not listed, add *N. pag.* after the date of
    publication. Then list the name of the site (italicized),
    Web., and the date of access. If print publication is not
    available, provide the name of the site (italicized), the

corporate or organizational site provider, *Web.*, and the date of access.

> Angelou, Maya. "Still I Rise." 1978. *Poetry Foundation.* Poetry Foundation, 2009. Web. 3 June 2009.

> Arnold, Matthew. "Dover Beach." 1867. *A Victorian Anthology, 1837-1895.* Ed. Edmund Clarence Stedman. Cambridge: Riverside, 1895. N. pag. *Bartleby.com.* Web. 18 Nov. 2008.

45. **Article in an Online Journal** Include the journal's volume and issue number, if available. If page numbers are listed, include them in the citation. If page numbers are not listed, add *n. pag.* after the date of publication. Then list *Web.* and the date of access. Treat journal articles located through Google Scholar or other full-text online databases like sources from library databases (see entry 32).

> Blumner, Jacob S. "A Writing Center-Education Department Collaboration: Training Teachers to Work One-on-One." *Praxis: A Writing Center Journal* 3.2 (2006): n. pag. Web. 27 Jan. 2009.

46. **Article in an Online Magazine**

> Singel, Ryan. "Spammer Slammer Targets Politics." *Wired News.* Wired, 14 Dec. 2006. Web. 2 Jan. 2009.

47. **Article in an Online Newspaper or Newswire**

> Jones, Meg. "Cashing in on Crayfish." *Milwaukee Journal Sentinel Online.* Milwaukee Journal Sentinel, 18 June 2009. Web. 19 June 2009.

48. **Article in an Online Dictionary, Encyclopedia, or Reference Database**

> "Onomatopoeia." *Merriam-Webster Online.* Merriam-Webster, 2009. Web. 1 June 2009.

> "Peru." *Encyclopaedia Britannica.* Encyclopaedia Britannica, 2009. Web. 12 Feb. 2009.

49. **Government Publication Online** Use GPO as the acronym for the United States Government Printing Office when listed as a publisher.

> United States. Cong. Senate. Committee on Foreign Relations. *Hearings on the Policy Options for Iraq.* 109th Cong., 1st sess. Washington: GPO, 2006.

United States Government Printing Office. Web. 18 Mar. 2009.

50. Online Version of a Biblical or Other Sacred Text

The Bible. King James Vers. *Blue Letter Bible.* Web. 28 Nov. 2008.

51. E-Mail Communication

Hampton, Hayes. "Poetry Event." Message to the author. 5 May 2009. E-mail.

52. Real-Time Communication/Instant Messaging (IM)
This format applies to online chat forums and instant messaging programs. Cite the name of the sender, the title of the discussion (if available), recipient of the message, and the date of the communication. Then include the medium of publication.

Campbell, David. Message to Michael Sterling. 29 Nov. 2008. Gmail Chat.

Kehrwald, Kevin. "Oscar Nominations." Message to the author. 20 Feb. 2009. Windows Live Messenger.

53. Podcast
If the podcast is downloaded to your computer or other audio device, indicate the file type, such as an *MP3 file.* If the podcast is listened to through an open Web site, list the podcast as a Web source.

Menendez, James. "BBC NewsPod." *BBC.* 16 June 2009. MP3 file.

Tracey, Elizabeth, and Rick Lange. "Week of May 15, 2009." *Johns Hopkins Medicine.* Johns Hopkins Medicine, 15 May 2009. Web. 29 May 2009.

Additional sources in print, audio, video, online, or other formats

54. Publication on CD-ROM or DVD
Follow available publication information with the medium, database title, database vendor, and date of publication.

Flanagan, Caitlin. "Bringing Up Baby." *New Yorker* 15 Nov. 2004: 46+. DVD-ROM. *The Complete* New Yorker. New Yorker. 2005.

Mattmer, Tobias. "Discovering Jane Austen." CD-ROM. *Discovering Authors.* Vers. 1.0. Gale. 1992.

MLA

55. **Computer Software/Video Game** References to computer software are similar to references to CD-ROM or DVD-ROM materials (see entry 54) except the medium type is placed at the end of the entry.

> *Sid Meier's Civilization IV*. 2K-Firaxis. 2005. CD-ROM.

56. **Television Program** Include the title of the episode (in quotation marks), the title of the program (italicized), the title of the series (if available, with no italicizing or quotation marks), the name of the network, the call letters and city of the local station (if relevant), the broadcast date and *Television*. If pertinent, add information such as the names of the performers, director, or narrator.

> "Final Grades." *The Wire*. HBO. 10 Dec. 2006. Television.

> *When Parents Are Deployed*. Narr. Cuba Gooding, Jr. PBS. SCETV, Columbia, 27 Dec. 2006. Television.

57. **Online Television Program** If viewed online, include the name of the Web site, corporate or organizational site provider, date of release, *Web.*, and date of access.

> "Every Man for Himself." *Lost*. Dir. Stephen Williams. Perf. Matthew Fox, Josh Holloway, and Evangeline Lilly. *ABC.com*. ABC, 25 Oct. 2006. Web. 28 Dec. 2006.

58. **Radio Program**

> "How to Live on $2 a Day." *On Point*. Narr. Tom Ashbrook. Natl. Public Radio. WBUR, Boston, 9 June 2009. Radio.

59. **Online Radio Program** If accessed online, include the name of the Web site, corporate or organizational site provider, date of release, *Web.*, and date of access.

> Gordon, Dick, narr. "The Women of Rwanda." *The Connection*. WBUR, 22 Apr. 2004. Web. 28 Dec. 2006.

60. **Sound Recording/CD** Depending on which you want to emphasize, cite the composer, conductor, or performer first. Then list the title (italicized); artist; manufacturer; year of issue (if unknown, write *n.d.* for "no date"); and medium (*CD*, *LP*, or *Audiocassette*). Place a comma between manufacturer and date, with periods following all other items.

> Perlman, Itzhak. *Mozart Violin Concertos nos. 3 and 5*. Wiener Philharmoniker Orch. Cond. James Levine. Deutsche Grammophon, 1983. LP.

> U2. "Magnificent." *No Line on the Horizon*. Interscope, 2009. CD.

61. **Sound Recording/MP3/Music Download** For MP3 files and other music downloads, indicate file type at the end of the entry.

> West, Kanye. "Love Lockdown." *808s and Heartbreak.* Roc-a-Fella, 2008. MP3 file.

62. **Film Viewed in a Theater** Begin a reference to a film with the title (italicized), and include the director, distributor, and year. You may also include the names of the screenwriter, performers, and producer. List *Film.* at the end of the entry. (See also entries 63–65.)

> *The Dark Knight.* Dir. Christopher Nolan. Perf. Christian Bale, Heath Ledger, and Aaron Eckhart. Warner, 2008. Film.

> *Pride and Prejudice.* By Jane Austen. Dir. Joe Wright. Perf. Keira Knightly and Matthew Macfadyen. Focus, 2005. Film.

63. **Film, Emphasis on the Director**

> Boyle, Danny, dir. *Slumdog Millionaire.* Perf. Dev Patel, Anil Kapoor, and Freida Pinto. Fox Searchlight, 2008. Film.

64. **Video Recording on Videocassette or DVD** Include the original release date for films re-released on video or DVD, when relevant. List the medium (*Videocasette.* or *DVD.*) at the end of the entry.

> *Spellbound.* Dir. Alfred Hitchcock. Perf. Gregory Peck and Ingrid Bergman. 1945. Criterion, 2002. DVD.

65. **Video Recording Posted Online** List the name or pseudonym of the person who posted the video recording, if available.

> Transfinitejoy. "The Protagonist and the Pterodactyl." *YouTube.* YouTube, 8 Dec. 2006. Web. 15 May 2009.

66. **Live Performance of a Play** Like a reference to a film (see entry 62), references to performances usually begin with the title and include similar information. Include the theater and city where the performance was given, separated by a comma and followed by a period, and the date of the performance. Add *Performance.* at the end of the entry.

> *Waiting for Godot*. By Samuel Beckett. Dir. Sean Mathias. Perf. Ian McKellen and Patrick Stewart. Theatre Royal Haymarket, London. 10 May 2009. Performance.

67. **Musical Composition** Cite like a book, beginning with the composer's name. Italicize the title of an opera, a ballet, or a piece of music with a name, but put quotation marks around the name of an individual song. If the composition is known only by number, form, or key, do not italicize or use quotation marks. If the composition is known only by number, form, or key, do not italicize or use quotation marks. Do not capitalize abbreviations such as *no.* and *op.* Include the composition date after the title. List the type of medium at the end of the entry.

> Mozart, Wolfgang Amadeus. *The Magic Flute*. 1791. London: Faber, 2001. Print.

68. **Work of Art** Begin with the artist's name, italicize the title of the work, and include the date of the work. Then list the medium of the work, followed by a period. Add the institution that houses the work or the person who owns it, followed by a comma, and the city in which it is located. If reproduced in a print source, omit the medium of composition and add the appropriate publication information, citing the page, slide, figure, or plate number. List *Print.* for works reproduced in a print source.

> Dalí, Salvador. *Forgotten Horizon*. 1936. Oil on wood. Tate Mod., London.

> Lichtenstein, Roy. *Drowning Girl*. 1963. Museum of Mod. Art, New York. *Roy Lichtenstein*. By Janis Hendrickson. Berlin: Taschen, 1988. 31. Print.

69. **Online Work of Art** Follow the information in entry 68, but add the appropriate publication information for the Web site on which an image of the work of art is posted.

> Monet, Claude. *Waterloo Bridge, London, at Sunset*. 1904. National Gallery of Art, Washington. *National Gallery of Art*. Web. 28 Dec. 2006.

70. **Photograph** Cite a photograph in a museum as a work of art. Cite a published photograph by indicating the name of the photographer and the publication information needed to locate the source (see entry 68).

MLA

> Gursky, Andreas. *Times Square, New York*. 1997.
> Photograph. Museum of Mod. Art, New York.

71. **Online Photograph** Follow the guidelines in entry 70, but add the appropriate publication information for the Web site on which the image is posted.

> Prather, Terry. *Don't Play with Your Food*. Photograph.
> *MSNBC*. MSNBC, 17 May 2009. Web. 1 June 2009.

72. **Personal Photograph** For a personal photograph, name the subject and location of your photo. Then include *Personal photograph by author* and the date of the photo, followed by the medium.

> Trafalgar Square, London. Personal photograph by author.
> 9 May 2009. JPEG file.

73. **Letter or Memo** For a letter sent to you, name the letter writer, followed by *Letter to the author* and the date. For a letter in an archival collection, include the name of the archive, followed by a period. Add the institution name and city. Cite a published letter like a work in an anthology (see entry 8), but include the date of the letter. Cite the medium of publication as *MS* (for manuscript) or *TS* (for typescript) if the document is unpublished.

> Blumen, Lado. Letter to Lui Han. 14 Oct. 1998. MS. Lado
> Blumen Papers. Minneapolis Museum of Art Lib.,
> Minneapolis.

> Johnson, Jeffrey. Letter to the author. 1 Apr. 2009. MS.

> Nafman, Theresa. Memo to Narragansett School Board.
> Narragansett High School, Boston. 3 May 2004. TS.

> West, Rebecca. "To Bertrand Russell." Sept. 1929.
> *Selected Letters of Rebecca West*. Ed. Bonnie Kime
> Scott. New Haven: Yale UP, 2000. 114-17. Print.

74. **Personal, Telephone, or E-Mail Interview** If you conducted the interview, start with the name of the person interviewed, the type of interview (*Personal interview, Telephone interview, E-mail interview*), and the date.

> Flannagan, Rebecca. Telephone interview. 3 Apr. 2006.

> Krier, April. Personal interview. 15 May 2009.

MLA

75. **Radio or Television Interview** Add the appropriate medium at the end of the entry.

> Geithner, Timothy. Interview with Charlie Rose. *The Charlie Rose Show*. PBS. SCETV, Columbia. 6 May 2009. Television.

76. **Online Radio or Television Interview** If accessed online, include the name of the Web site, the corporate or institutional site provider, the date of release, *Web.*, and the date of access.

> Carter, Jimmy. Interview with Terry Gross. *Fresh Air with Terry Gross*. NPR.com. Natl. Public Radio, 27 Nov. 2006. Web. 28 Dec. 2006.

77. **Map or Chart** Treat a map or chart like a book without an author, but add the descriptive label *Map* or *Chart*.

> *New York*. Map. Chicago: Rand, 1995. Print.

78. **Online Map or Chart** Name the map or chart title, followed by the descriptive label *Map* or *Chart*. Then include the name of the Web site, corporate or organizational site provider, date of publication, *Web.*, and the date of access.

> "Chicago." Map. *Mapquest*. Mapquest, 1 May 2009. Web. 1 May 2009.

79. **Cartoon or Comic Strip** Begin with the cartoonist's name, followed by the title of the cartoon or strip (if any) in quotation marks and a descriptive label (*Cartoon* or *Comic strip*), and conclude with the usual publication information. For a cartoon or comic strip found online, add the relevant Internet information.

> Amend, Bill. "FoxTrot." Comic strip. *Morning News* [Florence] 21 Dec. 2006: D3. Print.

80. **Online Cartoon or Comic Strip** Follow the guidelines in entry 79 for the artist, title, and descriptive label. Then include the name of the Web site, corporate or organizational site provider, date of publication, *Web.*, and the date of access.

> Lang, Bob. "Looking Out for Number One." Cartoon. *CNN.com*. Cable News Network, 11 May 2007. Web. 24 Aug. 2007.

81. **Advertisement** Begin with the name of the product, company, or institution that is the subject of the advertisement, followed by the descriptive label *Advertisement*. Conclude with the appropriate publication information and medium.

> Apple Computer. Advertisement. *Apple.com*. Apple Inc., 2006. Web. 28 Dec. 2006.

> Mercedes-Benz. Advertisement. CNN. 28 Dec. 2006. Television.

> Toyota Prius. Advertisement. *Entertainment Weekly* 29 May 2009: 43. Print.

82. **Lecture, Speech, or Address** Begin with the speaker's name, followed by the title of the presentation (if available) in quotation marks. Add the meeting and sponsoring organization, location, and date. Add a descriptive label such as *Address* or *Speech* to indicate the medium.

> Villanueva, Victor. "Blind: Talking of the New Racism." Intl. Writing Center Assn. Convention. Minneapolis Hyatt Regency, Minneapolis. 21 Oct. 2005. Address.

> Wiesel, Elie. Koger Center, U of South Carolina, Columbia. 12 Sept. 2006. Address.

83. **Online Lecture, Speech, or Address** Follow the guidelines in entry 82. Then include the name of the Web site, corporate or organizational site provider, date of publication, *Web.*, and date of access.

> Eisenhower, Dwight D. "D-Day Invasion Order." 5 June 1944. Speech. *History.com*. Arts and Entertainment Television Network, 2006. Web. 27 Dec. 2008.

> Friedman, Thomas. "The World Is Flat." Lecture. *MITWorld*. MIT, 16 May 2005. Web. 20 April 2009.

84. **Pamphlet** Cite a pamphlet like a book. If from a government agency, cite with the appropriate attribution.

> *How to Fit a Bicycle Helmet*. Arlington: Bicycle Helmet Safety Inst., 2006. Print.

> United States. Dept. of the Interior. Natl. Park Service. *The White House*. Washington: GPO, 2006. Print.

85. **Online Pamphlet** Follow the example in entry 84. Then include the name of the Web site, *Web.*, and the date of access.

> *Using Graphic Novels in the Classroom.* New York: Graphix-Scholastic, 2005. *Scholastic.* Web. 28 Apr. 2009.

86. **Comic Book** Writers and artists are co-creators of comic books. Start your entry with the creator whose work is most central to your project, following it with a label identifying the person's role. Italicize the comic title. List the issue number and then cite the publication information as you would cite a book (also see entry 23 for citing graphic novels).

> Heinberg, Allan, writer. *Wonder Woman.* Art by Terry Dodson. Issue 3. New York: DC, 2006. Print.

87. **Online Comic Book** Follow the example in entry 86. Include the name of the Web site, *Web.*, and the date of access.

> Ellis, Warren, writer. *Nextwave.* Art by Stuart Immonen. Issue 1. New York: Marvel, 2006. *Marvel Comics.* Web. 29 Dec. 2006.

88. **Online Published Dissertation**

> Maloney, Kathleen A. *Mirrored Images—English and India: Women's Educational Opportunities in Literature, 1844-1898.* Diss. Purdue U, 2002. Ann Arbor: UMI, 2002. *ProQuest.* Web. 28 Jan. 2009.

89. **Abstract of a Dissertation** Begin with the publication information for the original work, and then add the information for the journal in which the abstract appears. If accessed through a library subscription service, then add the name of the database, *Web.*, and the date of access.

> Groode, Tiffany A. "Biomass to Ethanol: Potential Production and Environmental Impacts." Diss. MIT, 2008. *DAI* 69.6 (2008): item AAT0820325. *ProQuest Dissertations and Theses.* Web. 29 Nov. 2008.

42d Sample pages

Follow the format shown here for the first two pages and the Works Cited page of an MLA-style research paper. A separate title page is not required in MLA style.

1 inch

1/2 inch

Bryant 1

Liza Bryant

Dr. Jennifer Kunka

English 200

24 April 2007

Crumbling Buildings and Broken Dreams:

South Carolina's Rural Students Deserve Better

Imagine you are walking into your new school, and as you start up the steps to go to the front door, the steps begin to creak and give way underneath your feet. Once inside, you walk down the hallway of a school built in the nineteenth century, and the sights do not get any better. You can focus only on the peeling paint chips and the rotting molding. The hallway smells like sewage, the water fountains do not work, and plywood patches cover the floor. Along with all of this, you are freezing because it is thirty degrees outside and the heating in the building does not work. You walk into your classroom, and students are bundled up in their jackets and gloves; they can barely pay attention to the teachers because they are trying to stay warm. Continuing to look around the classroom, you find that the desks are about to fall apart. Looking up, you see spots in the ceiling where there is water damage from the leaking roof.

double-s
text

1 inch

1 inch

1-inch bo
margi

1 inch

1/2 inch

Bryant 2

often make the decision to drop out. This educational problem, however, can be alleviated with additional funding from the state. The state of South Carolina expects to receive a budget surplus of $1 billion for 2007 (Adcox). The state legislature should use a significant portion of this money to make an investment in South Carolina's future by improving physical conditions in these rural schools and giving these students a true opportunity to succeed.

1 inch

1-inch

1-inch bo
margi

MLA

1 inch ↕   1/2 inch ↕

Bryant 8

Works Cited

Adcox, Seanna. "S.C. Senate Begins Work on State's
$7.3 Billion Budget." *State* [Columbia]. State, 9 Apr.
2007. Web. 15 Apr. 2007.

"Annual Average Unemployment Rates by County
(2001-2005)." *South Carolina Statistical Abstract*.
Office of Research and Statistics, South Carolina
State Budget and Control Board, 2007. Web. 12
Apr. 2007.

Drake, John. "Judge Rules in School Funding Case."
Associated Press State and Local Wire 29 Dec.
2005. *LexisNexis*. Web. 17 Apr. 2007.

---. "Publication Ranks SC's Graduation Rate Worst in
Nation." *Associated Press State and Local Wire* 20
June 2006. *LexisNexis*. Web. 17 Apr. 2007.

Ferillo, Bud, dir. *Corridor of Shame: The Neglect of
South Carolina's Rural Schools*. Ferillo & Assoc.,
2005. DVD.

Gladwell, Malcolm. *The Tipping Point: How Little
Things Can Make a Big Difference*. New York:
Little, 2000. Print.

Kropf, Schuyler. "Court Gives S.C. Schools Partial
Win." *Post and Courier* [Charleston] 30 Dec. 2005:
A1. Print.

National Dropout Prevention Center/Network. "Quick
Facts." *National Dropout Prevention
Center/Network*. National Dropout Prevention
Center/Network, 24 Mar. 2004. Web. 16 Apr. 2007.

South Carolina Kids Count. "Kids Count Reflects on
Judge Cooper's Ruling." *South Carolina Kids
Count*. South Carolina Kids Count, n.d. Web. 12
Apr. 2007.

double-space
text

1-inch ↔   1 inch ↔

(Proportions shown in the margins of the MLA paper
are not actual but have been adjusted to fit space
limitations of this book. Follow actual dimensions
indicated and your instructor's directions.)

1-inch ↕

43

Documenting in APA Style

The format prescribed by the **American Psychological Association (APA)** is used to document papers in fields such as psychology, sociology, business, economics, nursing, social work, and criminology. For APA format, follow the guidelines offered here and consult the *Publication Manual of the American Psychological Association,* 6th ed. (Washington: APA, 2010). Check for further updates on the APA Web site (apastyle.apa.org).

HINT

Features of APA Style

- The paper begins with a brief abstract or summary.
- For in-text citations, give the author's last name and the source's year of publication. For quoted material or other references to specific information in the original source, add a page (*p.*) number or paragraph (*para.*) number to guide readers to the original passage.
- In quotations, put signal words (see 40d) in past tense ("Smith reported") or present perfect tense ("as Smith has reported").
- A list of works mentioned in the paper is called References. In the References list at the end of the paper, give full publication information, alphabetized by author.
- Use full last names but only initials of first and middle names of authors.
- Capitalize only the first word and proper names in book and article titles, but capitalize all major words in journal titles. Use italics for book and journal titles; do not put article titles in quotation marks.
- Use the ampersand (&) instead of the word *and* with authors' names in parenthetical citations, tables, captions, and the References.

43a In-text citations

When you use APA format and refer to sources in your text, include the author's name, a comma, and then date of publication. For direct quotations or specific references to the original source, add another comma after the date. For print sources, include the page number, with *p.* (for page) before the number. For online or electronic sources, include the paragraph number, with *para.* (for paragraph) before the number.

Examples of APA In-Text Citations

1. Direct Quotations 218
2. Author's Name Given in the Text 218
3. Author's Name Not Given in the Text 218
4. Work by Multiple Authors 218
5. Group as Author 218
6. Unknown Author 218
7. Authors with the Same Last Name 219
8. Two or More Works in the Same Citation 219
9. Republished Work 219
10. Biblical and Classical Works 219
11. Specific Parts of a Source 219
12. Personal Communications 220
13. World Wide Web 220
14. Indirect Source 220

1. **Direct Quotations** When you quote a source, enclose the quote in quotation marks, and then give the author and year. For print sources, add *p.* and the page number. For online or electronic sources, add *para.* and the paragraph number. All quotations or specific references to the text must contain a page or paragraph number to guide readers to the original passage.

   In coastal areas, natural catastrophe insurance "is either impossible to come by or has skyrocketed past affordable" (Richter, 2006, p. 28). Many insurers "have simply stopped writing new homeowners' insurance policies in coastal counties" (Marlyebone, 2009, para. 4).

2. **Author's Name Given in the Text** Cite only the year of publication in parentheses. If the year appears in the sentence, don't add parenthetical information. If you refer to the same study again in the paragraph with the source's name, you don't have to cite the year again if it is clear that the same study is being referred to.

When Patel (2008) reproduced the study, she noted an increase in levels of carbon dioxide. Patel also noted a corresponding decrease in oxygen levels.

3. **Author's Name Not Given in the Text** Cite the name and year, separated by a comma.

In a recent study of response times (Chung, 2005), no change was noticed.

4. **Work by Multiple Authors** For two authors, cite both names every time you refer to the source. Use *and* in the text, but use an ampersand (&) in parenthetical material, tables, captions, and the References list.

Best and Wickham (2007) noted that their data refuted the results of a similar study on oxygen molecules (Singh & Wong, 2006).

For three, four, or five authors, include all authors (and date) the first time you cite the source. For later references to the same work, use only the first author's name and *et al.* (for "and others"), with no underlining or italics.

Egan, Parker, Koch, and Romstein (2007) reviewed the historical effects of economic recessions. Later, when Phu et al. (2009) continued their study of recessions, they developed indicators to measure future economic trends.

For six or more authors, cite only the first author and *et al.* and the year for all references.

Mokach et al. (2006) noted no improvement in norms for participant scores.

5. **Group as Author** Usually, the name of the group that serves as the author (for example, a government agency or a corporation) is spelled out each time it appears in a citation. However, if the name is long but easily identified by its abbreviation, you can give the abbreviation in parentheses when the entire name first appears and then refer to the group by its abbreviated name in additional references.

In 1992, when the National Institutes of Mental Health (NIMH) prepared its report, no field data on this epidemic were available. However, NIMH agreed that future reports would correct this deficiency.

6. **Unknown Author** When a work has no author indicated, cite the first few words of the title in quotation marks and the year.

> One recent article ("Safe as Houses," 2009) speculated on the collapse of the housing market.

7. **Authors with the Same Last Name** When two or more authors in the References have the same last name, include their initials in text citations.

> After J. D. Humphrey (2009) reviewed the initial study (F. M. Humphrey, 2007), a new report was issued.

8. **Two or More Works in the Same Citation** When two or more works are cited within the same parentheses, arrange them in the order in which they appear in the References list, and separate them with semicolons.

> Several studies (Balfour, 2009; Figa, 2005; Phi & Janovich, 2008) reported similar behavior patterns in such cases.

9. **Republished Work** If you are using a version of a source originally published in a different year, include in your in-text citation both the original date of publication and the publication date from the version you consulted, separated by a slash.

> The evolutionary development of species is a complex process (Darwin, 1859/2009).

10. **Biblical and Classical Works** Reference entries are not necessary for major classical works such as the Bible and ancient Greek and Roman works, but identify the version you used in the first citation in your text. If appropriate, in each citation, include the part (book, chapter, lines).

> When Abraham saw three men passing his tent, he asked them to stop and not pass by him (Gen. 18:3, Revised Standard Version).

> The most recent translation (Homer, trans. 2008) reveals a new perspective on this issue.

11. **Specific Parts of a Source** To cite a specific part of a source, include the page, chapter, figure, or table. Use the abbreviation *p.* (for "page") but no abbreviation for "Chapter."

> Previous research on pandemic flu did not consider this factor (Chang & Ramanda, 2007, p. 108), but recently Takai (2009, Chapter 9) investigated this phenomenon.

For an electronic source that contains no page number, use the abbreviation for paragraph (*para.*)

followed by the paragraph number. When no paragraph number is given, cite the heading and the number of the paragraph following it.

> The two methods showed a significant difference (Smith, 2000, para. 2) when repeated with a different age group.

> No further study indicated any change in the results (Pappas, 2007, Conclusion section, para. 5).

12. **Personal Communications** Personal communications, such as letters, memos, telephone conversations, and electronic communications, such as e-mail, discussion groups, and messages on electronic bulletin boards, are not archived. Because the data can't be recovered, these are included only in the text, not in the References list. Include the initials and last name of the communicator and as exact a date as possible. (For electronic sources that can be documented, see 43c.)

> According to P. P. Roy (personal communication, July 21, 2009), that outcome is likely.

13. **World Wide Web** To cite a Web site in the text (but not a specific document), include the Web address. See 43c for more information.

> Consult the Web site for the American Psychological Association (http://apastyle.apa.org) for updates on how to cite Internet sources.

14. **Indirect Source** If you locate a passage in a source but the passage is quoted from or attributed to another original source, you should try to locate that original source and cite it in your paper. If that original source is out of print or not available to you, cite the source you consulted in your References list. Then mention the original source in the text of your paper and make reference to the source you consulted in your in-text citation.

> Goran's theory (as cited in Eames, 2009, p. 67) discusses the connections between criminality and social stimuli.

43b Footnotes

In your paper, you may need footnotes to expand on content and to acknowledge copyrighted material. Content footnotes add important information that can't be integrated into the text, but they are distracting. So use them only if they strengthen the discussion. Copyright permission footnotes refer to the sources of quotations and other copyrighted materials. Number the footnotes consecutively with superscript Arabic numerals (1, 2, 3, etc.). Include the footnotes at the bottom of the pages on which they appear, or list all footnotes together on a separate page after the References.

43c References list

Arrange all entries in alphabetical order by the author's last name; for several works by one author, arrange by year of publication with the earliest one first (see entry 25 for an example). For each entry in the list, the first line begins at the left margin and all following lines are indented five spaces. Start the References list on a new page, with the word *References* centered at the top of the page, and double-space all entries.

APA

TRY THIS

To Format Titles in APA Style

Capitalize only the first word of the title and subtitle, the first word after a colon, and any proper nouns. Italicize book titles, Web site titles, journal titles, and volume numbers of journals. Titles of articles, book chapters, and pages on Web sites should not be italicized or surrounded by quotation marks.

HINT

Formatting Reference Entries for Electronic Sources

Follow these guidelines for creating your References list.

Author names Include the name(s) of the author(s) in the same format used for books and journals.

Date of publication Include the date in parentheses following the name(s) of the author(s), followed by a period. If no date is available, write (n.d.) for "no date."

Titles Do not use italics when listing names of articles and pages within Web sites. Use italics for titles of books, periodicals, and most whole Web sites.

Volume and issue numbers For periodicals such as journals and magazines, include the volume and issue number in your entry if each issue of the publication starts with page 1. If the pagination continues from issue to issue, no issue number is needed.

DOIs Some publications such as journal articles, books, and technical reports are now identified by DOI (Digital Object Identifier) numbers. A DOI is a unique code assigned to that publication. Regardless of where the publication was accessed, the DOI will remain the same. If the publication has been assigned a DOI, include the DOI number after the publication information (see entries 1 and 22). If you access the publication online, list the DOI instead of the URL.

Retrieval information A retrieval line generally begins with "Retrieved from" and the URL. In some cases, a retrieval line is not necessary, but in other cases, more information may be needed:

- **URL** Include the full URL for works accessed online that do not have DOIs. Include the home page URL (up to the first /) when accessing materials available only by search or subscription. Give the full URL for pages on sites that are difficult to search or for posts to blogs or online message boards. If you have to divide the URL onto two or more lines, break the address before slashes and punctuation marks (except within "http://"), and never add a hyphen. Write the URL like the rest of your text; do not use underlining, italics, angle brackets, or an end period.

- **Date of retrieval** Include the date you accessed the material only if the item is very likely to be updated or changed (see entry 46).

- **Databases** Include the names of databases in the retrieval line only if the source is rare, a print version is difficult to locate, or the material is available only on a small number of databases. Otherwise, for materials located on widely available databases, including library subscription services, do not include a retrieval line (see entries 7 and 16).

Examples of APA References

PERIODICALS

1. Journal Article with a DOI—One Author 224
2. Journal Article with a DOI – Two to Seven Authors 224
3. Journal Article with a DOI—More Than Seven Authors 225
4. Article in a Journal Paginated Continuously—No DOI 225
5. Article in a Journal Paginated Separately by Issue—No DOI 225
6. Article from an Online Journal—No DOI 225
7. Journal Article with No DOI from an Online Database, Library Database, or Subscription Service 226
8. Article in a Monthly or Bimonthly Magazine 226
9. Article in a Weekly or Biweekly Magazine 226
10. Magazine Article from an Online Database, Library Database, or Subscription Service 226
11. Article in an Online Magazine 226
12. Exclusive Online Magazine Content 227
13. Article in a Newspaper 227
14. Unsigned Article 227
15. Article in an Online Newspaper 227
16. Newspaper Article from an Online Database, Library Database, or Subscription Service 227
17. Editorial 227
18. Letter to the Editor 227
19. Review of a Work 228
20. Published Interview 228
21. Abstract Accessed Online 228

BOOKS AND REPORTS

22. Book with a DOI 228
23. Book with No DOI 228
24. Book Accessed Online 228
25. More Than One Work by the Same Author 228
26. Republished Work 229
27. Anthology, Scholarly Collection, or Work That Names an Editor 229
28. Article or Chapter in an Anthology, Scholarly Collection, or Work That Names an Editor 229
29. Second or Later Edition 229
30. Work That Names a Translator 229
31. Work by a Group or Corporate Author 229
32. Work That Has More Than One Volume 229
33. Introduction, Foreword, Preface, or Afterword 230
34. Government Publication 230
35. Signed Article in a Dictionary, Encyclopedia, or Reference Book 230
36. Unsigned Article in a Dictionary, Encyclopedia, or Reference Book 230

APA

37. Online Dictionary, Encyclopedia, or Reference Book Article 230
38. Biblical and Classical Works 230
39. Technical or Research Report 230
40. Technical or Research Report Accessed Online 231
41. U.S. Government Report Available from the GPO (Government Printing Office) Access Database 231
42. Published Dissertation Accessed from a Database 231

WEB SOURCES

43. Page on a Web Site 231
44. Chapter or Section of an Internet Document 231
45. Posting on a Blog 232
46. Wiki Article 232
47. E-Mail and Instant Messaging (IM) 232

SOURCES IN MULTIMEDIA AND OTHER FORMATS

48. Personal, Telephone, and E-Mail Interviews 232
49. Television Series 232
50. Episode from a Television Series 232
51. Television Series Episode Podcast 233
52. Motion Picture Released Theatrically 233
53. DVD 233
54. Online Video Recording 233
55. Radio Broadcast 233
56. Audio Podcast 233
57. Audio Recording on CD 233
58. Music Recording on CD or MP3 233
59. Print or Online Map 233
60. Lecture Notes or Multimedia Slides 234
61. Online Lecture, Speech, or Address 234
62. Computer Program or Software 234

Examples of APA References

Please note that all entries should be double-spaced on your References page.

Periodicals

1. **Journal Article with a DOI – One Author**

   Shelton, D. (2009). Leadership, education, achievement, and development: A nursing intervention for prevention of youthful offending behavior. *Journal of the American Psychiatric Nurses Association, 14,* 429–441. doi:10.1177/1078390308327049

2. **Journal Article with a DOI – Two to Seven Authors**

   Lorber, M. F., & Egeland, B. (2009). Infancy parenting and externalizing psychopathology from childhood through adulthood: Developmental trends. *Developmental Psychology, 45,* 909–912. doi:10.1037/a0015675

Anderson, C. B., Hughes, S. O., & Fuemmeler, B. F. (2009). Parent-child attitude congruence on type and intensity of physical activity: Testing multiple mediators of sedentary behavior in older children. *Health Psychology, 28,* 428–438. doi: 10.1037/a0014522

3. **Journal Article with a DOI – More Than Seven Authors** List the first six authors followed by an ellipsis (three periods) and the final author's name.

> Nelson, P. T., Abner, E. L., Schmitt, F. A., Kryscio, R. J., Jicha, G. A., Santacruz, K., . . . Markesbery, W. R. (2009). Brains with medial temporal lobe neurofibrillary tangles but no neuritic amyloid plaques are a diagnostic dilemma but may have pathogenetic aspects distinct from Alzheimer's disease. *Journal of Neuropathology and Experimental Neurology, 68,* 774–784. doi: 10.1097/NEN.0b013e3181aacbe9

4. **Article in a Journal Paginated Continuously – No DOI** If the journal is paginated continuously from issue to issue, include the volume number but do not add the issue number.

> Pasnak, R., Cooke, W. D., & Hendricks, C. (2006). Enhancing academic performance by strengthening class-inclusion reasoning. *Journal of Psychology, 140,* 603–613.

5. **Article in a Journal Paginated Separately by Issue – No DOI** If each of the journal issues is paginated beginning with 1, include the issue number in parentheses after the volume number.

> Cubitt, S. (2006). Grayscale video and the shift to color. *Art Journal, 65*(3), 40–53.

6. **Article from an Online Journal – No DOI** Add a retrieval line with the Web address (URL) for the article. List just the home page URL if the site has a search function.

> Brooks, R. (2009). Young people and political participation: An analysis of European Union policies. *Sociological Research Online, 14*(1). Retrieved from http://www .socresonline.org.uk

APA

7. **Journal Article with No DOI from an Online Database, Library Database, or Subscription Service** If the article does not have a DOI but is widely available through library databases and subscription services, cite it like a print journal article and do not name the database. Name the database *only* if the source is rare or is available on a small number of databases.

> Richter, A. (2006). Insurance catastrophe. *Journal of Property Management, 71*(6), 28–32.

> Wright, W. K. (1916). Psychology and the war. *Psychological Bulletin, 13*(12), 462–466. Retrieved from PsycINFO database.

8. **Article in a Monthly or Bimonthly Magazine** Include the publication month after the year. Include the volume number in italics after the magazine title. If each issue of the magazine begins with page 1, add the issue number in parentheses after the volume number.

> Roberts, D. (2006, June). Below the rim. *Smithsonian, 37*(3), 54–65.

9. **Article in a Weekly or Biweekly Magazine** Include the publication month and day after the year. Include the volume number in italics after the magazine title. If each issue of the magazine begins with page 1, add the issue number in parentheses after the volume number.

> Hersh, S. M. (2009, April 6). Syria calling. *The New Yorker, 85*(8), 26–32.

10. **Magazine Article from an Online Database, Library Database, or Subscription Service** Follow the same citation format you would use for a print magazine. Add a retrieval line that names the database only if the source is rare or available on a small number of databases.

> Yang, J. L. (2009, April 27). Gang green. *Fortune, 159*(8), 12.

> Trollope, A. (1861). The civil service as a profession. *The Cornhill Magazine, 3*, 214–228. Retrieved from the Wellesley Index of Victorian Periodicals.

11. **Article in an Online Magazine** If a volume and issue number are available, add them after the online magazine title.

> Monson, K. (2009, May 18). The ultimate Twitter toolkit. *PCMag.com*. Retrieved from http://www.pcmag.com

12. **Exclusive Online Magazine Content** Use this format for online content not available in the print version of a magazine.

> Graeber, C. (2009, May 22). Remember Pearl Harbor? This lock breaker does [Online exclusive]. *Wired, 17*(6). Retrieved from http://www.wired.com/techbiz/people /magazine/17-06/ff_keymaster_showa

13. **Article in a Newspaper** For newspaper articles, use *p.* (for a single page) or *pp.* (for multiple pages) before the page numbers. If the article appears on multiple disconnected pages, list each page number separated by a comma.

> Leonnig, C. D. (2009, July 27). Infectious diseases study site questioned. *The Washington Post,* pp. A1, A14.

14. **Unsigned Article** Place the title of the article before the date of publication.

> U.S. assigns terror score to international travelers. (2006, December 1). *The New York Times,* p. A28.

15. **Article in an Online Newspaper** Include the URL for the newspaper's home page.

> Mann, L. (2009, May 15). Meet the modern rowhouse. *Chicago Tribune.* Retrieved from http://www .chicagotribune.com

16. **Newspaper Article from an Online Database, Library Database, or Subscription Service** Follow the same citation format you would use for a newspaper article. Add a retrieval line that names the database *only* if the source is rare or available on a small number of databases.

> Martin. J. (2009, May 19). Tornado hunters roam the Plains. *USA Today,* p. A3.

> Smith, C. S. (1898, July 3). Wartime prosperity. *The New York Times,* p. 18. Retrieved from The Historical New York Times database.

17. **Editorial** Insert the word *Editorial* in brackets after the title of the article.

> Friedman, T. L. (2009, July 1). Just do it [Editorial]. *The New York Times,* p. A33.

18. **Letter to the Editor** Insert *Letter to the editor* in brackets after the title.

> White, L. J. (2009, July 24). No monopoly on credit wisdom [Letter to the editor]. *The Financial Times,* p. 6.

APA

19. **Review of a Work** If the review is untitled, use the material in brackets as the title and indicate whether the review is of a book, film, or video; the brackets indicate the material is a description of form and content, not a title.

> Epstein, P. R. (2006). [Review of the motion picture *An Inconvenient Truth*]. *British Medical Journal, 332,* 1397.

20. **Published Interview** Cite published interviews like articles in journals, newspapers, and magazines, and list the interviewer as the author.

> Worth, J. (2006, November). Punk rock capitalism? *New Internationalist, 395,* 16–17.

21. **Abstract Accessed Online**

> Madachy, R., Boehm, B., & Lane, J. A. (2006). Assessing hybrid incremental processes for SISOS development. *USC Center for Systems and Software Engineering.* Abstract retrieved from http://sunset .usc.edu

Books and reports

22. **Book with a DOI** If the book has been assigned a digital object identifier (DOI), omit the publication city and publisher and add the DOI after the book title.

> Bianchi, D. W., Crombleholme, T. M., D'Alton, M. E., & Malone, F. (2010). *Fetology: Diagnosis and management of the fetal patient.* doi:10.1036/ 0071442014

23. **Book with No DOI**

> Anderson, C. (2006). *The long tail: Why the future of business is selling less of more.* New York, NY: Hyperion.

24. **Book Accessed Online** If the book has a DOI, use the format for entry 22 instead.

> James, W. (1907). *Pragmatism.* Retrieved from http://www .gutenberg.org

25. **More Than One Work by the Same Author** Include the author's name in each reference and arrange by year of publication, the earliest first.

Gladwell, M. (2005). *Blink: The power of thinking without thinking.* New York, NY: Little, Brown.

Gladwell, M. (2008). *Outliers: The story of success.* New York, NY: Little, Brown.

26. **Republished Work**

Darwin, C. (2009). *On the origin of species* (W. Bynum, Ed.). New York, NY: Penguin. (Original work published 1859)

27. **Anthology, Scholarly Collection, or Work That Names an Editor**

Brettell, C. B., & Sargent, C. F. (Eds.). (2008). *Gender in cross-cultural perspective* (5th ed.). Upper Saddle River, NJ: Prentice Hall.

28. **Article or Chapter in an Anthology, Scholarly Collection, or Work That Names an Editor**

Ball, J. D., & Peake, T. H. (2006). Brief psychotherapy in the U.S. military: Principles and applications. In C. H. Kennedy & E. A. Zillmer (Eds.), *Military psychology: Clinical and operational applications* (pp. 61–73). New York, NY: Guilford Press.

29. **Second or Later Edition** Place the number of the edition in parentheses after the book title. If the book is a revised edition, instead of a number, place *Rev. ed.* in parentheses after the book title.

Drafke, M. (2008). *The human side of organizations* (10th ed.). Upper Saddle River, NJ: Prentice Hall.

30. **Work That Names a Translator**

Bourdieu, P. (1984). *Distinction: A social critique on the judgement of taste* (R. Nice, Trans.). Cambridge, MA: Harvard University Press. (Original work published 1979)

31. **Work by a Group or Corporate Author**

American Medical Association. (2009). *Principles of CPT coding* (6th ed). Chicago, IL: Author.

32. **Work That Has More Than One Volume**

Neely, A., Bourne, M., Mills, J., Platts, K., & Richards, H. (2002). *Strategy and performance* (Vols. 1–3). Cambridge, United Kingdom: Cambridge University Press.

33. **Introduction, Foreword, Preface, or Afterword** List the author of the section first. Include the page numbers after the title of the book.

> Annan, K. (2003). Foreword. In N. Mandela, *In his own words* (pp. xiii–xiv). New York, NY: Little, Brown.

34. **Government Publication**

> Office of the President. (2008). *Budget of the United States government, fiscal year 2009*. Washington, DC: U.S. Government Printing Office.

35. **Signed Article in a Dictionary, Encyclopedia, or Reference Book**

> Miller, C. (2002). Informed consent. In M. Herzen & W. Sledge (Eds.), *Encyclopedia of psychotherapy* (Vol. 2, pp. 17–24). San Diego, CA: Elsevier Science.

36. **Unsigned Article in a Dictionary, Encyclopedia, or Reference Book** If using a multivolume work, add the volume number after the book title (see entry 12).

> Whizzbang. (2008). In *Webster's new college dictionary* (3rd ed., p. 1290). Boston, MA: Houghton Mifflin Harcourt.

37. **Online Dictionary, Encyclopedia, or Reference Book Article**

> Vermeil. (2009). In *Encyclopaedia Britannica online*. Retrieved from http://www.britannica.com

38. **Biblical and Classical Works** Major classical works, such as the Bible and ancient Greek and Roman works, are not listed in the References. Instead, they are cited in the paper when referred to. See 43a for in-text citation format and examples.

39. **Technical or Research Report** If there is a report number, include it in parentheses after the title. If the report has been assigned a digital object identifier (DOI), omit the publication city and publisher and add the DOI at the end of the entry.

> Arquilla, J., & Ronfeldt, D. (2001). *Networks and netwars: The future of terror, crime, and militancy* (Report No. MR-1382-OSD). doi:10.1222/ 0833030302

40. **Technical or Research Report Accessed Online** If there is a report number, include it in parentheses after the title. After "Retrieved from," include the name of the publisher unless the publisher is also the corporate or organizational author of the report. If there is a DOI number, include this instead of the retrieval line.

> Johnson, R. D., & Lewis, R. J. (2009). Determination of etomidate in human postmortem fluids and tissues (Report No. DOT/FAA/AM-09/3). Retrieved from the Federal Aviation Administration website: http://www .faa.gov/library/reports/medical/oamtechreports /2000s/media/200903.pdf

41. **U.S. Government Report Available from the GPO (Government Printing Office) Access Database**

> U.S. General Accounting Office. (2003, May 15). *Rebuilding Iraq* (Publication No. GAO-03-792R). Retrieved from the GPO Access database.

42. **Published Dissertation Accessed from a Database** Add the dissertation file number at the end of the entry.

> Negre, F. (2005). *Biosynthesis and regulation of floral scent in snapdragon and petunia flowers.* Retrieved from ProQuest Digital Dissertations. (AAT 3210759)

Web sources

43. **Page on a Web Site** Add the date of access to the retrieval line only if the URL or content is likely to change. Include the URL for only the home page if the site has a search function.

> Boyles, S. (2009, July 31). Forehead lift cures migraine patients. *WebMD.* Retrieved from http://www .webmd.com

> Mullis, K. B. (2009). Polymerase chain reaction. *Kary Mullis.* Retrieved from http://www.karymullis.com /pcr.shtml

44. **Chapter or Section of an Internet Document**

> Commission on the Intelligence Capabilities of the United States Regarding Weapons of Mass Destruction. (2005, March 31). Case study: Iraq. In *Report to the President* (chap. 1). Retrieved from http://www.wmd .gov/report/report.html

45. **Posting on a Blog**

> Finchsigmate, K. (2007, January 3). More fishie science
> [Web log post]. Retrieved from http://www.thechemblog
> .com/?p=354

46. **Wiki Article** Wikis are Web sites that are written and edited by many people. Assess the credibility of such sources before including them in your work. Wikis are likely to be updated, so include the retrieval date in your entry.

> Monopoly. (2006, July 14). Retrieved April 13, 2009, from
> The Economics Wiki: http://economics.wikia.com
> /wiki/Monopoly

47. **E-Mail and Instant Messaging (IM)** Personal e-mail, instant messaging, and other electronic communications that are not archived are identified as personal communications in the paper and are not listed in the References. See example 12 in Chapter 43a.

Sources in multimedia and other formats

48. **Personal, Telephone, and E-Mail Interviews** Personal, telephone, and e-mail interviews are not included in the References. Instead, use a parenthetical citation in the text. See entry 20 for citing a published interview.

49. **Television Series** Start with the creator's name and then, in parentheses, the person's function (for example, *Producer*). After the title, insert *Television series* enclosed in brackets, followed by a period. Add the place the broadcast originated from, a colon, and the broadcasting network.

> Abams, J. J., Burk, B., Cuse, C., & Lindelof, D. (Executive
> producers). (2004–2009). *Lost* [Television series].
> New York, NY: ABC.

50. **Episode from a Television Series**

> Armus, A., Foster, N. K. (Writers), & Dawson, R. (Director).
> (2007, February 12). Run! [Television series episode].
> In A. Arkush & T. Kring (Producers), *Heroes*. New York,
> NY: NBC.

51. **Television Series Episode Podcast**

> Young, R. (Writer/Director/Producer), & Smith, H. (Writer). (2004, November 16). Is Wal-Mart good for America? [Television series episode podcast]. In D. Fanning & M. Sullivan (Executive producers), *Frontline*. Retrieved from http://www.pbs.org

52. **Motion Picture Released Theatrically**

> Reitman, J. (Writer/Director), & Sacks, D. O. (Producer). (2006). *Thank you for smoking* [Motion picture]. United States: Fox Searchlight.

53. **DVD**

> Allen, W. (Writer/Director), Jaffe, C. H., & Rollins, J. (Producers). (2006). *Match point* [DVD]. United States: Dreamworks. (Original release date 2005)

54. **Online Video Recording**

> Voltz, S., & Grobe, F. (2006). The Diet Coke and Mentos experiments [Video file]. Retrieved from http://www.eepybird.com/dcm1.html

55. **Radio Broadcast**

> Amari, C., & Wolski, R. (Producers). (2004, May 29). *Twilight time* [Radio program]. Chicago, IL: WGN Radio.

56. **Audio Podcast**

> Inskeep, S. (Host). (2007, June 8). Bono presses G-8 leaders on Africa aid [Audio podcast]. *Morning Edition*. Retrieved from http://www.npr.org

> Ryssdal, K. (Host). (2009, July 28). *Marketplace* [Audio podcast]. Available from iTunes.

57. **Audio Recording on CD**

> Sedaris, D. (Speaker). (2003, October 9). *David Sedaris live at Carnegie Hall* [CD]. New York, NY: Little, Brown.

58. **Music Recording on CD or MP3**

> Mayer, J. (2006). Waiting on the world to change. On *Continuum* [CD]. New York, NY: Aware/Columbia.

> West, K. (2007). Stronger [MP3]. Available from iTunes.

59. **Print or Online Map**

> *Georgia*. (2004). [Map]. Skokie, IL: Rand McNally.

> *San Diego*. (2009). [Map]. Retrieved from http://www.mapquest.com

APA

60. Lecture Notes or Multimedia Slides

> Bracchini, Y. (2009, February 23). *Understanding your blood values.* [PowerPoint slides]. Retrieved from http:// www.houstoncancerinstitute.com/Bracchini _bloodvalues2009.ppt

61. Online Lecture, Speech, or Address

> Ganz, M. (2009, March 19). *Distributed leadership in the Obama campaign.* Lecture at MIT. Cambridge, MA. Retrieved from http://mitworld.mit.edu

62. Computer Program or Software Reference entries are unnecessary for most popular software programs. This citation format applies only to specialized software programs.

> CursorFX (Version 2.01) [Computer software]. (2009). Retrieved from http://www.stardock.com

43d Sample pages

Follow the format shown here for a title page, abstract, first page of the paper, and first page of the References list. For all pages, leave a margin of at least one inch on all sides.

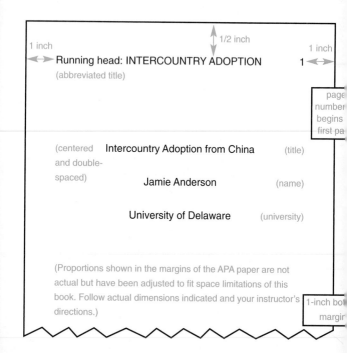

1 inch
1/2 inch
1 inch
→ Running head: INTERCOUNTRY ADOPTION 1 ←→
(abbreviated title)

page number begins first pa

(centered and double-spaced)
Intercountry Adoption from China (title)

Jamie Anderson (name)

University of Delaware (university)

(Proportions shown in the margins of the APA paper are not actual but have been adjusted to fit space limitations of this book. Follow actual dimensions indicated and your instructor's directions.)

1-inch bot margin

1/2 inch

1 inch

Abstract

Adoption of children from other countries by American families has increased dramatically since World War II, and in the past decade, adoptions of Chinese children have risen from a few hundred to over 5,000. Studies on the effects of intercountry adoption from China reveal both positive and negative results. Negatives include identity confusion, racism, and developmental delays. With understanding and support, however, adoptive parents can overcome these obstacles. In addition to published research, personal experiences of real adoptive families are cited. Intercountry adoption is found to be a generally positive experience for both parents and children.

double-
space text

1 inch

1 inch

1/2 inch

1 inch

Intercountry Adoption from China

Intercountry adoption, the process of adopting children from across international borders, has been taking place in the United States since the years immediately following World War II. According to Rojewski and Rojewski (2001), there were 7,948 intercountry adoptions in the United States in 1989; in 1998, that number rose to 15,774, accounting for 12% to 13% of all adoptions (p. 3). Even more impressive has been the extreme growth in number of adoptions from China. In 1992, only 201 children were brought into the United States from China. By 2000, that number had increased to 5,053 children (p. 3). Studies on the process and effects of intercountry adoption from China have revealed both positive and negative

double-
space text

1 inch

1 inch

bottom
margin

APA

1/2 inch

1 inch

References

Dickinson, A. (2002, August 26). Bicultural kids:
Parents who adopt children of a different ethnicity
are enjoying the best of both worlds. *Time, 160*(9),
B1, B3.

Gravois, J. (2004, January 16). Bringing up babes.
Slate. Retrieved from http://www.slate.com

Rojewski, J. W., & Rojewski, J. L. (2001). *Intercountry
adoption from China.* Westport, CT: Bergin &
Garvey.

Tan, X. T., Marfo, K., & Dedrick, R. F. (2007). Special
needs adoption from China: Exploring child-level
indicators, adoptive family characteristics, and
correlates of behavioral adjustment. *Children and
Youth Services Review, 29*(10), 1269–1285.
doi:10.1016/j.childyouth.2007.05.001

Tessler, R., Gamache, G., & Liu, L. (1999). *West
meets East: Americans adopt Chinese children.*
Westport, CT: Bergin & Garvey.

Transracial and transcultural adoption. (2002, March 3).
National adoption information clearinghouse.
Retrieved from http://www.calib.com

Triseliotis, J. (1993). Intercountry adoption: In whose
best interest? In M. Humphrey & H. Humphrey
(Eds.), *Intercountry adoption: Practical experiences*
(pp. 119–137). New York, NY: Tavistock/Routledge.

Vonk, M. E. (2001, July). Cultural competence for
transracial adoptive parents. *Social Work, 46,*
246–255.

double
space

1 inch

1 inch

1 inch

Chicago Manual of Style (CM)

In disciplines such as history and other humanities, the preferred style is that of *The Chicago Manual of Style* (15th ed., 2003), which is also explained in *A Manual for Writers of Term Papers, Theses, and Dissertations* (7th ed., 2007), by Kate L. Turabian et al.

When you use CM style, you may use notes or endnotes to acknowledge sources in the text, or you may use in-text citations that refer the reader to a bibliography at the end of the paper.

Numbered notes

- **Numbering in the text.** Numbered notes indicate publication information and add explanations and other material that would otherwise interrupt the main text. Number citations consecutively with superscript numbers ([1]). Put the note number at the end of the sentence or end of a clause immediately following the punctuation mark. Don't insert a space between the punctuation mark and the superscript number.

   > The violence in the Raj at that time was more pronounced than it had been in the previous conflict.[4] As Peter Holman has noted, "The military police were at a loss to stem the tide of bloodshed."[5]

- **Placing notes.** List notes at the bottom of the page as footnotes or at the end of the essay as endnotes.

- **Spacing notes.** Single-space within each note, and insert one blank line between each note. Indent the first line of each note the same space that you indent paragraphs.

- **Ordering the parts of notes.** Begin with the author's first and last names, add the title, and then include the publishing information and page numbers.

- **Punctuating, capitalizing, and abbreviating.** Use commas between elements, and put publishing information within parentheses. Include the page number, but omit the abbreviation *p.* or *pp.* Italicize titles of books and periodicals. Capitalize titles of articles, books, and journals. Use quotation marks around titles of periodical articles and sections of books.

- **Using a bibliography page.** The use of a bibliography page is optional with the use of notes.

Ordering Notes in a Paper The first time you cite a source, include the authors' full names, followed by a comma; the full title, followed by a comma; publication information, enclosed in parentheses; and the page or pages being cited, omitting *p.* or *pp.* Later citations include authors' last names, a shortened version of the title, and page numbers.

Use *Ibid.* to refer to the work in the directly preceding note or, if the page is different, use *Ibid.* followed by a comma and the page number.

> 6. Peter Holman, *The History of the Raj: Nineteenth and Twentieth Centuries* (New York: Dorset Press, 1996), 18.
> 7. Martin Joos, *The Five Clocks* (New York: Harcourt, Brace, 1962), 5.
> 8. Holman, *History of the Raj*, 34–36.
> 9. Ibid., 72.

Author-date citation format

The author-date citation format requires both in-text citations and a bibliography page. For in-text citations:

- Up to three authors are cited by last name. If there are four or more authors, list only the first author's last name, followed by *et al.* or *and others*.

- The date of publication is given next, with no intervening punctuation.

- If a page number is required, it is given following a comma.

(Patel 2004, 18)	(Baez et al. 2004, 244)
(Newhouse and Zuzu 1889)	As explained by Patel (2004, 18), . . .

For online or electronic works without page numbers, indicate the section title (if available) under which the specific reference can be located:

(Quinn 2006, under "Espionage")

Bibliography in CM style

Title your list "Bibliography," "Works Cited," or "References." In the bibliography, list authors with last name first. Elements in the bibliography are separated by periods.

Start the first line of each entry at the left margin, and indent all other lines in the entry. Single-space within each entry, and insert one blank line between each entry. Italicize titles of books and periodicals. Use quotation marks around titles of periodicals and sections of books.

Examples of CM-Style Notes and Bibliography

BOOKS

1. One Author 240
2. Two Authors 240
3. Three Authors 240
4. Four or More Authors 240
5. Book with an Unknown Author 241
6. Book with an Editor 241
7. Second or Later Edition 241
8. Reprinted Book 241
9. Selection or Book Chapter in an Anthology/Scholarly Collection 241
10. Multivolume Book 242
11. Book with a Title within the Title 242
12. Government Publication 242
13. Article in a Reference Book 242
14. Biblical or Other Scriptural Reference 242

PERIODICALS

15. Article in a Journal 243
16. Article in a Magazine 243
17. Article in a Newspaper 243
18. Book Review 243

ONLINE AND ELECTRONIC SOURCES

19. Article from a Print Journal, Magazine, or Newspaper Located in a Library Database or Subscription Service 243
20. Entire Web Site 244
21. Page on a Web Site 244
22. Article from an Online Journal, Magazine, or Newspaper 244
23. Entire Blog 245
24. Posting on a Blog 245
25. Online Government Document 245
26. E-Mail Message or Posting to a Mailing List 245
27. Software 245
28. Podcast, MP3, or Other Downloaded Material 246

CM

OTHER SOURCES

29. Unpublished
    Dissertation 246

30. Television
    Interview 246

31. Personal or Telephone
    Interview 246

32. Film on Videotape or
    DVD 246

33. Sound Recording 246

34. Source Quoted from
    Another Source 247

35. Television Episode 247

36. Advertisement 247

Books

In the following examples, *N* stands for note format and *B* stands for bibliography format

1. **One Author**

   N: 1. Seymour M. Hersh, *Chain of Command: The Road from 9/11 to Abu Ghraib* (New York: HarperCollins, 2004), 97.

   B: Hersh, Seymour M. *Chain of Command: The Road from 9/11 to Abu Ghraib.* New York: HarperCollins, 2004.

2. **Two Authors**

   N: 2. Shoshana Felman and Dori Laub, *Testimony: Crises of Witnessing in Literature, Psychoanalysis, and History* (New York: Routledge, 1992), 57.

   B: Felman, Shoshana, and Dori Laub. *Testimony: Crises of Witnessing in Literature, Psychoanalysis, and History.* New York: Routledge, 1992.

3. **Three Authors**

   N: 3. Glen Stout, Charles Vitchers, and Robert Gray, *Nine Months at Ground Zero: The Story of the Brotherhood of Workers Who Took On a Job like No Other* (New York: Scribner, 2006), 90–91.

   B: Stout, Glen, Charles Vitchers, and Robert Gray. *Nine Months at Ground Zero: The Story of the Brotherhood of Workers Who Took On a Job like No Other.* New York: Scribner, 2006.

4. **Four or More Authors** In the notes format, list the first author and add *et al.* or *and others* with no intervening punctuation.

   N: 4. James A. Baker III et al., *The Iraq Study Group Report: The Way Forward—a New Approach* (New York: Vintage, 2006), 27.

In the bibliography format, list all authors for a work with between four and ten authors. If the work has eleven or more authors, list the first seven authors and add *et al.*

B: Baker, James A., III, Lee H. Hamilton, Lawrence S. Eagleburger, Vernon E. Jordan Jr., Edwin Meese III, Sandra Day O'Connor, Leon E. Panetta, William J. Perry, Charles S. Robb, and Alan K. Simpson. *The Iraq Study Group Report: The Way Forward—a New Approach.* New York: Vintage, 2006.

5. **Book with an Unknown Author**

N: 5. *The Second World War: A World in Flames* (Oxford: Osprey, 2004), 30–31.

B: *The Second World War: A World in Flames.* Oxford: Osprey, 2004.

6. **Book with an Editor**

N: 6. Nancy P. McKee and Linda Stone, eds., *Readings on Gender and Culture in America* (Upper Saddle River, NJ: Prentice Hall, 2002), 1–2.

B: McKee, Nancy P., and Linda Stone, eds. *Readings on Gender and Culture in America.* Upper Saddle River, NJ: Prentice Hall, 2002.

7. **Second or Later Edition**

N: 7. Nancy Bonvillain, *Women and Men: Cultural Constructs of Gender,* 3rd ed. (Upper Saddle River, NJ: Prentice Hall, 2001), 39–41.

B: Bonvillain, Nancy. *Women and Men: Cultural Constructs of Gender.* 3rd ed. Upper Saddle River, NJ: Prentice Hall, 2001.

8. **Reprinted Book**

N: 8. Edith Wharton, *House of Mirth* (1905; repr., New York: Penguin, 1986), 64–65.

B: Wharton, Edith. *House of Mirth.* 1905. Reprint, New York: Penguin, 1986.

9. **Selection or Book Chapter in an Anthology/Scholarly Collection**

N: 9. Stuart Moulthrop, "No War Machine," in *Reading Matters: Narratives in the New Media Ecology,* ed. Joseph Tabbi and Michael Wutz (Ithaca, NY: Cornell University Press, 1997), 280.

B: Moulthrop, Stuart. "No War Machine." In *Reading Matters: Narratives in the New Media Ecology,* edited by Joseph Tabbi and Michael Wutz, 269–92. Ithaca, NY: Cornell University Press, 1997.

10. **Multivolume Book** In the notes format, when citing a book without an individual volume title, omit the volume number after the book title. Instead, after the facts of publication, insert the volume number, followed by a colon, and the page numbers (e.g., 2:45–96).

N: 10. Roy T. Matthews and F. Dewitt Platt, *The Western Humanities,* vol. 2, *The Renaissance to the Present*, 5th ed. (New York: McGraw-Hill, 2004), 297–98.

B: Matthews, Roy T., and F. Dewitt Platt. *The Western Humanities*. Vol. 2, *The Renaissance to the Present*. 5th ed. New York: McGraw-Hill, 2004.

11. **Book with a Title within the Title**

N: 11. Rebello, Stephen, *Alfred Hitchcock and the Making of "Psycho"* (New York: St. Martin's Griffin, 1998), 60.

B: Rebello, Stephen. *Alfred Hitchcock and the Making of "Psycho."* New York: St. Martin's Griffin, 1998.

12. **Government Publication**

N: 12. Office of the President, *Budget of the United States Government, Fiscal Year 2007* (Washington, DC: Government Printing Office, 2006), 11.

B: Office of the President. *Budget of the United States Government, Fiscal Year 2007*. Washington, DC: Government Printing Office, 2006.

13. **Article in a Reference Book** Don't include the volume or page number. Instead, cite the term in the reference book under which the information is contained. Use the abbreviation *s.v.* for *sub verbo,* meaning "under the word," and place the term in quotation marks. Well-known reference books are not listed in the bibliography as long as the title is cited in the text.

N: 13. *Encyclopaedia Britannica,* 15th ed., s.v. "Parks, Rosa."

14. **Biblical or Other Scriptural Reference** Include the book (abbreviated with no underlining or italics), chapter, and verse, but no page number. Scriptural references are usually cited in the notes or in the parenthetical citation.

N: 14. Gen. 21:14–18.

Periodicals

15. **Article in a Journal** If no issue number is available, place the year of publication in parentheses directly after the volume number.

   N: 15. Fredrik Logevall, "Lyndon Johnson and Vietnam," *Presidential Studies Quarterly* 34, no. 1 (2004): 102.

   B: Logevall, Fredrik. "Lyndon Johnson and Vietnam." *Presidential Studies Quarterly* 34, no. 1 (2004): 100–12.

16. **Article in a Magazine** Referenced page numbers should be included in the notes entry; page numbers for the full article are optional for the bibliographic entry.

   N: 16. George Packer, "Knowing the Enemy," *New Yorker*, December 18, 2006, 62.

   B: Packer, George. "Knowing the Enemy." *New Yorker*, December 18, 2006, 60–69.

17. **Article in a Newspaper** No page numbers are listed. If you are citing a specific edition of the paper, you may add a comma after the year and list the edition (e.g., late edition, Southeast edition), followed by a period.

   N: 17. Somini Sengupta, "Interests Drive U.S. to Back a Nuclear India." *New York Times*, December 10, 2006.

   B: Sengupta, Somini. "Interests Drive U.S. to Back a Nuclear India." *New York Times*, December 10, 2006.

18. **Book Review**

   N: 18. Kevin Warwick, review of *Beyond the Image Machine: A History of Visual Technologies*, by David Tomas, *Modernism/Modernity* 13 (January 2006): 213.

   B: Warwick, Kevin. Review of *Beyond the Image Machine: A History of Visual Technologies*, by David Tomas. *Modernism/Modernity* 13 (January 2006): 212–14.

Online and electronic sources

19. **Article from a Print Journal, Magazine, or Newspaper Located in a Library Database or Subscription Service** Follow the citation format for the print version of the text, and then provide the electronic address to the entry page of the database or subscription service, usually the URL up to the first slash (/).

CM

N: 19. Bill Powell, "When Outlaws Get the Bomb," *Time*, October 23, 2006, 32, http://find.galegroup.com/ (accessed January 2, 2009).

B: Powell, Bill. "When Outlaws Get the Bomb." *Time*, October 23, 2006, 32. http://find.galegroup.com/ (accessed January 2, 2009).

20. **Entire Web Site** Unless the name of the Web site is the name of an online journal, magazine, newspaper, or book, don't italicize it.

N: 20. San Diego Zoo, http://www.sandiegozoo.org/ (accessed March 21, 2009).

B: San Diego Zoo. http://www.sandiegozoo.org/ (accessed March 21, 2009).

21. **Page on a Web Site** Unless the name of the Web site is the name of an online journal, magazine, newspaper, or book, don't italicize it.

N: 21. Andrew Hollinger, "United States Holocaust Museum Decries Eviction of Aid Agencies in Darfur and Southern Sudan," United States Holocaust Memorial Museum (March 5, 2009), http://www.ushmm.org/ museum/press/archives/detail.php?category=03-coc& content= 2009-03-05 (accessed March 29, 2009).

B: Hollinger, Andrew. "United States Holocaust Museum Decries Eviction of Aid Agencies in Darfur and Southern Sudan." United States Holocaust Memorial Museum. March 5, 2009. http://www.ushmm.org/ museum/press/archives/detail.php?category= 03-coc& content=2009-03-05 (accessed March 29, 2009).

22. **Article from an Online Journal, Magazine, or Newspaper** Follow the guidelines for the print version of the source. Then add the full electronic address and the access date.

N: 22. Dinesh Joseph Wadiwel, "Sovereignty, Torture, and Blood: Tracing Genealogies and Rethinking Politics," *Borderlands* 5, no. 1 (May 2006), http://www .borderlandsejournal.adelaide.edu.au/vol5no1_2006/ wadiwel_blood.htm (accessed December 23, 2006).

B: Wadiwel, Dinesh Joseph. "Sovereignty, Torture, and Blood: Tracing Genealogies and Rethinking Politics." *Borderlands* 5, no. 1 (May 2006). http:// www.borderlandsejournal.adelaide.edu.au/vol5no1 _2006/wadiwel_blood.htm (accessed December 23, 2006).

23. **Entire Blog**

> **N:**   23. Political Cortex: Brain Food for the Body Politic, http://www.politicalcortex.com/ (accessed February 20, 2009).
>
> **B:**   Political Cortex: Brain Food for the Body Politic. http://www.politicalcortex.com/ (accessed February 20, 2009).

24. **Posting on a Blog** If the author's real name is unknown, add *pseud.* in square brackets.

> **N:**   24. Arnold [pseud.], comment on "Close," The Little Professor, comment posted December 28, 2006, http://littleprofessor.typepad.com/the_little_professor/2006/12/close.html#comments (accessed January 2, 2007).
>
> **B:**   Arnold [pseud.]. Comment on "Close." The Little Professor. December 28, 2006. http://littleprofessor.typepad.com/the_little_professor/2006/12/close.html#comments (accessed January 2, 2007).

25. **Online Government Document**

> **N:**   25. National Council on Disability, *Creating Livable Communities* (Washington, DC: National Council on Disability, October 31, 2006), 10, http://www.ncd.gov/newsroom/publications/2006/pdf/livable_communities.pdf (accessed January 3, 2007).
>
> **B:**   National Council on Disability. *Creating Livable Communities*. Washington, DC: National Council on Disability, October 31, 2006. http://www.ncd.gov/newsroom/publications/2006/pdf/livable_communities.pdf (accessed January 3, 2007).

26. **E-Mail Message or Posting to a Mailing List** E-mail messages and postings to mailing lists usually appear only in the notes or parenthetical citations, not in the bibliography. Add an electronic address and access date at the end of the entry if the posting is archived on a Web site.

> **N:**   26. Dora Dodger-Gilbert, e-mail message to Veterinary Questions and Viewpoints mailing list, January 3, 2009.
>   27. Daniel Kaplan, e-mail message to the author, September 23, 2009.

27. **Software**

> **N:**   28. *All-Movie Guide*, CD-ROM (Corel, 1996).
>
> **B:**   *All-Movie Guide*. CD-ROM. Corel, 1996.

28. **Podcast, MP3, or Other Downloaded Material** Add the provider and file format at the end of the entry.

N: 29. Melvyn Bragg, Roger Crowley, Judith Herrin, and Colin Imber, "The Siege of Constantinople," *BBC Radio 4: In Our Time* (December 28, 2006), iTunes MP3.
     30. Kanye West, *Late Registration* (New York: Roc-a-Fella Records, 2005), iTunes MP3.

B: Bragg, Melvyn, Roger Crowley, Judith Herrin, and Colin Imber. "The Siege of Constantinople." *BBC Radio 4: In Our Time*. December 28, 2006. iTunes MP3.
     West, Kanye. *Late Registration*. New York: Roc-a-Fella Records, 2005. iTunes MP3.

Other sources

29. **Unpublished Dissertation**

N: 31. Arnold Mayniew, "Historical Perceptions of Royal Prerogative" (PhD diss., University of Illinois, 1991), 32–37.

B: Mayniew, Arnold. "Historical Perceptions of Royal Prerogative." PhD diss., University of Illinois, 1991.

30. **Television Interview**

N: 32. Barack Obama, interview by Tim Russert, *Meet the Press*, NBC, October 22, 2006.

B: Obama, Barack. Interview by Tim Russert. *Meet the Press*. NBC. October 22, 2006.

31. **Personal or Telephone Interview** In the author-date format, personal communications are acknowledged in the text but not in the bibliography.

N: 33. Kenneth Autrey, interview by the author, October 24, 2009, Florence, South Carolina.
     34. John Sutton, telephone interview by the author, December 1, 2008.

32. **Film on Videotape or DVD**

N: 35. *Good Night, and Good Luck*, DVD, directed by George Clooney (2005; Burbank, CA: Warner Home Video, 2006).

B: *Good Night, and Good Luck*. DVD. Directed by George Clooney. 2005. Burbank, CA: Warner Home Video, 2006.

33. **Sound Recording** Include the product number (often located on the spine of a CD) at the end of the entry.

N: 36. Johann Sebastian Bach, *Four Concerti for Various Instruments*, Orchestra of St. Luke's, dir. Michael Feldman, Musical Heritage Society, CD 512268T.

B: Bach, Johann Sebastian. *Four Concerti for Various Instruments*. Orchestra of St. Luke's, dir. Michael Feldman. Musical Heritage Society, CD 512268T.

34. **Source Quoted from Another Source** Quotations from secondary sources should ordinarily be avoided. If, however, the original source is unavailable, list both sources in the entry.

N: 37. H. H. Dubs, "An Ancient Chinese Mystery Cult," *Harvard Theological Review* 35 (1942): 223, quoted in Susan Naquin, *Millenarian Rebellion in China: The Eight Trigrams Uprising of 1813* (New Haven, CT: Yale University Press, 1976), 288.

B: Dubs, H. H. "An Ancient Chinese Mystery Cult." *Harvard Theological Review* 35 (1942): 223. Quoted in Susan Naquin, *Millenarian Rebellion in China: The Eight Trigrams Uprising of 1813*. New Haven, CT: Yale University Press, 1976, 288.

35. **Television Episode**

N: 38. *Lost*, Episode no. 509, directed by Jack Bender and written by Brian K. Vaughan and Paul Zbyszewski, ABC, March 18, 2009.

B: *Lost*. Episode no. 509. Directed by Jack Bender and written by Brian K. Vaughan and Paul Zbyszewski. ABC. March 18, 2009.

36. **Advertisement** List advertisements in the bibliography only if they are retrievable.

N: 39. Sony Bravia, "Play-Doh," television advertisement, Fallon London, directed by Juan Cabral, 2008.

B: Sony Bravia. "Play-Doh." Television advertisement. Fallon London, directed by Juan Cabral, 2008.

CM

Council of Science Editors (CSE) Style

Writers in the physical and life sciences follow Council of Science Editors (CSE) style, found in *Scientific Style and Format: The CSE Manual for Authors, Editors, and Publishers* (7th ed., 2006). The *CSE Manual* offers three documentation styles: *name-year*, *citation-sequence*, and *citation-name*.

1. **Name-Year Format** Authors' names and publication dates are included in parenthetical citations in the text, closely resembling *Chicago Manual* name-date style (see Chapter 44).

   In-Text Citation

   > The earlier studies done on this virus (Fong and Townes 1992; Mindlin 2004) reported similar results. However, one of these studies (Mindlin 2004) noted a mutated strain.

   In the list of references at the end of the paper, list names alphabetically with the date after the name. Journal titles are abbreviated, without periods.

   Reference List Entry

   > Fong L, Townes HC. 1992. Viral longevity. Biol Rep. 27(2):129-45.

2. **Citation-Sequence Style** References may instead be cited by means of in-text superscript numbers (numbers set above the line, such as [1] and [2]) that refer to a list of numbered references at the end of the paper. The references are numbered in the order in which they are cited in the text, and later references to the same work use the original number. When you have two or more sources cited at once, put the numbers in sequence, separated with commas but no spaces.

   In-Text Citation

   > Early studies on this virus [1,4,7] reported similar results, but a new study [9] noted a mutation.

In the list of references, the entries are listed in the order in which they are cited in the paper, not alphabetically.

Reference List Entry

> 1. Fong L, Townes HC. Viral longevity. Biol Rep. 1992;27(2): 129-45.

3. **Citation-Name Style** In this style, all sources are first listed on the References page in alphabetical order by authors' names and then assigned a number in sequence. These numbers correspond to in-text superscript numbers. Other than the change in numbering, the in-text and the reference list citation formats are the same as that used for the citation-sequence style.

CSE references list

At the end of the paper, include a list titled "References" or "Cited References." The placement of the date depends on which style you use.

- **Name-date style.** Put the date after the author's name. Arrange the list alphabetically by last names. Do not indent any lines in the entries.

- **Citation-sequence and citation-name styles.** For books, put the date after the publisher's name. For periodicals, put the date after the periodical name. Arrange the list by number. Put the number at the left margin, followed by a period and a space and then the authors' names.

References in CSE style

Use periods between major divisions of the entry.

Author	Start with the last name first, no comma, and initials without periods for first and middle names. Separate authors' names with commas. End the list of authors' names with a period.
Title	For books and article titles, capitalize only the first word and proper nouns. Do not underline, italicize, or use quotation marks. For journals,

abbreviate titles and capitalize all major words.

City of publication (state abbreviation): publisher; publication date

Include a semicolon and a space between the name of the publisher and the date. Use a semicolon with no space between the date and volume number of the journal. Abbreviate months. End with a period.

Pages

For books, you may include the total number of pages, with *p.* after the number. End the entry with a period. For journal articles, show the page numbers and end with a period.

Examples of CSE Format for a Reference List

1. Book with One Author 250
2. Book with More Than One Author 250
3. Anthology, Scholarly Collection, or Work That Names an Editor 251
4. Article or Chapter in an Anthology, Scholarly Collection, or Work That Names an Editor 251
5. Work by a Group or Corporate Author 251
6. Article in a Journal or Magazine 251
7. Article in a Newspaper 251
8. Journal Article in a Library Database or Subscription Service 251
9. Article in an Online Journal 253
10. Entire Web Site 252
11. E-Mail and Instant Messaging (IM) 252

All numbered references shown are in the citation-sequence format. References should be single-spaced, with a blank line between each entry.

1. **Book with One Author**

    1. Woit P. Not even wrong: the failure of string theory and the search for unity in physical law. New York: Basic Books; 2006. 291 p.

2. **Book with More Than One Author** If there are more than ten authors, list the first ten and add *et al.* or *and others*.

2. French S, Krause D. Identity in physics: a historical, philosophical, and format analysis. New York: Oxford University Press; 2006. 422 p.

3. **Anthology, Scholarly Collection, or Work That Names an Editor**

   3. Fraser LH, Keddy PA, editors. The world's largest wetlands: ecology and conservation. New York: Cambridge University Press; 2005. 488 p.

4. **Article or Chapter in an Anthology, Scholarly Collection, or Work That Names an Editor**

   4. Terborgh J. The green world hypothesis revisited. In: Ray JC, Redford KH, Steneck RS, Berger J, editors. Large carnivores and the conservation of biodiversity. Washington (DC): Island Press; 2005. p 82-99.

5. **Work by a Group or Corporate Author**

   5. Council of Science Editors, Style Manual Committee. Scientific style and format: the CSE manual for authors, editors, and publishers. 7th ed. Reston (VA): The Council; 2006. 658 p.

6. **Article in a Journal or Magazine**

   6. Wang Y, Wang R. Imaging using parallel integrals in optical projection tomography. Phys Med Biol. 2006;51(12): 6023-32.

7. **Article in a Newspaper** Provide the page number and column number of the beginning of the article. If there is no author, begin the entry with the article title.

   7. Edwards H. Aquarium shows off new views. Seattle Times (Metro Ed.). 2007 Jun 15;Sect. A:1 (col.1).

8. **Journal Article in a Library Database or Subscription Service**

   8. Hulme M, Turnpenny J. Understanding and managing climate change: the UK experience. Geog J [Internet]. 2004 [cited 2009 Mar 23];170(2):105-15. Available from: http://www.fmarion.edu/academics/journalarticlesanddatabases after clicking InfoTrac and then clicking Expanded Academic ASAP and searching by article title.

9. **Article in an Online Journal**

   9. Pribram KH. What makes humanity humane. J Biomed Discov Collab [Internet]. 2006 Nov 29 [cited 2009 Mar 23];1(14):1-7. Available from: http://www.j-biomed-discovery.com/content/pdf/1747-5333-1-14.pdf

10. **Entire Web Site**

> 10. Gray W. Tropical meteorology project [Internet]. c1994-2003. Fort Collins: Colorado State University; [updated 2009 Mar 5; cited 2009 Mar 23]. Available from: http://hurricane.atmos.colostate.edu/

11. **E-Mail and Instant Messaging (IM)** Personal e-mail, instant messaging, and other personal communications are identified in the body of the paper and are not listed in the References.

Glossary of Usage

This list includes words and phrases you may be uncertain about when writing. If you have questions about words not included here, try the index at the back of this book to see whether the word is discussed elsewhere. You can also check a recently published dictionary.

A, An Use *a* before words beginning with a consonant and before words beginning with a vowel that sounds like a consonant:

a cat   a house   a one-way street   a union   a history

Use *an* before words that begin with a vowel and before words with a silent *h*.

an egg   an ice cube   an hour   an honor

Accept, Except *Accept*, a verb, means *to agree to, to believe*, or *to receive*.

The detective **accepted** his account of the event.

Except, a verb, means *to exclude or leave out*, and *except*, a preposition, means *leaving out*.

Because he did not know the answers, he was **excepted** from the list of contestants and asked to leave.

Except for brussels sprouts, I eat most vegetables.

Advice, Advise *Advice* is a noun, and *advise* is a verb.

She always offers too much **advice**.

Would you **advise** me about choosing the right course?

Affect, Effect Most frequently, *affect*, which means *to influence*, is used as a verb, and *effect*, which means *a result*, is used as a noun.

The weather **affects** my ability to study.

What **effect** does coffee have on your concentration?

However, *effect*, meaning *to cause* or *bring about*, is also used as a verb.

The new traffic enforcement laws **effected** a change in people's driving habits.

Common phrases with *effect* include the following:

in effect   to that effect

Ain't This is a nonstandard way of saying *am not, is not, has not, have not*, and so on.

All Ready, Already *All ready* means *prepared*; *already* means *before* or *by this time*.

The courses for the meal are **all ready** to be served.

When I got home, she was **already** there.

253

All Right, Alright *All right* is two words, not one. *Alright* is an incorrect form.

All Together, Altogether *All together* means *in a group*, and *altogether* means *entirely, totally*.

> We were **all together** again after having separate vacations.

> He was not **altogether** happy about the outcome of the test.

Alot, A Lot *Alot* is an incorrect form of *a lot*.

a.m., p.m. (*or*) A.M., P.M. Use these with numbers, not as substitutes for the words *morning* or *evening*.

> We meet every ~~a.m.~~ for an exercise class.
> *morning at 9*

Among, Between Use *among* when referring to three or more things and *between* when referring to two things.

> The decision was discussed **among** all the members of the committee.

> I had to decide **between** the chocolate mousse pie and the almond ice cream.

Amount, Number Use *amount* for things or ideas that are general or abstract and cannot be counted. For example, *furniture* is a general term and cannot be counted. That is, we cannot say *one furniture* or *two furnitures*. Use *number* for things that can be counted (for example, *four chairs* or *three tables*).

> He had a huge **amount** of work to finish before the deadline.

> A **number** of people saw the accident.

An See the entry for **a, an**.

And Although some people discourage the use of *and* as the first word in a sentence, it is an acceptable word with which to begin a sentence.

And Etc. Adding *and* is redundant because *et* means *and* in Latin. See the entry for **etc**.

Anybody, Any Body See the entry for **anyone, any one**.

Anyone, Any One *Anyone* means *any person at all*. *Any one* refers to a specific person or thing in a group. There are similar distinctions for other words ending in -*body* and -*one* (for example, *everybody, every body, anybody, any body, someone,* and *some one*).

> The teacher asked if **anyone** knew the answer.

> **Any one** of those children could have taken the ball.

Anyways, Anywheres These are nonstandard forms for *anyway* and *anywhere*.

As, As If, As Though, Like Use *as* in a comparison (not *like*) when there is an equality intended or when the meaning is *in the function of*.

> Celia acted **as** (not *like*) the leader when the group was getting organized. (Celia = leader)

Use *as if* or *as though* for the subjunctive.

> He spent his money **as if** (*or* **as though**) he were rich.

Use *like* in a comparison (not *as*) when the meaning is *in the manner of* or *to the same degree as*.

The boy swam **like** a fish.

Don't use *like* as the opening word in a clause in formal writing:

Informal: **Like** I thought, he was unable to predict the weather.

Formal: **As** I thought, he was unable to predict the weather.

Assure, Ensure, Insure   *Assure* means *to declare* or *promise*, *ensure* means *to make safe* or *certain*, and *insure* means *to protect with a contract of insurance*.

I **assure** you that I am trying to find your lost package.

Some people claim that eating properly **ensures** good health.

This insurance policy also **insures** my car against theft.

Awful, Awfully   *Awful* is an adjective meaning *inspiring awe* or *extremely unpleasant*.

He was involved in an **awful** accident.

Awfully is an adverb used in very informal writing to mean *very*. Avoid it in formal writing.

Informal: The dog was **awfully** dirty.

Awhile, A While   *Awhile* is an adverb meaning *a short time* and modifies a verb:

He talked **awhile** and then left.

A while is an article with the noun *while* and means *a period of time*:

I'll be there in **a while**.

Bad, Badly   *Bad* is an adjective and is used after linking verbs. *Badly* is an adverb. (See 16a.)

The wheat crop looked **bad** (not *badly*) because of lack of rain.

There was a **bad** flood last summer.

The building was **badly** constructed and unable to withstand the strong winds.

Beside, Besides   *Beside* is a preposition meaning *at the side of, compared with*, or *having nothing to do with*. *Besides* is a preposition meaning *in addition to* or *other than*. *Besides* as an adverb means *also* or *moreover*. Don't confuse *beside* with *besides*.

That is **beside** the point.

Besides the radio, they had no other means of contact with the outside world.

Besides, I enjoyed the concert.

Between, Among   See the entry for **among, between**.

Breath, Breathe   *Breath* is a noun, and *breathe* is a verb.

She held her **breath** when she dived into the water.

Learn to **breathe** deeply when you swim.

But   Although some people discourage the use of *but* as the first word in a sentence, it is an acceptable word with which to begin a sentence.

Can, May   *Can* is a verb that expresses ability, knowledge, or capacity:

He **can** play both the violin and the cello.

May is a verb that expresses possibility or permission. Careful writers avoid using *can* to mean *permission*:

May [not *can*] I sit here?

Can't Hardly   This is incorrect because it is a double negative.

She ~~can't~~ ^{can} hardly hear normal voice levels.

Choose, Chose   *Choose* is the present tense of the verb, and *chose* is the past tense:

Jennie should **choose** strawberry ice cream.

Yesterday, she **chose** strawberry-flavored popcorn.

Cite, Site   *Cite* is a verb that means *to quote an authority or source*; *site* is a noun referring to *a place*.

Be sure to **cite** your sources in the paper.

That is the **site** of the new city swimming pool, and its Web **site** has information about its hours.

Cloth, Clothe   *Cloth* is a noun, and *clothe* is a verb.

Here is some **cloth** for a new scarf.

His paycheck helps feed and **clothe** many people in his family.

Compared to, Compared with   Use *compared to* when showing that two things are alike. Use *compared with* when showing similarities and differences.

The speaker **compared** the economy **to** a roller coaster because both have sudden ups and downs.

The detective **compared** the fingerprints **with** other sets from a previous crime.

Could of   This is incorrect. Instead use *could have*.

Data   This is the plural form of *datum*. In informal usage, *data* is used as a singular noun, with a singular verb. However, because dictionaries do not accept this, treat *data* as a plural form in academic writing.

Informal: The **data** is inconclusive.

Formal: The **data** are inconclusive.

Different from, Different than   *Different from* is always correct, but some writers use *different than* if a clause follows this phrase.

This program is **different from** the others.

That is a **different** result **than** they predicted.

Done   The past tense forms of the verb *do* are *did* and *done*. *Did* is the simple form that needs no additional verb as a helper. *Done* is the past form that requires the helper *have*. Some writers make the mistake of interchanging *did* and *done*.

They ~~done~~ ^{did} it again. (*or*) They ~~done~~ ^{have done} it again.

Effect, Affect   See the entry for **affect, effect**.

Ensure   See the entry for **assure, ensure, insure**.

Etc.   This is an abbreviation of the Latin *et cetera*, meaning *and the rest*. Because it should be used sparingly if at all in formal academic writing, substitute other phrases such as *and so forth* or *and so on*.

Everybody, Every Body   See the entry for **anyone, any one**.

Everyone, Every One   See the entry for **anyone, any one**.

Except, Accept   See the entry for **accept, except**.

Farther, Further   Although some writers use these words inter-changeably, dictionary definitions differentiate them. *Farther* is used when actual distance is involved, and *further* is used to mean *to a greater extent, more.*

> The house is **farther** from the road than I realized.

> That was **furthest** from my thoughts at the time.

Fewer, Less   *Fewer* is used for things that can be counted (*fewer trees, fewer people*), and *less* is used for ideas, abstractions, things that are thought of collectively rather than separately (*less trouble, less furniture*), and things that are measured by amount, not num-ber (*less milk, less fuel*).

Fun   This noun is used informally as an adjective.

> **Informal:**   They had a **fun** time.

Goes, Says   *Goes* is a nonstandard form of *says.*

> Whenever I give him a book to read, he ~~goes~~, "What's it about?"
> *says*

Gone, Went   Past tense forms of the verb *go. Went* is the simple form that needs no additional verb as a helper. *Gone* is the past form that requires the helper *have.* Some writers make the mis-take of interchanging *went* and *gone.* (See section 14b.)

> *went (or) have gone*
> They ~~gone~~ away yesterday.

Good, Well   *Good* is an adjective and therefore describes only nouns. *Well* is an adverb and therefore describes adjectives, other adverbs, and verbs. The word *well* is used as an adjective only in the sense of *in good health.* (See 16a.)

> *well*   *well*
> The stereo works ~~good~~. I feel ~~good~~.

> She is a **good** driver.

Got, Have   *Got* is the past tense of *get* and should not be used in place of *have.* Similarly, *got to* should not be used as a substitute for *must. Have got to* is an informal substitute for *must.*

> *have*
> Do you ~~got~~ any pennies for the meter?

> *must*
> I ~~got to~~ go now.

> **Informal:**   You **have got to** see that movie.

Great   This adjective is overworked in its formal meaning of *very enjoyable, good,* or *wonderful* and should be reserved for its more exact meanings such as *remarkable, intense, high degree of,* and so on.

> **Informal:**   That was a **great** movie.

More exact uses of *great*:

> The vaccine was a **great** discovery.

> The map went into **great** detail.

Have, Got   See the entry for **got, have**.

Have, Of *Have*, not *of*, should follow verbs such as *could*, *might*, *must*, and *should*.

> *have*
> They should ~~of~~ called by now.

Hisself This is a nonstandard substitute for *himself*.

Hopefully This adverb means *in a hopeful way*. Many people consider the meaning *it is to be hoped* as unacceptable.

> **Often considered unacceptable:** **Hopefully**, it will not rain tonight.
>
> **Acceptable:** He listened **hopefully** for the knock at the door.

I Although some people discourage the use of *I* in formal essays, it is acceptable. If you wish to eliminate the use of *I*, see Chapter 5 on passive verbs.

Imply, Infer Some writers use these interchangeably, but careful writers maintain the distinction between the two words. *Imply* means *to suggest without stating directly, to hint*. *Infer* means *to reach an opinion from facts or reasoning*.

> The tone of her voice **implied** he was stupid.
>
> The anthropologist **inferred** this was a burial site for prehistoric people.

Insure See the entry for **assure, ensure, insure**.

Irregardless This is an incorrect form of the word *regardless*.

Is When, Is Why, Is Where, Is Because These are incorrect forms for definitions. See Chapter 7 and the Glossary of Grammatical Terms on faulty predication.

> **Faulty predication:** Nervousness is when my palms sweat.
>
> **Revised:** When I am nervous, my palms sweat.
>
> *(or)*
>
> Nervousness is a state of being very uneasy or agitated that causes the palms to sweat.

Its, It's *Its* is a personal pronoun in the possessive case. *It's* is a contraction for *it is*.

> The kitten licked **its** paw.
>
> **It's** a good time for a vacation.

Kind, Sort These two forms are singular and should be used with *this* or *that* when a singular noun follows. Use *kinds* or *sorts* with *these* or *those* when the noun that follows is plural.

> **This kind** of cloud indicates heavy rain.
>
> **These sorts** of plants are regarded as weeds.

Lay, Lie *Lay* is a verb that needs an object and should not be used in place of *lie*, a verb that takes no direct object. (See 14b.)

> *lie*
> He should ~~lay~~ down and rest awhile.

> *lay*
> You can ~~lie~~ that package on the front table.

Leave, Let *Leave* means *to go away*, and *let* means *to permit*. It is incorrect to use *leave* when you mean *let*.

> *Let*
> ~~Leave~~ me get that for you.

Less, Fewer   See the entry for **fewer, less**.

Let, Leave   See the entry for **leave, let**.

Like, As   See the entry for **as, as if, like**.

Like for   The phrase "I'd like for you to do that" is incorrect. Omit *for*.

May, Can   See the entry for **can, may**.

Most   It is incorrect to use *most* as a substitute for *almost*.

Nowheres   This is an incorrect form of *nowhere*.

Number, Amount   See the entry for **amount, number**.

Of, Have   See the entry for **have, of**.

Off of   It is incorrect to write *off of* for *off* in a phrase such as *off the table*.

O.K., OK, Okay   These can be used informally but should not be used in formal or academic writing.

Reason . . . Because   This is redundant. Instead of *because*, use *that*.

The reason she dropped the course is ~~because~~ *that* she couldn't keep up with the homework.

Less wordy revision: She dropped the course **because** she couldn't keep up with the homework.

Reason Why   Using *why* is redundant. Drop the word *why*.

The reason ~~why~~ I called is to remind you of your promise.

Saw, Seen   Past tense forms of the verb *see*. *Saw* is the simple form that needs no additional verb as a helper. *Seen* is the past form that requires the helper *have*. Some writers make the mistake of interchanging *saw* and *seen*. (See 14b.)

They ~~seen~~ *saw* it happen. (*or*) They ~~seen~~ *have seen* it happen.

Set, Sit   *Set* means *to place* and is followed by a direct object. *Sit* means *to be seated*. It is incorrect to substitute *set* for *sit*.

Come in and ~~set~~ *sit* down.

~~Sit~~ *Set* the flowers on the table.

Should of   This is incorrect. Instead use *should have*.

Sit, Set   See the entry for **set, sit**.

Site, Cite   See the entry for **cite, site**.

Somebody, Some Body   See the entry for **anyone, any one**.

Someone, Some One   See the entry for **anyone, any one**.

Sort, Kind   See the entry for **kind, sort**.

Such   This is an overworked word when used in place of *very* or *extremely*.

Suppose to, Use to   These are nonstandard forms for *supposed to* and *used to*.

Sure The use of *sure* as an adverb is informal. Careful writers use *surely* instead.

> **Informal:** I **sure** hope you can join us.

> **Revised:** I **surely** hope you can join us.

Than, Then *Than* is a conjunction introducing the second element in comparison. *Then* is an adverb meaning *at that time, next, after that, also,* or *in that case.*

> She is taller **than** I am.

> He picked up the ticket and **then** left the house.

That There, This Here, These Here, Those There These are incorrect forms for *that, this, these, those.*

That, Which Use *that* for essential clauses and *which* for nonessential clauses. Some writers, however, also use *which* for essential clauses. (See 20c.)

Their, There, They're *Their* is a possessive pronoun; *there* means *in, at,* or *to that place*; and *they're* is a contraction for *they are.*

> **Their** house has been sold.

> **There** is the parking lot.

> **They're** both good swimmers.

Theirself, Theirselves, Themself These are all incorrect forms for *themselves.*

Them It is incorrect to use this in place of either the pronoun *these* or *those.*

> Look at ~~them~~ those apples.

Then, Than See the entry for **than, then.**

Thusly This is an incorrect substitute for *thus.*

To, Too, Two *To* is a preposition, *too* is an adverb meaning *very* or *also,* and *two* is a number.

> He brought his bass guitar **to** the party.

> He brought his drums **too**.

> He had **two** music stands.

Toward, Towards Both are accepted forms with the same meaning, although *toward* is preferred in American usage.

Use to This is incorrect for the modal meaning *formerly.* Instead, use *used to.*

Use to, Suppose to See the entry for **suppose to, use to.**

Want for Omit the incorrect *for* in phrases such as "I want *for* you to come here."

Well, Good See the entry for **good, well.**

Went, Gone See the entry for **gone, went.**

Where It is incorrect to use *where* to mean *when* or *that.*

> The Fourth of July is a holiday ~~where~~ when the town council shoots off fireworks.

> I see ~~where~~ that there is now a ban on shooting panthers.

Where...at   This is a redundant form. Omit *at*.

This is where the picnic is ~~at~~.

Which, That   See the entry for **that, which**.

While, Awhile   See the entry for **awhile, a while**.

Who, Whom   Use *who* for the subjective case; use *whom* for the objective case.

He is the person **who** signs that form.

He is the person **whom** I asked for help.

Who's, Whose   *Who's* is a contraction for *who is*; *whose* is a possessive pronoun.

Who's included on that list?

Whose wristwatch is this?

Your, You're   *Your* is a possessive pronoun; *you're* is a contraction for *you are*.

Your hands are cold.

You're a great success.

Glossary of Grammatical Terms

Absolutes   Words or phrases that modify whole sentences rather than parts of sentences or individual words. An absolute phrase, which consists of a noun and participle, can be placed anywhere in the sentence but needs to be set off from the sentence by commas.

The snow having finally stopped, the football game began.
(absolute phrase)

Abstract Nouns   See Chapter 32.

Active Voice   See **Voice**.

Adjective Clauses   See **Dependent Clauses**.

Adjectives   See 16a.

Adverb Clauses   See **Dependent Clauses**.

Adverbs   See 16a.

Agreement   See 14a.

Antecedents   Words or groups of words to which pronouns refer.

When the **bell** was rung, **it** sounded very loudly.

(*Bell* is the antecedent of *it*.)

Antonyms   Words with opposite meanings.

Word	Antonym
hot	cold
fast	slow

Appositives   Nonessential phrases and clauses that follow nouns and identify or explain them. (See 20c.)

My uncle, **who lives in Wyoming**, is taking windsurfing
(appositive)
lessons in Florida.

Articles   See **Noun Determiners** and Chapter 33.

Auxiliary Verbs   Verbs used with main verbs in verb phrases.

should be going   **has** taken
(auxiliary verb)   (auxiliary verb)

Cardinal Numbers   See **Noun Determiners**.

Case   See 15a.

Clauses   Groups of related words that contain both subjects and predicates and function either as sentences or as parts of sentences. Clauses are either independent (or main) or dependent (or subordinate). (See Chapter 13 and 20b, 20c.)

Collective Nouns   Nouns that refer to groups of people or things, such as a *committee, team*, or *jury*. When the group includes a number of members acting as a unit and is the subject of the sentence, the verb is also singular.

The **jury** has made a decision.

Comma Splices   Punctuation errors in which two or more independent clauses in compound sentences are separated only by commas and no coordinating conjunctions. (See 13a.)

Jessie said he could not help, that was typical of his responses to requests.
but (or);

Common Nouns   See Chapter 32.

Comparative   See 16b.

Complement   When linking verbs link subjects to adjectives or nouns, the adjectives or nouns are complements.

Phyllis was **tired**.
(complement)

She became a **musician**.
(complement)

Complex Sentences   Sentences with at least one independent clause and at least one dependent clause arranged in any order.

Compound-Complex Sentences   Sentences with at least two independent clauses and at least one dependent clause arranged in any order.

Compound Nouns   Words such as *swimming pool, dropout, roommate*, and *stepmother*, formed of more than one word that could stand on its own.

Compound Sentences   Sentences with two or more independent clauses and no dependent clauses. (See Chapter 13.)

Conjunctions   Words that connect other words, phrases, and clauses in sentences. *Coordinating conjunctions* connect independent clauses; *subordinating conjunctions* connect dependent or subordinating clauses with independent or main clauses.

Coordinating conjunctions:	and, but, for, or, nor, so, yet
Some subordinating conjunctions:	after, although, because, if, since, until, while

Conjunctive Adverbs   Words that begin or join independent clauses. (See Chapter 20.)

consequently, however, therefore, thus, moreover

Connotation   The attitudes and emotional overtones beyond the direct definition of a word. For example, the words *plump* and *fat* both mean *fleshy*, but *plump* has a more positive connotation than *fat*.

Consistency   See Chapter 18.

Coordinating Conjunctions   See **Conjunctions**.

Coordination   Equal importance. Two independent clauses in the same sentence are coordinate because they have equal importance and the same emphasis.

Correlative Conjunctions   Words that work in pairs and give emphasis.

both . . . and	neither . . . nor	either . . . or
not . . . but also		

Dangling Modifiers   See 17a.

Declarative Mood   See **Mood**.

Demonstrative Pronouns   Pronouns that refer to things. (See **Noun Determiners**.)

Denotation   The explicit dictionary definition of a word, as opposed to the connotation of a word. (See **Connotation**.)

Dependent Clauses (Subordinate Clauses)   Clauses that cannot stand alone as complete sentences. (See Chapters 19, 20.) There are two kinds of dependent clauses: adverb clauses and adjective clauses.

Adverb clauses begin with subordinating conjunctions such as *after, if, because, while, when*.

Adjective clauses tell more about nouns or pronouns in sentences and begin with words such as *who, which, that, whose, whom*.

Determiner   See **Noun Determiners**.

Diagrams   See **Sentence Diagrams**.

Direct Discourse   See **Mode of Discourse**.

Direct/Indirect Quotations   Direct quotations are the exact words said by someone or the exact words in print that are being copied. Indirect quotations are not the exact words but the rephrasing or summarizing of someone else's words. (See 23a.)

Direct Objects   Nouns or pronouns that follow a transitive verb and complete the meaning or receive the action of the verb. The direct object answers the question *what?* or *whom?*

Ellipsis   See 24h.

Essential and Nonessential Clauses and Phrases   *Essential* (also called *restrictive*) clauses and phrases appear after nouns and are necessary or essential to complete the meaning of the sentence. *Nonessential* (also called *nonrestrictive*) clauses and phrases appear after nouns and add extra information, but that information can be removed from the sentence without altering the meaning. (See 20c.)

Apples **that are green** are not sweet.
(essential clause)

Golden Delicious apples, **which are yellow**, are sweet.
(nonessential clause)

Excessive Coordination   Situation that occurs when too many equal clauses are strung together with coordinators into one sentence.

Excessive Subordination   Situation that occurs when too many subordinate clauses are strung together in a complex sentence.

Faulty Coordination   Situation that occurs when two clauses that are unequal in importance or that have little or no connection to each other are combined in one sentence and written as independent clauses.

Faulty Parallelism   See Chapter 8.

Faulty Predication   See Chapter 7.

Fragments   Groups of words punctuated as sentences that either do not have both a subject and a complete verb or that are dependent clauses. (See Chapter 12.)

Whenever we wanted to pick fresh fruit while we were staying on my

, we would head for the orchard with buckets
grandmother's farm.

Fused Sentences   Punctuation errors (also called *run-ons*) in which there is no punctuation between independent clauses in the sentence. (See 13b.)

Jennifer never learned how to ask politely she just took what she wanted.

Gerunds   Verbal forms ending in -*ing* that function as nouns. (See **Phrases** and **Verbals**.)

Arnon enjoys **cooking**.
(gerund)

Jogging is another of his pastimes.
(gerund)

Homonyms   Words that sound alike but are spelled differently and have different meanings. (See 29c.)

hear/here   passed/past   buy/by

Idioms   Expressions meaning something beyond the simple definition or literal translation into another language. For example, idioms such as "short and sweet" or "wearing his heart on his sleeve" are expressions in English that cannot be translated literally into another language. (See 14b.)

Imperative Mood   See **Mood**.

Indefinite Pronouns   Pronouns that make indefinite reference to nouns.

anyone, everyone, nobody, something

Independent Clauses   Clauses that can stand alone as complete sentences because they do not depend on other clauses to complete their meanings. (See 23a.)

Indirect Discourse   See **Mode of Discourse**.

Indirect Objects   Words that follow transitive verbs and come before direct objects. They indicate the one to whom or for whom something is given, said, or done and answer the questions to *what?* or to *whom?* Indirect objects can always be inverted to a prepositional phrase beginning with *to* or *for*.

Alice gave **me** some money.
    (indirect object)

Inverted: Alice gave some money to me.

Infinitives   Phrases made up of the present form of the verb preceded by *to*. Infinitives can have subjects, objects, complements, or modifiers.

Everyone wanted **to swim** in the new pool.
    (infinitive)

Intensifiers   Modifying words used for emphasis.

She **most certainly** did fix that car!
   (intensifiers)

Interjections   Words used as exclamations.

Oh, I don't think I want to know about that.
(interjection)

Interrogative Pronouns   Pronouns used in questions.

who, whose, whom, which, that

Intransitive Verbs   See **Verbs**.

Irregular Verbs   See 14b.

Jargon   See Chapter 10.

Linking Verbs   See 14a.

Misplaced Modifiers   See 17b.

Modal Verbs   See 31c.

Mode of Discourse   See 23a.

Modifiers   See Chapter 17.

Mood   See 14b.

Nonessential Clauses and Phrases   See **Essential and Non-essential Clauses and Phrases**.

Nonrestrictive Clauses and Phrases   See **Essential and Nonessential Clauses and Phrases**.

Noun Clauses   See 14a.

Noun Determiners   Words that signal that a noun is about to follow. They stand next to their nouns or can be separated by adjectives. Some noun determiners can also function as nouns. There are five types of noun determiners:

1. Articles: definite: *the*; indefinite: *a, an*

2. Demonstratives: *this, that, these, those*

3. Possessives: *my, our, your, his, her, its, their*

4. Cardinal numbers: *one, two, three*, and so on

5. Miscellaneous: *all, another, each, every, much*, and many others

Noun Phrases   See **Phrases**.

Nouns   Words that name people, places, things, and ideas and have plural or possessive endings. Nouns function as subjects, direct objects, predicate nominatives, objects of prepositions, and indirect objects.

Number   The quantity expressed by a noun or pronoun, either singular (one) or plural (more than one).

Object Complements   The adjectives in predicates modifying the object of the verb (not the subject).

> The enlargement makes the picture **clear**.
>
> (object complement)

Objective Case of Pronouns   See 15a.

Object of the Preposition   The noun following the preposition. The preposition, its object, and any modifiers make up the prepositional phrase.

> For **Daniel**
>
> (object of the preposition *for*)
>
> She knocked twice **on the big wooden door**.
>
> (prepositional phrase)

Objects   See **Direct Objects** and **Object Complements**.

Parallel Construction   See Chapter 6.

Parenthetical Elements   Nonessential words, phrases, and clauses set off by commas, dashes, or parentheses.

Participles   Verb forms that may be part of the complete verb or function as adjectives or adverbs. The present participle ends in *-ing*, and the past participle usually ends in *-ed, -d, -n,* or *-t*. (See **Phrases**.)

> **Present participles:** *running, sleeping, digging*
>
> She is **running** for mayor in this campaign.
>
> (present participle)
>
> **Past participles:**   *walked, deleted, chosen*
>
> The candidate **elected** will take office in January.
>
> (past participle)

Parts of Speech   The eight classes into which words are grouped according to their function, place, meaning, and use in a sentence: nouns, pronouns, verbs, adjectives, adverbs, prepositions, conjunctions, and interjections.

Passive Voice   See **Voice**.

Past Participle   See **Participles**.

Perfect Progressive Tense   See **Verb Tenses**.

Perfect Tenses   See **Verb Tenses**.

Person   See 15a.

Personal Pronouns   See 15a.

Phrases   Groups of related words without subjects and predicates.

Verb phrases function as verbs.

> She **has been eating** too much sugar.
> (verb phrase)

Noun phrases function as nouns.

> **A major winter storm** hit **the eastern coast of Maine**.
> (noun phrase)   (noun phrase)

Prepositional phrases usually function as modifiers.

> That book **of hers** is overdue at the library.
> (prepositional phrase)

Participial phrases, gerund phrases, infinitive phrases, appositive phrases, and absolute phrases function as adjectives, adverbs, or nouns.

Participial phrase:	I saw people **staring at my peculiar-looking haircut.**
Gerund phrase:	**Making copies of videotapes** can be illegal.
Infinitive phrase:	He likes **to give expensive presents.**
Appositive phrase:	You ought to see Dr. Elman, **a dermatologist.**
Absolute phrase:	**The test done,** he sighed with relief.

Possessive Pronouns   See **Personal Pronouns, Noun Determiners**, and 15a.

Predicate Adjectives   See **Subject Complements**.

Predicate Nominatives   See **Subject Complements**.

Predication   Words or groups of words that express action or state of beginning in a sentence and consist of one or more verbs, plus any complements or modifiers.

Prefixes   Word parts added to the beginnings of words.

Prefix	Word
bio- (life)	biography
mis- (wrong, bad)	misspell

Prepositional Phrases   See **Phrases**.

Prepositions   Words that link and relate their objects (usually nouns or pronouns) to some other word or words in a sentence. Prepositions usually precede their objects but may follow the objects and appear at the end of the sentence.

> The server gave the check **to my date** by mistake.
> (prepositional phrase)

> I wonder **what** she is asking **for**.
> (object of the preposition) (preposition)

Progressive Tenses   See **Verb Tenses**.

Pronoun Case   See **Subjective, Objective**, and **Possessive Cases** and 15a.

Pronouns   Words that substitute for nouns. (See 15a.) Pronouns should refer to previously stated nouns, called *antecedents*.

> When **Josh** came in, **he** brought some firewood.
> (antecedent)   (pronoun)

There are seven forms of pronouns: personal, possessive, reflexive, interrogative, demonstrative, indefinite, and relative.

Proper Nouns See 25a.

Reflexive Pronouns Pronouns that show that someone or some thing in the sentence is acting for itself or on itself. Because reflexive pronoun must refer to a word in a sentence, it is not th subject or direct object. If used to show emphasis, reflexive pronouns are called intensive pronouns.

Singular	Plural
First person: *myself*	First person: *ourselves*
Second person: *yourself*	Second person: *yourselves*
Third person: *himself, herself, itself*	Third person: *themselves*

> She returned the book **herself** rather than giving it to
> (reflexive pronoun)
> her roommate to bring back.

Relative Pronouns Pronouns that show the relationship of a dependent clause to a noun in the sentence. Relative pronoun substitute for nouns already mentioned in sentences and introduce adjective or noun clauses and include *that, which, who whom,* and *whose.*

> This was the movie **that** won the Academy Award.

Restrictive Clauses and Phrases See **Essential and Non essential Clauses and Phrases**.

Run-On Sentences See **Fused Sentences** and 13b.

Sentence Diagrams A method of showing relationships within a sentence.

Sentence Fragment See **Fragment**.

Sentences Groups of words that have at least one independen clause (a complete unit of thought with a subject and predicate). Sentences can be classified by their structure as simple, compound complex, and compound-complex.

Simple:	one independent clause
Compound:	two or more independent clauses
Complex:	one or more independent clauses and one or more dependent clauses
Compound-complex:	two or more independent clauses and one or more dependent clauses

Sentences can also be classified by their function as declarative interrogative, imperative, and exclamatory.

Declarative:	makes a statement
Interrogative:	asks a question
Imperative:	issues a command
Exclamatory:	makes an exclamation

Simple Sentence See **Sentences**.

Simple Tenses See **Verb Tenses**.

Split Infinitives   Phrases in which modifiers are inserted between *to* and the verb. Some people object to split infinitives, but others consider them grammatically acceptable.

to quickly turn   to easily reach   to forcefully enter

Subject   The word or words in a sentence that act or are acted on by the verb or are linked by the verb to another word or words in the sentence. The *simple subject* includes only the noun or other main word or words, and the *complete subject* includes all the modifiers with the subject.

Harvey objected to his roommate's alarm going off at 9:00 a.m.

(Harvey is the subject.)

Every single one of the people in the room heard her giggle.

(The simple subject is *one*; the complete subject is the whole phrase.)

Subject Complement   The noun or adjective in the predicate (predicate noun or adjective) that refers to the same entity as the subject in sentences with linking verbs, such as *is/are, feel, look, smell, sound, taste*, and *seem*.

She feels **happy**.

(subject complement)

He is a **pharmacist**.

(subject complement)

Subjective Case of Pronouns   See **Personal Pronouns** and 15a.

Subjunctive Mood   See **Mood**.

Subordinating Conjunctions   Words such as *although, if, until*, and *when* that join two clauses and subordinate one to the other.

She is late. She overslept.

She is late **because** she overslept.

Subordination   The act of placing one clause in a subordinate or dependent relationship to another in a sentence because it is less important and is dependent for its meaning on the other clause.

Suffixes   Word parts added to the ends of words.

Suffix	Word
-ful	careful
-less	nameless

Superlative Forms of Adjectives and Adverbs   See 16a and b.

Synonyms   Words with similar meanings.

Word	Synonym
damp	moist
pretty	attractive

Tense   See **Verb Tense**.

Tone   See Chapter 10.

Transitions   Words in sentences that show relationships between sentences and paragraphs. (See Chapter 8.)

Transitive Verbs   See **Verbs**.

Verbals   Words that are derived from verbs but do not act as verbs in sentences. Three types of verbals are infinitives, participles, and gerunds.

Infinitives:	*to* + verb
to wind,	to say

Participles:	Words used as modifiers or with helping verbs. The present participle ends in *-ing*, and many past participles end in *-ed*.

The dog is **panting**.
(present participle)

He bought only **used** clothing.
(past participle)

Gerunds:	Present participles used as nouns.

Smiling was not a natural act for her.
(gerund)

Verb Conjugations   The forms of verbs in various tenses. (See Chapter 31.)

Verb Phrases   See **Verbs**.

Verbs   Words or groups of words (verb phrases) in predicates that express action, show a state of being, or act as a link between the subject and the rest of the predicate. Verbs change form to show time (tense), mood, and voice and are classified as transitive, intransitive, and linking verbs. (See 14b and Chapter 31)

Transitive verbs:	Require objects to complete the predicate.

He **cut** the cardboard **box** with his knife.
(transitive verb)   (object)

Intransitive verbs:	Do not require objects.

My ancient cat often **lies** on the porch.
(intransitive verb)

Linking verbs:	Link the subject to the following noun or adjective.

The trees **are** bare.
(linking verb)

Verb Tenses   The times indicated by the verb forms in the past, present, or future. (See Chapter 31.)

Voice   Verbs are either in the *active* or *passive* voice. (See Chapter 5.) Voice can also refer to levels of formality used in writing. (See Chapter 10).

Index

a/an, 119
Abbreviations, 102–105
  periods with, 89
Active/passive verbs, 25–26
Addresses, commas with, 78
Adjectives, 59–62
  commas with, 77
Adverbs, 60–62
American Psychological
  Association. *See* APA style
American style in writing,
  112–113
APA format
  for books, 150
  for citing a journal article with
    a DOI from a library
    database, 152
  for citing an article from an
    Internet source, 153
  for magazines, 151
  headings and subheadings,
    179–180
  order of pages, 178
APA style, 216–236
  features of, 216
  footnotes, 220–221
  in-text citations, 217–220
  references list, 221–234
  sample pages, 234–236
  see also APA format; Works
    Cited list (MLA)
Apostrophes, 79–81
  misplaced, 14
Arguments, persuasive, 9–11
Articles in grammar, 119–120
Articles in periodicals
  APA style, 225–229
  bibliographic citations for,
    152, 153
  Chicago Manual of Style
    (CM), 245
  MLA style, 199–201

Bar graphs, 175
between, except, with, 53
Bibliographic citations,
  149–153
  evaluating, 157–160
  for books, 150

in *Chicago Manual of Style*
  (CM), 239–240
for citing a journal article with
  a DOI from a library
  database, 152
for citing an article from an
  Internet source, 153
for magazines, 151
Blogs, 137
Books
  APA style, 229–232
  bibliographic citations for, 150
  Chicago Manual of Style (CM),
    examples, 240–242
  Internet, 137, 142
  MLA style, 194–199
Books in Print, 133
Boolean terms, 139
Brackets, 91

Capitalization, 96–98
Cases of pronouns, 52–56
CD-ROM, 133
Chicago Manual of Style (CM),
  237–247
  author-date citation format,
    238
  bibliography, 239–240
  examples, 239–247
    articles in periodicals, 243
    books, 240–242
    online and electronic
      sources, 243–246
    other sources, 246–247
  numbered notes, 237–238
Citation sequence style in
  Council of Science Editors
  (CSE) style, 248–249
Clarity in sentence choices,
  21–24
  double negative, 21–22
  familiar-to-unfamiliar
    information, 22–23
  intended subject buried, 23–24
  positive instead of negative, 21
  verbs instead of nouns, 23
Clauses and phrases, as
  subjects, 47
Colons, 88–89

Combining sentences, 32
Commas, 73–79
  errors with, 14
Comma splices, 44–45
Common knowledge and
      plagiarism, 163
Common nouns, 96
Comparisons in adjectives and
      adverbs, 61–62
Complex sentences, 73
Compound constructions, 54
Compound sentences, 44, 73
  semicolons in, 82
Conciseness, 32–33
Consistency in document
      design, 173
Contractions, apostrophes
      with, 81
Contrasting design elements
      for emphasis, 173
Council of Science Editors (CSE)
      style, 248–252
  citation sequence style,
      248–249
  name-year format, 248
  reference list style, 249–252
Count/noncount nouns, 118
Cultural differences regarding
      plagiarism, 162–163
Current news and publications,
      Internet, 137

Dangling modifiers, 62–64
Dashes, 90–91
Dates, commas with, 77
Dependent clauses, 74
Dialogue, quotation marks
      with, 85
Digital object identifier (DOI)
      numbers, 223
Direct quotations, quotation
      marks with, 84
Document design, 173–180
  bar graphs, 175
  consistency, 173
  contrasting design elements
      for emphasis, 173
  flowcharts, 176
  fonts, 179
  headings and subheadings,
      173–174, 179–180
  images, 174
  indentations, 179
  line graphs, 175
  line spacing, 177
  lists, 174
  maps, 176
  margins, 178

order of pages, 178
  page numbers and
      identification, 179
  page preparation, 177–180
  paper, 177
  pie charts, 175
  tables, 176
  titles and title pages, 178–179
  visuals, 174–177
  white space, 173
Documentation, 181–252
  APA style, 217–238
  Chicago Manual of Style (CM),
      239–249
  Council of Science Editors
      (CSE) style, 248–252
  MLA style, 183–216
Double negatives, 21–22

E-books, 142
Ellipsis, 91–92
End punctuation, 89–90
Endnotes, MLA style, 189
English as a second language
      (ESL). *See* Multilingual
      speakers
Essential and nonessential
      words and clauses, 76
Euphemisms, 35
Exclamation points, 90

Familiar-to-unfamiliar
      information, 22–23
"FAN BOYS," (*for, and, nor, but,
      or, yet, so*), 75
Fillers, 32
First person, 65–66
Flowcharts, 176
Fonts, 179
Footnotes, APA style, 220–221
Foreign words and phrases,
      italics for, 100
Formal tone, 33–34
Fragments, sentence, 14, 42–43
Fused (run-on) sentences, 14,
      44, 45
Future tenses of verbs, 115–116

Geographical names, commas
      with, 78
Government sources, Internet,
      136, 143–144

Headings and subheadings,
      173–174, 179–180
Higher-order concerns (HOCs) in
      writing, 3–13
Hyphens, 86–88

Idioms, 123–124

ie/ei, 106

Images in document design, 174

Indefinite pronouns, 36, 58

Indentations, 179

Independent clauses, 42, 44, 73
  colons with, 88
  commas between, 75

Indirect quotations and
  quotation marks, 84

Inflated expressions, 35

Informal tone, 34

Information that requires
  documentation, 163

Internet, 136–140. *See also* Web
  resources
  bibliographic citations for, 153
  blogs, 137
  Boolean terms, 139
  current news and
    publications, 137
  government sources, 136,
    143–144
  library databases, 128
  newsgroups and
    E-mail lists, 137
  older books, 137
  online books (e-books), 142
  online library catalogs and
    databases, 136–137,
    140–141
  online media/images/art/
    photographs, 145
  search engines, 128,
    138, 141
  writers' resources, 140

Interrupting words or phrases,
  commas with, 78

In-text citations
  APA style, 217–220
  MLA style, 183–189

Introductory words/phrases/
  clauses, commas after,
  75–76

Italics, 99–100

Jargon, 34–35

Keyword searches, 133

Later-order concerns (LOCs)
  in writing, 13–14

Legal documents and quotation
  marks, 85

Letters used as examples, italics
  for, 100

LexisNexis, 134

Library databases, Internet, 128

*Library of Congress Subject
  Headings*, 133

Likert scales, 147

Line graphs, 175

Line spacing, 177

Lists
  capitals in, 98
  in document design, 174

Magazines, bibliographic
  citations for, 151

*Manual for Writers of Term
  Papers, Theses, and
  Dissertations*
  (Turabian), 237

Maps, 176

Margins, 178

Mechanics, 93–108
  abbreviations, 102–105
  capitalization, 96–98
  italics, 99–100
  numbers, 100–102
  spelling, 105–108

Minor titles, quotation marks
  for, 85

Misplaced modifiers, 64

MLA format
  for books, 150
  for citing a journal article
    with a DOI from a
    library database, 152
  for citing an article from an
    Internet source, 153
  for magazines, 151
  headings and
    subheadings, 179
  order of pages, 178

MLA style, 183–215
  endnotes, 189
  in-text citations
    (parenthetical
    references), 184–189
  major features of, 183
  parts of the citation format,
    183–184
  sample pages, 213–215
  see also MLA format;
    Works Cited list (MLA)

Modern Language Association.
  See MLA style

Modifiers, 62–65
  dangling, 62–64
  misplaced, 64
  split infinitives, 65

Multilingual speakers (ESL),
  109–124
  American style in writing,
    112–113

Multilingual speakers (*continued*)
    articles, 119–120
    count/noncount nouns, 118
    idioms, 123–124
    omitted and repeated words,
        122–123
    prepositions, 120–121
    verbs, 114–117
    Web sources for learning
        English as a second
        language, 113–114
Multiple-choice questions, 147

Name-year format in Council of
    Science Editors (CSE)
    style, 248
Newsgroups and E-mail lists,
    Internet, 137
Nonsexist language, 35–36
Nouns, count/noncount, 118
Number, and pronouns, 57–59
Numbered notes, in *Chicago
    Manual of Style* (CM),
    237–238
Numbers, 100–102
    commas with, 78
    spelling out and figures,
        100–103

Objective case of pronouns, 53
Omitted words, 122–123
    and ellipsis, 91–92
Online and electronic sources,
    Chicago Manual of Style
    (CM) examples, 243–246
Online books (e-books), 142
Online library catalogs and
    databases, 136–137,
    140–141
Online media/images/art/
    photographs, 145
Online tools for writing, 15
Oral and multimedia
    presentations, 15–18
    content, 116
    delivery, 16, 18
    designing multimedia
        presentations, 18
    organizing multimedia
        presentations, 16–17
    planning, 15–16

Pages in document design,
    178–180
Paper in document design, 177
Paragraph development, 7
Parallelism, 26–27
Paraphrasing, 167–168

Parentheses, 91
Parenthetical references. *See*
    In-text citations
Parts of larger works, quotation
    marks for, 85
Past tenses of verbs, 115
Perfect tenses of verbs, 114
Periods, 89
Pie charts, 175
Plagiarism, 161–165
    avoiding, 161–162
    checking work for, 164–165
    common knowledge, 163
    cultural differences regarding,
        162–163
    examples, 164
    information that requires
        documentation, 163
Plurals and apostrophes,
    81, 108
Poetry quotations, quotation
    marks with, 85
Portfolios, 12–13
Possessive case of pronouns,
    53, 54
Possessives, apostrophes with,
    79–80
PowerPoint, 16
Predication, faulty, 27–28
Prepositions, 120–121
    of place, 121
    of time, 121
    to show logical relationship, 121
Present tenses of verbs, 114–115
Presentation portfolio, 13
Primary (firsthand) sources, 131,
    145–153
Process portfolio, 12
Progressive tenses of verbs, 114
Pronoun references, 14
Pronouns, 52–59
    after *than* or *as*, 55
    and compound subjects, 58
    antecedents of, 56
    case before *we* or *us*, 55–56
    cases of, 52–56
    case with *to* + verb
        (infinitive), 56
    in compound constructions, 54
    indefinite, 58
    number, 57–59
    objective case of, 53
    possessive, 53, 54
    reflexive, 54
    subjective case of, 53
    vague, 56–57
    who/which/that, 58
    who/whom, 55

Proofreading, 13–14, 106
Proper nouns, capitalization of, 96–98
Prose quotations, quotation marks with, 84–85
Publication Manual of the American Psychological Association, 217. *See also* APA style
Punctuation, 69–92
  apostrophes, 79–81
  brackets, 91
  colons, 88–89
  commas, 73–79
  dashes, 90–91
  exclamation points, 90
  hyphens, 86–88
  omitted words (ellipsis), 91–92
  parentheses, 91
  periods, 89
  question marks, 90
  quotation marks, 84–86
  semicolons, 73–74, 82–83
  sentence punctuation patterns, 73–74
  slashes, 91

Question marks, 90
Questions, closed and open, 147
Quotation marks, 84–86
  colons after, 89
  semicolons with, 83
Quotations
  capitals in, 98
  commas with, 78

Readers' Guide to Periodical Literature, 133
References list
  APA style, 221–234
  Council of Science Editors (CSE) style, 248–252
Reflexive case of pronouns, 54
Religious works
  and italics, 99
  and quotation marks, 85
Repeated words, 122–123
Repetition, 32
Research, 125–180
  audience, 129
  Boolean terms, 139
  document design, 173–180
  evaluating content, 160–161
  evaluating print and online sources, 154–161
  integrating sources, 170–173
  Internet sources, 128, 136–140

interviews, 147–148
library databases, 128
library sources, 132–135
note-taking, 149
observations, 146
online news sites, 128
paraphrasing, 167–168
primary (firsthand) sources, 131, 145–153
purpose of writing, 129
quoting, 168–169
reference guides, 128
secondary sources, 131–132
signal words and phrases, 170
sources of information, 131–153
summarizing, 165–168
surveys, 146–147
thesis statement, 130–131
topic selection, 128–131
  see also Bibliographic citations; Document design; Plagiarism; Web resources

Sample pages
  APA style, 234–236
  MLA style, 213–215
Scientific Style and Format: The CSE Manual for Authors, Editors, and Publishers, 248
Search engines, 128, 138, 141
Secondary sources, 131–132
Second person, 65–66
Semicolons, 73–74, 82–83
Sentence choices, 19–30
  active/passive verbs, 25–26
  parallelism, 26–27
  predication, faulty, 27–28
  transitions, 29–30
  variety, 24–25
  see also Clarity in sentence choices
Sentence fragments, 42–43
Sentence grammar, 37–67
  comma splices, 44–45
  compound sentences, 44
  fragments, 14, 42–43
  fused (run-on) sentences, 14, 44, 45
  subjects and verbs, 45–51
Sentences
  capitals in, 98
  combining, 32
  complex, 73
  compound, 73
  punctuation patterns, 73–74
  simple, 73

Series and lists
commas in, 77
semicolons in, 83
Shifts, 65–67
in person or number, 65–66
in tone, 67
in verb tense, 66
Simple sentences, 73
Slang, 34
Slashes, 91
Specialized language, 34
Spell checkers, 105–106
Spelling, 105–108
aids for, 105
doubling consonants, 107
errors in, 14
final silent -e, 107
ie/ei, 106
plurals, 107–108
proofreading, 106
rules, 105
sound-alike words
(homonyms), 108
spell checkers, 105–106
Split infinitives, 65
Subheadings, 173–174, 179–180
Subjective case of pronouns, 53
Subject-verb agreement, 14,
45–50
Subjects
buried, 23–24, 47
clauses and phrases, 47
collective nouns and amounts
as, 48
compound, 47, 58
indefinites as, 48
linking verbs and, 49
or and either/or in, 47
plural words as, 48–49
subject-verb agreement, 45–50
titles, company names, words,
and quotations as, 49
who, which, that, and one of
as, 49–50
Subjects and verbs, 45–51
Summarizing, 165–168
Survey questions, 146–147

Tables, 176
than or as, 55
the, 119–120
them, these, those, 53
Thesis statement, 5–6, 130–131
Third person, 65–66
Titles, italics for, 99
Titles and title pages, 178–179
Titles of people, abbreviating,
102–105

Tone, 34
Trademarked names used as
words, italics for, 100
Transitions in writing, 7–8,
29–30
True/false and yes/no
questions, 147
Turabian, Kate L., *Manual
for Writers of Term
Papers, Theses, and
Dissertations*, 239

Unnecessary apostrophes, 81
Unnecessary colons, 89
Unnecessary commas, 78–79
Unnecessary quotation
marks, 86
Unnecessary semicolons, 83
Unnecessary words, 32–33
URLs, 223

Vague pronouns, 56–57
Various discipline sources,
133–136
Verb endings, problems with, 14
Verbs, 114–117
helping verbs with main
verbs, 116
-ing and to plus verb form, 117
instead of nouns, 23
irregular, 50–51
lie/lay and sit/set, 51–52
modal verbs, 116
mood, 52
regular, 50
subject-verb agreement, 45–50
two-word (phrasal) verbs,
116–117
voice, 52
Verbs and subjects, 45–51
Verb tenses, 114–116
problems with, 14
Visuals in document design,
174–177
Voice and formality, 33–35

we or *us*, 55–56
Web resources
domain name and registrant,
156–157
evaluating, 155–156
for learning English as a
second language, 113–114
well, 61
White space in document
design, 173
who, which, that, 33, 58
who/whom, 55

Words
  dividing at end of a line, 88
  italics for emphasizing, 100
  omitted and repeated words,
      122–123
  quotation marks for, 85
Works Cited list *see* APA format;
      APA style; References list,
      221–234
  electronic sources format,
      221–222
  examples of, 224–234
    articles in periodicals,
        224–228
    books and reports, 228–231
    multimedia and other
        formats, 232–234
    Web sources, 231–232
  title format, 221
  see APA format; APA style
Works Cited list (MLA), 189–213
  basic Web site sources, 192
  books in print, 190
  examples of, 192–213
    articles in periodicals,
        199–201
    books, 194–199
    electronic sources, 201
    Internet sources, 201–206
    print/audio/video/online/
        other formats, 206–213
  magazines, 190

media, 190
newspapers, 190
online library databases
    or subscription
    services, 191
print sources posted
    online, 192
scholarly journals, 190
see also MLA format; MLA
    style
Writers' resources, Internet, 140
Writing, 1–14
  about literature, 11–12
  arguments, persuasive, 9–11
  audience, 4
  conclusions, 8–9
  document revisions, 13
  grammatical problems, 15
  higher-order concerns (HOCs),
      3–13
  introductions, 7–8
  later-order concerns (LOCs),
      13–14
  online tools, 15
  organization, 7
  paragraph development, 7
  portfolios, 12–13
  proofreading, 13–14
  thesis, 5–6
  topic, 4–5
  transitions, 7–8
Writing style, 31–36